A LOOK AT
U.S. MILITARY SERVICE SPORTS
1952-1958

Photo: Fort Ord, CA, 1957; no identifying information included with photo (1).

Disclaimer: This work is an historical study based on archival research and is not affiliated with or endorsed by the U.S. Department of Defense or any military branch.

Publisher: Goodrich Fine Books

ISBN: 979-8-218-86868-0

Author Note: Please note that *all words* and work product in this book (except for the cover, which was produced by the impressive Raelene Mack, and pre-printed photo captions), including the writing, editing, and formatting, is the product of the author's hand, and the author's hand only. *No AI was used in the writing or production of this book.*

ACKNOWLEDGEMENTS

Thank you to the ever-helpful librarians and staff at Jefferson County, Alabama and Huntsville-Madison County, Alabama public libraries for your support. It is greatly appreciated!

Thank you to Raelene Mack of Assist Graphics, once again, for the incredible book cover!

Thank you to the amazing used bookstores where I was able to find rare and high-quality books for my research, which was immensely helpful in compiling this Service Sports resource. Notable stores included the gigantic Second Story Books in Rockville, MD; 2nd & Charles in Hoover, AL; Mr. K's Used Books in Greenville, SC; and McKay's in Knoxville, TN.

Thank you again to Paul W. Bryant Museum curator and photo archivist, Brad Green, at the great University of Alabama, Tuscaloosa, for his helpful generosity and sharing of some superb archival documentation pertaining to 1950s Alabama sports. Roll Tide!

Thank you to Evangeline Marie Giaconia and Jada Yolich from University Archives at the University of Maryland for their amazing help in finding documentation supporting the Terrapin Connection section. The documents and photos were amazing!

Thank you to Fort Benning for preserving historical structures and making them accessible to the public.

Thank you again to Christopher Malpass from Inter-Library Loan and Document Services at UNC Wilmington, North Carolina, who graciously provided scanned copies of many pages of the rare *1954 Armed Forces Sports Almanac* pertaining to football and basketball Service Sports.

Thank you to U.S. Military veterans who served, and continue to serve, America with honor and pride.

Thank you to my family, from whose help and support and confidence in me I could not do without.

This book is dedicated to Mike Gilotti of Hoover, Alabama – husband, father, tank commander. U.S. Army Iraq combat vet.

Justice was not served.

Rest in Peace, American Hero.

"The Army today offers the most vigorous and flexible sports program in its history."

-    SP1 Wallace J. Kissel, *Army Times*, 4 January 1958

CONTENTS

INTRODUCTION

The United States Military Service Sports program of the last century offered a wide array of recreational options, such as track and field, basketball, contact sports and non-contact sports, and team sports as well as individual sporting activities. All major branches were included in the Service Sport programs, and servicemen and women were strongly encouraged by senior command staff to participate for the benefit of general health and optimum military performance.

Major sports like football, basketball, and baseball were very popular, and attracted sometimes large military and civilian crowds. The Service Sports teams, football in particular, were often strongly competitive and could (and did) sometimes favorably compete against some of the best college, and even professional teams, in the country.

Did you know, for example, that San Diego Chargers legendary NFL Hall of Fame coach, Don Coryell, inventor of "Air Coryell" passing attacks, coached Service Sports powerhouse Fort Ord in 1956, leading the team to a title, and to become the only undefeated service team in the nation that season?

The weight of evidence in my research leads me to believe that the Mid-1950s, post-Korean Armistice, was the pinnacle time period of U. S. Military Service Sports in the 20th Century, in terms of interest, talent, support, and organized structure.

Service Sports in the 1950s were grouped by areas of command, most notably Europe, Continental United States (CONUS), and Far East (Japan and Korea). This book addresses 1950s CONUS Service Sports, particularly football, which had a very robust and exciting presence in America. Post-Armistice Far East Service Sports were previously documented in *The Forgotten Athletes of the American Forces Far East*, released by Goodrich Fine Books in 2025.

This book will primarily focus on Service Sports from 1952 to 1958 in the continental United States, when major sports were fully supported and active.

Information contained within these pages (sources documented in the bibliography) was obtained from numerous resources, including National Archives II in College Park, Maryland; personal documentation; local library archives and resources; internet research; archival newspapers such as *Stars and Stripes* and *Army Times*, and other miscellaneous sources.

My goal for this book is to fill the gap – the gap of information left out of nearly every Service Sports alumni's biography or obituary. Military and sports historians have been shortchanged, because many notable athletic accomplishments may have occurred during a subject athlete's time of service, unbeknownst in whole or in part to the surviving family, relatives, or friends.

For example, a personal biography might give a long list of the player's sports accomplishments, and then somewhere in the middle it might say, "His athletic career was interrupted by two years of military service," with no enlightenment as to what happened during those two years. My goal is to provide that explanation, where possible.

This is plausibly the first comprehensive long-form documentation of the incredibly competitive CONUS U.S. Military Service Sports programs from the mid-1950s. The athletes and domestic Service Sports competitions were worthy of memorializing.

Join me in getting to know those who came before us!

Notes on images.

Original/primary documents were scanned by the author, and the quality of the physical scan varied depending on the quality of the original document. Photos were selected based on historical value and quality; if a photo was selected, it was the best available.

POST-KOREAN WAR AMERICA

Korean hostilities ended 27 July 1953 with the Armistice signing, but the war was never officially ended. The main focus of this book is the immediate post-Korean War period because many high-level athletes had entered the military during wartime, either through draft or enlistment, and were subsequently available for Service Sports participation once the fighting stopped.

Somewhat surprisingly, published evidence shows that some Service Sports programs were active *during* the war, even in the Far East, though apparently at a reduced level.

Post-Armistice, those remaining in the military from wartime, or those who had subsequently been drafted (or enlisted), filled the Service Sports participation ranks, leading to the pinnacle of Service Sports popularity and quality in the Far East, in the Continental United States, and in a variety of U.S. military installation locations. We honor those who served and participated in Service Sports post-war, while at the same time acknowledging tremendous losses suffered by America during the Korean War in defense of freedom.

General Maxwell D. Taylor relieved Lt. Gen. Van Fleet as Eighth Army Commander on 11 February 1953. Truce documents were signed on 27 July (2).

> "The Armistice does not mean that the war is over," General Taylor told his men that day. "The Armistice is just a suspension of hostilities – an interruption in the shooting. It may or may not be preparatory to a permanent peace; in itself it does not end the war."

A book titled *History of the United States Army* (3) says, "The years from Korea to Vietnam represented a period of fundamental reappraisal for the Armed Forces," noting that atomic power was now in play and would dictate all military decisions going forward. The author claimed the expense of the new nuclear program had forced a reduction of six Army divisions.

Eisenhower pushed legislation to allow citizens to serve part of their military commitment in the reserves or National Guard (Author note: My father came from the National Guard to serve active duty in Korea in the mid-1950s; see: *The Forgotten Athletes of the American Forces Far East*).

Photo: General Mark Clark signs the Korean War Armistice Agreement July 1953 (4).

Following the Korean War, the Eisenhower administration developed the concept of "massive retaliation," which implied use of nuclear weapons. The political aftermath of the Korean conflict changed the world's power balance; while North Korean communists were suppressed (the Korean People's Army never fought above corps-level after Inchon), China grew in power and influence and the U.S. economy expanded significantly during the war (4), thus allowing for the buildup of defense systems.

Author Clarence G. Oliver, Jr., a Korean War veteran, writes in *Tony Dufflebag* (5), "The fact that the war in Korea wasn't on the minds of most people back in the United States was a surprise to us." Citizens stateside didn't seem to care that soldiers had just returned from combat, and it was an abrupt change from total focus on the war while in Korea to mundane problems back home.

Despite apparent indifference from the general populace, returning soldiers were treated to a large crowd of friends and family waiting for them at Fort Sill, Oklahoma, according to Oliver (Fort Sill, you will see, played a large role in post-Korean War Service Sports). Soldiers like Mr. Oliver often returned with only a small amount of cash, and were therefore in immediate need of a job.

"Most of us who participated in that war to stop the spread of Communism are proud of being part of that idealistic effort. Mission accomplished."

Despite additional monetary and personnel strains on the American military, authors Larry Schweikert and Michael Allen in *A Patriots History of the United States* (6) referred to the post-war period as one of can-do optimism and problem-solving confidence in America.

Dwight D. Eisenhower, for example, had retired from the Army in 1952 to run for president; his credentials were obvious, and, according to the authors, "Americans considered military service a training ground for the presidency."

Eisenhower won the presidency by an electoral landslide over Adlai Stevenson (twice!), and rewarded his voters with low inflation and virtually full employment (6), though Cold War, culture issues (which would become very evident in the 1960s), and atomic force considerations were always in the background, militarily and politically.

5

The 1950s were a time of suburban development and expansion, and business and educational achievement soared; at the same time, traditional family structures remained largely intact, which helped support a cohesive and functional society.

As the interstate highway system and auto ownership grew (the 1956 National Highway Act built tens of thousands of interstate miles), road travel for leisure became easier and therefore more popular. Road travel, of course, allowed sports fans to access their favorite teams in sometimes far-flung cities.

The mid-1950s national setting was favorable for robust and thriving CONUS Service Sports.

CONUS SERVICE SPORTS HISTORY

CONUS U.S. Military Service Sports were exceedingly popular in the mid-1950s, particularly American-style football, which often drew thousands of fans and invited widespread mainstream-media attention. Powerhouse military post football teams, such as those of the now-defunct Fort Ord, dominated competition with talented players, both well-known and lesser-known. Not only were teams like Fort Ord dominant in Service Sports leagues, they were also sometimes ranked among the best NCAA major-college teams.

The U.S. Army described the history of the Morale, Welfare, and Recreation (MWR) program within which Special Services sports programs operated (7):

> Between 1946 and 1955, the core recreation programs were established and staffed by a combination of active-duty military and civilians. Until the mid-1980s, it was active duty enlisted Soldiers and officers who held military occupational specialties in Special Services and were assigned at every level of command who made up MWR.

Special Services had been placed under the command of the Adjutant General's Office in 1950. A Seventh Division publication from the mid-1950s (undated) stated (2):

> Korea is the only command in the Army where division level sports competition is permitted. Brigade and company level sports are likewise emphasized.

The 1950s were an era where if you didn't attend sporting events in person, it was unlikely that you would see many games, since it was a time in which there was not a wide variety of live-televised games, though there were substantial print-media reviews of previous day's contests. The 1961 *Sports Broadcasting Act*, which held that leagues could pool their broadcasting rights without violating federal anti-trust laws (8), helped to accelerate the availability of televised games to the public.

Photo: 22 October 1942, Pre-Flight football, [NARA] RG 80, General Records Department of the Navy 1804-1983.

The 1950s were a time when the team was considered first and foremost over the individual; focus was on individuals working as a unit - promoting success of the team as a whole.

This mindset shifted in later decades with the rise of individual fame, which did not replace the team concept but ran parallel to it. Author David Halberstam pointed out in *Playing for Keeps, Michael Jordan and the World He Made,* the result of the rise of alternative media such as ESPN in the mid-1980s: "As the league and network became co-conspirators in the promotion of stars, a major new direction, barely understood at the time, was being charted for the league. It was part of a larger new phenomenon taking place in sports, and society in general, but most nakedly and obviously in basketball (9)."

The initial public reaction to this cultural change was one of disdain for the glorification of the individual; however, the trend gained momentum, and the new emphasis on individuals versus the team propelled athletes to unimagined levels of fame and fortune.

THE ASCENT OF MILITARY SERVICE TEAMS

Author Douglas Stark's book, *Wartime Basketball* (10), entailed discussion of the "Emergence of a National Sport during World War II," but also touched on the post-war "military pipeline."

Stark opined, "Service teams turned out some darn good players in the postwar years." He gave the example of Joe Perry, who went straight from Alameda Naval Training Station to stardom with the 49ers. Hall-of-Famer, "Night Train" Lane (*Richard Lane - Fort Ord, LA Rams, Chicago Cardinals*) did likewise post-Army service.

D. (Night Train) Lane

Another example was "Big Daddy" Lipscomb, who had learned his football in the Marines and went on to become an NFL Pro Bowl athlete (*Gene Lipscomb – Camp Pendleton, Los Angeles Rams, Baltimore Colts, Pittsburgh Steelers*).

Green Bay Packers fullback Howie Ferguson, a product of Navy football, was the number two rusher in the NFL in 1955. 1956 Los Angeles Rams rookie, "Touchdown Tommy" Wilson, earned a spot with the professionals following his service with Shaw Air Force Base. Wilson went on to set a then-NFL record of 223 yards gained in a single game.

"The training they got in service ball enabled them to carve out successful pro careers."

The Forgotten Athletes of the American Forces Far East (11) reported that San Diego had been a hotbed for service football in the late 1920s and early 1930s. Battle Force of the Navy held the Army All-Stars scoreless in 1931, 17-0, and again the following year, 32-0. Both games had been played in front of crowds of 70,000 in Berkeley, California, but Battle Force also defeated the Marines in 1931, 1932, and 1933 in front of capacity crowds at their home turf at Balboa Stadium in San Diego (11).

Battle Force coach Tom Hamilton, a former Naval Academy All-American, suggested that the Battle Force teams were better than two previous teams from the NCAA he had coached, Naval Academy and Pitt. High praise, indeed.

Football Archaeology (12) reported on 4 October 2022 that service football teams "played colleges large and small" during the two world wars, and that the "tradition continued in the 1950s, though most service teams played one another exclusively."

Service Sports "produced some excellent football teams, partly because Uncle Sam drafted NFL and former college players like everyone else." The sometimes-tremendous talent in the Service Sports programs is noted, though the overall talent level was not always consistent. Fort Ord appeared to be the exception, having been loaded with college and pro talent, leading them to, among other successes, victories in the "Salad Bowl" and "Poinsettia Bowl" national service bowl matchups.

Football Archaeology noted on 15 October 2021 (13) that the 1956 Eglin Air Force Base football team had a roster which included multiple gifted athletes, including Jim Dooley of the Chicago Bears, Max McGee of the Green Bay Packers, and Zeke Bratkowski, also of the Chicago Bears.

"Military bases of the 1950s fielded football teams for morale and public relations purposes … the military did not recruit for athletic ability … most had a mix of high school, college, and professional athletes … only three of the forty-six men named to the 1956 All-Service teams … had not played college football."

Photo: Jim Dooley, from Eglin AFE to Chicago Bears, teaming up with Army A'l-Star Rick Casares (14).

Eglin mostly played military teams and was overlooked by college teams; however, Eglin's exploits had been covered by local media in the Southeast, including by *The Command Courier* reporter and Airman First Class, Hunter S. Thompson (Yes, *that* Hunter S. Thompson).

Jim Dooley's departure after having served his time in the military, however, diminished Eglin's chances for a Service Sports national championship. Dooley, McGee, and Bratkowski went on to solid professional football careers following their separation from service, including participating in title games and Super Bowls.

Photo: Seventh Division football, undated – ca. 1950s (15).

FORT BENNING'S JIM BROWN, MULTI-SPORT & HOLLYWOOD STAR

Perhaps the most well-known athlete to spend time in Service Sports was Jim Brown, stationed at Fort Benning, Georgia. Brown's athletic accomplishments are hard to overstate; he was one of the greatest all-around athletes of our age.

Georgia-born Brown ended up in New York, where his schooling took place. He was a natural, gifted athlete who starred in lacrosse, basketball, football, track and field, and really anything he tried. In baseball, he was scouted and eventually offered a contract by the Yankees - which he declined - preferring to focus his talents elsewhere.

Brown played football and lacrosse at Syracuse and was outstanding at each. His college play led to his having been drafted by the Cleveland Browns of the NFL, where he ended up spending his entire career (16). He played from 1957 to 1965, including for the NFL championship in 1964. He was a nine-time Pro-Bowl honoree, and a three-time NFL MVP. He averaged an astonishing 100+ yards per game for his entire career.

CLEVELAND BROWNS

Aug. 29 at L. A.—8:15 P.M.
Coach: Paul Brown
Pub. Director: Harold Sauerbrei

Sept. 28 at L. A.—1:35 P.M.
Home Field: Cleve. Mun. Stadium
1957 Record: W 9 L 2 T 1

1958 Schedule
Sept. 28 Rams (A)
Oct. 5 Steelers (A)
Oct. 12 Cards (H)
Oct. 19 Steelers (H)
Oct. 26 Cards (A)
Nov. 2 Giants (H)
Nov. 9 Lions (H)
Nov. 16 'Skins (A)
Nov. 23 Eagles (H)
Nov. 30 'Skins (H)
Dec. 7 Eagles (A)
Dec. 14 Giants (A)

Top Scorers: Lou Groza—*(1st-T) 77 pts., 32 XPs, 15 FGs.
Jim Brown—(8th-T) 60 pts., 10 TDs.

Top Runners: Jim Brown—(1st) 202 atts., 942 yds., 4.7 avg.
Chet Hanulak—(22nd-T) 125 atts., 375 yds., 3.0 avg.

Top Passers: Tommy O'Connell—(1st) 110 atts., 63 comp., 1229 yds., 9 TDs.
Milt Plum—(15th) 76 atts., 41 comp., 590 yds., 2 TDs.

Top Receivers: Darrel Brewster—(14th) 30 for 614 yds., 2 TDs.
Pres Carpenter—(21st) 27 for 298 yds., 2 TDs.
*(NFL Finish)

Sporting News and *New York Daily News* called Jim Brown the greatest football player of all time. His fame didn't end with football. Brown went to Hollywood following his football career, starring in movies and TV shows.

Writer Chris Carlson called Brown a flawed man, though a great athlete (17).

While at Syracuse, "He delivered an athletic career so comprehensive that he is one of a handful of people who could credibly claim to be the greatest athlete who ever lived."

Syracuse teammate Jim Ridlon said that Brown's assets were not just physical; "He had an iron mind when it came to being successful at a task. He always focused on the goal."

Focusing on the goal sounds like a military objective. Brown took his varied and sundry skills to Fort Benning, as archival news articles reveal.

Brown, however, wrestled with personal demons; he had been arrested six times, "usually on charges of violence against women … The history of these claims over multiple decades and Brown's own admission to slapping multiple women makes it impossible to summarize … a life that paired such greatness with such flaws."

HALFBACK JIMMY BROWN OF SYRACUSE IS THE KEY FIGURE IN POWERFUL RUNNING ATTACK

Photo: Jim Brown at Syracuse, 1956 (18).

Though Jim Brown appeared in military sports news in the 1950s, it is not clear whether or not he played service football given the evidence reviewed.

The 15 March 1958 *Army Times* reported (19) that "All-Pro football star Jim Brown of the Cleveland Browns scored 25 points as Benning beat Campbell" in basketball, at Fort Benning, though teammate Dick Long outdid him with 33 points. Jesse White led Campbell (Kentucky) with 22 points. Fort Benning prevailed over Campbell, 98-78.

Another *Army Times* article, of 19 April 1958, mentioned Jim Brown (20), this time for a track meet in which Benning fell to Fort Campbell. Campbell defeated Benning and Redstone Arsenal 103-70-7. Benning had three teams in the tournament, accumulating 70 points for second place. "Doughboy Jim Brown, Cleveland Browns and All-American halfback from Syracuse, was high scorer with 15 1/2 points."

Jim Brown: College star, Service Sports star, and NFL star. One of the greatest athletes of all time. A complicated and flawed man, whose contributions to sport must be acknowledged. Can we separate personal behavior from athletic accomplishments? I'll let the reader decide.

Mr. Brown passed away in 2023 at age 87. Rest in Peace, soldier.

VIBRANT 1950s SERVICE SPORTS

1950s Service Sports were robust and vibrant, particularly when it came to military football. CONUS Service Sport football was attracting large crowds and offered enormous talent, but Far East football championship attendance exploded in 1958 with the availability of the then-new Japan National Stadium. The 1958 championship "Rice Bowl" game in the then-new stadium boosted attendance from 42,000 the previous year to an epic 78,000 fans who showed up in 1958 to witness the clash between Air Force and Army all-stars. It was the largest-ever football crowd outside of the continental United States up to that time (21).

Though Service Academies continued their football programs, and still thrive to this day, "football teams comprised of active-duty personnel (Service Sports) largely disappeared in the 1960s." The 1950s were indeed a special time for U. S. Military Service Sports programs.

FORT ORD MEETS LOS ANGELES RAMS, 1955

The 1953 Fort Ord football team was the top-rated service team in the nation (22), having won their 11th straight game by beating the Seattle Ramblers semi-pro team 28-0 in front of 9000 fans in the Queen City Bowl game. The great Ollie Matson had been virtually unstoppable that season, having heavily contributed to Ord's 402 points on the season, as opposed to their opponent's meager 43 points. "Matson had shown the fans why he was voted All-American, All-Pro, and All-Army."

Ord's Pro Backfield

THIS FORT ORD, Calif., backfield could be one of the greatest ever in service ball. From left: Jim Powers, former USC quarterback and safetyman for the San Francisco 49ers; Oregon State's Dave Mann, Army Times All-Army selection last year and now owned by the Chicago Cards; Oregon State's Sam Baker, with the Washington Redskins last year; and Ollie Matson, one of football's greatest players. Matson won All-American honors with the University of San Francisco, All-Pro honors with the Chicago Cards, and was named "most valuable player" on last year's Army Times All-Army team. Mann and Matson will be available to Ord for only part of the season.

Photo: Fort Ord Pro Backfield (before Matson's eligibility expired), 1954 Army Times (23).

Ord had earned the right to meet Great Lakes Navy on New Year's Day in the Salad Bowl in Phoenix, Arizona.

By the time 1955 rolled around, Ord had clearly established itself as a dominant force in Service Sports football. The Rams were in for a challenge, despite the absence of Matson, who had completed his military service and moved on to the pros.

On 30 July 1955, the Los Angeles Rams, led by quarterback Norm Van Brocklin, faced off against the mighty Ord Warriors, then led by quarterback Jimmy Powers, in Long Beach, CA.

Strong as they were, the Warriors were overmatched by the professional Rams team, falling 44-17 at Veterans Memorial Stadium.

Rams' history is detailed on their team website, noting that they had been a powerhouse in 1950, having amassed 5000 yards for the season, thanks in large part to quarterbacks Bob Waterfield and Van Brocklin (24).

Rams receiver Tom Fears set a record in 1950 with 84 pass receptions, and the Rams scored an astonishing 466 points on the season (including one game with 70 points on the board). Despite the impressive numbers, new-franchise Cleveland Browns sent the Rams home with a loss in the championship game by a two-point margin, 30-28.

The following year, however, the Rams reversed 1950 results by sending Cleveland packing with a 24-17 loss. A 73-yard Van Brocklin-to-Fears touchdown pass had decisively put the game out of reach for the Browns.

The Rams would go on to become one of the NFL's most storied franchises, though even in the 1950s they were a severe test even for the remarkable Fort Ord talent.

At the time of the Ord game, Dan Reeves was the Rams owner along with entertainer Bob Hope and others, and Sid Gillman was the head coach. Reserved-seat game tickets were a whopping $3.90.

OFFICIAL PROGRAM
PRICE 25¢
(Including Tax)

SATURDAY
JULY 30, 1955

JOIN
See Page 23

LOS ANGELES RAMS
VS
FORT ORD ARMY

In the Rams vs. Ord game program, short "Meet the Rams" biographies were offered, with Norm Van Brocklin's saying that he had been NFL passing champion or runner-up the previous five seasons. He passed for 554 yards in one game against the New York Yankees (yes, Yankees pro football). "The Van Brocklin-Bill Wade combination at quarterback provides the Rams with the greatest aerial one-two punch in professional football today."

The same section noted that Skeets Quinlan, Rams halfback, had been a Marine all-service halfback with the San Diego team.

Ord's complete roster included eight former professional players and all except one were former college football players.

The Rams/Ord game program included an article from sports columnist Dick Zehms of the *Press-Telegram*, who said that new Rams coach Gillman had come from the University of Cincinnati, and would receive "baptism under fire" in the game.

NEW RAM COACHING STAFF, left to right: Joe Madro, offensive line coach; Joe Thomas, defensive line coach; Sid Gillman, head coach; Lowell Storm, end coach; Jack Faulkner, backfield coach.

Fort Ord's Warriors were "no pushover," though this was the third annual game between the teams and the Rams had defeated the Warriors in the previous two games, 24-0 in 1953, and, from Ord's perspective, a respectable 34-13 in 1954.

The game program said that Ord did not care about Coach Gillman's past successes; they wanted a win, and they were a team on their way to a service championship.

> Uncle Sam's military gridders ... are not the ones to be awed by their opposition, for among them are players from the pro ranks ... Rudy Bukich, who at one stage of his post-college career was a Ram quarterback backing up "Dutch" Van Brocklin, is now pitching pigskins for the Warrior camp.

19

In the same game program, Dave Lewis of the *Long Beach Independent* and *Press-Telegram* said that the Rams would face the "star studded" Fort Ord Warriors in the "season's first major football game played in this country."

Mr. Lewis said that in past games the Rams had to deal with "the great Ollie Matson," who "in the past two games reeled off three of the greatest runs ever seen in this or any other stadium." He noted that Matson had since moved on to the NFL's Chicago Cardinals. Despite the loss of Matson, Fort Ord "once again is loaded with name stars, including nine pro aces and a host of topflight collegians."

Though Fort Ord fell to the Rams, they proved beyond doubt their Service Sports team was competitive at the highest level.

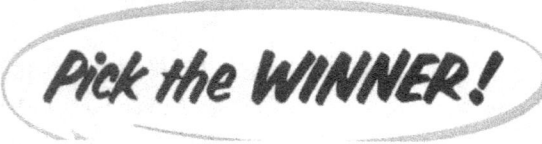

Los Angeles Rams' Halfback Paul (Tank) Younger cuts back for a good gain behind a wave of rough and ready Ram blockers. Today, keep your eyes on the speedy Ram backs and their hard-charging lines for top-notch football.

THE LOS ANGELES RAMS
(PROBABLE STARTING LINEUP)

No.	Name	Position
80	TOM FEARS	LE
73	BOB CROSS	LT
61	DUANE PUTNAM	LG
50	LEON McLAUGHLIN	C
63	JOHN HOCK	RG
70	CHARLEY TOOGOOD	RT
89	BOB LONG	RE
11	NORM VAN BROCKLIN	QB
21	SKEET QUINLAN	LH
82	BOB BOYD	RH
23	TOM McCORMICK	FB

The Ram Squad

3 Burroughs, qb	57 Paul, g
9 Wade, B., qb	58 Griffin, c
11 Van Brocklin, qb	61 Putnam, g
18 Clayton, hb	62 McFadin, t
20 Lewis, e	63 Hock, g
21 Quinlan, hb	64 West, g
22 Haynes, hb	65 Hauser, t
23 McCormick, fb	66 Thompson, g
24 Nygaard, hb	67 Richter, g
28 Meyers, hb	70 Toogood, t
29 Dwyer, hb	71 Dahms, t
31 Wade, D., hb	72 Ellena, g
32 Towler, fb	73 Cross, t
35 Younger, hb	74 Delavan, g
36 Stelle, hb	75 Fouch, t
41 Hoffman, fb	76 Svare, e
42 Bowers, hb	78 Lipscomb, t
43 Sherman, hb	79 Holtzman, t
46 Tharp, hb	80 Fears, e
47 Webb, hb	81 Miller, e
48 Taylor, hb	82 Boyd, e
49 Hughes, hb	84 Robustelli, e
50 McLaughlin, c	89 Long, e
55 Beatty, e	

THE FORT ORD WARRIORS
(PROBABLE STARTING LINEUP)

Nc.	Name	Position
..	RON MILLER	LE
..	GERALD PERRY	LT
..	CHARLES KAAIHUE	LG
..	JIM DUBLINSKI	C
..	GERALD BENN	RG
..	BOB PEVIANI	RT
..	DEWEY BRUNDAGE	RE
..	RUDY BUKICH	QB
..	PAUL CAMERON	LH
..	ALEX BURL	RH
..	SAM BAKER	FB

The Warrior Squad

15 Bills, hb	36 Nyman, g
16 Spence, hb	37 Kaaihue, g
17 Callahan, qb	38 Reinhart, qb
18 Amico, hb	39 Nix, e
19 Burl, hb	40 Baker, fb
20 Bukich, qb	41 Peviani, t
21 Hicks, qb	42 Benn, t
22 Braghetta, fb	43 Atthowe, e
24 Dutcher, g	44 Halladay, g
25 Powers, qb	45 Eberling, t
26 Wacholz, e	46 Miller, e
27 Standard, fb	47 Barnes, e
28 Foster, e	48 Jerome, t
29 Arias, g	49 Brundage, e
30 Dattola, hb	50 Dublinski, c
31 Kallem, g	51 Biglen, t
32 Rancatore, g	52 French, t
33 Reid, c	53 Grant, c
34 Cameron, hb	54 Perry, t
35 Whyte, fb	

FROM SERVICE FOOTBALL TO NFL

The New York Giants NFL franchise, among others, benefited immensely from Service football talent upon completion of their service obligations. Some had previously played in the NFL, and yet others had their NFL participation interrupted by a military draft.

NFL teams seen most often as destinations for Service stars included the Chicago Bears, the Cleveland Browns and the New York Giants. Close behind were the Philadelphia Eagles and Pittsburgh Steelers. The Chicago Cardinals had been Chicago's second team through the 50s, and they eventually morphed into today's Arizona Cardinals after leaving Chicago in 1959 (with an interim stop in St. Louis).

The NFL was considerably smaller in the 1950s (though this suggests teams had the luxury of being more selective in who they chose to fill their rosters); the existing teams were: Baltimore Colts, Chicago Bears, Chicago Cardinals, Cleveland Browns, Detroit Lions, Green Bay Packers, Los Angeles Rams, New York Giants, New York Yanks, Philadelphia Eagles, Pittsburgh Steelers, Washington Redskins, Dallas Texans, and the San Francisco 49ers (25).

Many of the below-named service stars had been All-Army first or second team, All-Service, or Service Sports Tournament MVPs. They were the cream of the crop of service football. Note: Some played for multiple teams; this is not an exhaustive list.

The Giants drafted, acquired, or made offers to service stars such as Rosey Grier (1955), Yale Lary, Hal Mitchell, Joe Ramona, Leo Miles, Charlie Maloy, John McMullen, Alex Litman, and Don Heinrich (1954), among others.

The Browns picked up or made offers to service stars such as Bolling ace Tommy O'Connell, Bob "Tiny" Goss, Bill Quinlan, Jim Greer, Bill Rayfield, Willie Davis, Phil Stewart, Curry Juneau, Don Shula, Frank Catski, Ed Soergel, Jim Brown (*first player chosen, 1957*), and others.

23

The Chicago Bears amassed talent such as Jim Dooley (*first player selected, 1952*), Zeke Bratkowski, Rick Casares, Joe Ryan, Lee Hermsen, Ted Daffer (*roster 1954*), and others.

CHICAGO CARDINALS

Sept. 6 at Seattle—2:00 P.M.

Coach: Frank Ivy

Pub. Director: Ed McGuire

Nov. 30 at Chicago—1:05 P.M.

Home Field: Comiskey Park

1957 Record: W 3 L 9

1958 Schedule
Sept. 28 Giants (At Buffalo, N.Y.)
Oct. 4 'Skins (H)
Oct. 12 Browns (A)
Oct. 19 Giants (A)
Oct. 26 Browns (H)
Nov. 2 Eagles (H)
Nov. 9 'Skins (A)
Nov. 16 Eagles (A)
Nov. 23 Steelers (H)
Nov. 30 Rams (H)
Dec. 7 Bears (A)
Dec. 13 Steelers (A)

Top Scorers: Ollie Matson—*(10th-T) 54 pts., 9 TDs.
Pat Summerall—(15th-T) 42 pts., 24 XPs, 6 FGs.

Top Runners: Ollie Matson—(6th) 134 atts., 577 yds., 4.3 avg.
Johnny Olszewski—(32nd) 83 atts., 271 yds., 3.3 avg.

Top Passers: Lamar McHan—(5th) 200 atts., 87 comp., 1568 yds., 10 TDs.
Ted Marchibroda—(19th) 45 atts., 15 comp., 238 yds., 1 TD.

Top Receivers: Gern Nagler—(20th) 27 for 475 yds., 4 TDs.
Woodley Lewis—(30th) 21 for 424 yds., 5 TDs.

*(NFL Finish)

The Colts acquired Dick Szymanski (All-Army) in 1955, and Heisman winner Billy Vessels was picked up in 1956 (Note: Vessels had initially been drafted in 1953). Great Lakes star Bernie Flowers was also on the Colts' roster in 1956.

Steelers talent included George Tarasovich, Paul Cameron, Bob Luna, Jack Stephans, and others. The Eagles boasted stars such as John Michels, Don Holleder, John Bredice, Winifred Tillery, Ollie Matson, and others.

The Rams acquired "Big Daddy" Lipscomb in 1953, and in 1956, the Colts picked him up for "the $100 waiver price" (25).

The St. Louis Cardinals made Ollie Matson the first player chosen in 1952; "Matson was an Olympic medalist and a spectacular halfback from the University of San Francisco" (25), but Matson entered the Army just before the 1953 NFL season.

24

GENE LIPSCOMB Tackle 6'6" 288 Miller (Det.) High

A rare bargain picked up on waivers from the Los Angeles Rams in 1956, "Big Daddy" jumped into the defensive lineup immediately and has been a solid rock in the Colts' line. He broke in as a defensive end with the Rams in 1953 and might possibly be shifted to a linebacking spot this fall to take advantage of his wide range . . . he led the team with 135 tackles, 54 more than the number two man. One of the few pros to make the grade without college experience, he played two seasons in the Marine Corps at Camp Pendleton. Now lives in Baltimore. Born: August 9, 1931.

In *Giants Among Men* (26), author Jack Cavanaugh said that Tommy O'Connell's play with the Browns surprised the Giants in their 9 December 1956 meeting in Yankee Stadium in unruly weather, which included rain and snow, limiting fan turnout to 27,707.

> O'Connell surprised the Giants with his play in the 24-7 victory. A journeyman at best, he had been a backup quarterback with the Bears during his rookie year of 1953, but then served the next two years in the army (sic) during the Korean War (*Ed. – post Korean War*). When he returned in 1956, he was cut by the Bears owner and coach on the grounds that, at five-feet-ten, O'Connell was too short to play quarterback. Apparently Papa Bear Halas got the impression that O'Connell had shrunk during his military service, since he was still the same height as when he had played with the Bears in 1953.

Despite the challenging conditions, O'Connell surpassed the Giant's expectations. O'Connell had been the third quarterback of the Browns' season, following loss of George Ratterman and Babe Parilli to injuries. The Browns were 10 ½ point underdogs, but "to the astonishment of the small crowd," the Browns outplayed the Giants and handing them a decisive defeat. "He was amazing," Paul Brown said of O'Connell. "He was calm and poised throughout the game."

One would have to conclude that O'Connell had honed his skills and gained enough confidence with his military football experience to bring the fruits of that improvement back to the NFL.

25

What a different time it was. Author Cavanaugh wrote that when the 1956 season ended, Giants players left New York and headed home to attend to their "off-season jobs." Sam Huff would bag groceries in a local market. Frank Gifford, the man who had just finished fifth in the league in rushing, first in rushing-yards-per-carry, and third in receiving, would sell insurance. Other players went home to similar mundane jobs. For perspective, Redskins players averaged $8000 per year salary - more than Army wages, but less than other careers.

The Giants were 1956 NFL champions, and all players would return to the team except two - one being Rosey Grier, who was drafted into the Army, though he had been expected back in a year or so. His position was to be filled by the capable Jim Katcavage, but his absence would be felt, continued author Cavanaugh. "He may have ballooned to over 300 pounds during the 1956 season, but even so he was remarkably fast and nimble."

Jim Katcavage   **Dayton**   **22**   **230**   **6'3"**

Katcavage is a four-star football player who may become one of the greats of the game. As a rookie last year he filled in at either defensive end and at tackle. A real crasher, nightmare to enemy passers. May be shifted to defensive tackle this season. Has just completed six months active Army service. No. 4 draft pick, 1956. Single. Home town Philadelphia. Birthday, Oct. 28.

Sam Huff said Grier was as fast as any lineman who played the game. He could catch fast runners, and "when he set his mind to getting the quarterback, not many linemen could stop him." Despite his ferocity on the field, Grier was known to be gentle off the field and he kept teammates entertained. He would be missed during his absence from the Giants, but little did they know his skills would not deteriorate, thanks to Army football.

There was a Paul "Bear" Bryant connection to service sports and the NFL through his popular overseas service football clinics in 1955, along with Maryland's coach, Jim Tatum, and Michigan State's Hugh Daugherty (27); Bryant helped some service football players reach their NFL dreams.

Bryant had coached at Alabama, Kentucky, Maryland and Texas A&M, and of course he encountered some players who would also experience participation in Service Sports. One such player was Bob Fry, who played under Coach Bryant at Kentucky, and ultimately ended up in the NFL.

The original Fearsome Foursome—Robustelli, Modzelewski, Katcavage, and Grier—coming off the field after another patented goal-line stand for the Giants.
DIAMOND IMAGES

Photo: Giants Among Men (26).

Bob Fry was born on 11 November 1930 in Cincinnati, Ohio, and passed away on 10 November 2019 in Wilmington, North Carolina. He was a natural athlete, and his talents were recognized early, earning him a scholarship at the University of Kentucky to play football for Coach Bryant following his high school graduation in 1949.

Bryant's Wildcats were good - really good. In 1950, Kentucky earned a place in the Sugar Bowl (back when bowl games *really* meant something, as there weren't as many of them) and beat Oklahoma 13-7. Fry entered at the right time; he immediately became a member of a national championship team.

Fry's athleticism allowed him to perform double-duty by playing with the Kentucky basketball freshman team, alongside Naismith Hall of Famers Cliff Hagen and Frank Ramsey (28).

Bob played football in the Cotton Bowl Classic, and had twice been named All-SEC. Coach Bryant named Fry to his All-Time Team, according to Fry's obituary.

The L.A. Rams drafted Fry out of college in 1953 at the tackle position. Fry was traded to the Cowboys in 1960, where he was the first tackle to start for the new team. He retired from professional football in 1964 with a solid professional record, though his desire to be around football continued, leading him to become a line coach for the Falcons, Steelers and Jets.

Interestingly, Fry's obituary, though detailed, is silent as to his military service, however, *Army Times* reported on 9 October 1954 that Bob Fry, "with the Los Angeles Rams," had played football for Fort Monmouth in New Jersey (29).

The article reported that Fry's Monmouth Signaleers opened their (home) 1954 season with a matchup against PhibLant (Little Creek) Gators at Greely Field in front of 7000 fans. Monmouth was victorious, with a 15-7 win over the Gators.

```
1954  (5-6-0)
9/     scrimmage        Bainbridge Naval Base
9/11   scrimmage     at Upsala College
9/18   W 46-13       at Ashland Miners (at Pottsville, Pa.) (pro)  4,000 (exhibition) (benefit)
10/1   W 15-7           Little Creek Amphibs (Norfolk) (H)  7,000
10/8   W 13-7           Fort Eustis (H) (night)  5,500
10/15  L 13-20          Parris Island Marines (H) (night)
10/23  L  7-22       at Fort Belvoir Engineers, Pullen Field  6,500
10/29  L  0-28       at Fort Lee (Va.) at Nowak Field  5,500
11/5   W 26-0        at Parris Island, Donohue Field
11/12  L 18-38          Bolling A.F.B. (H) (night)  5,500
11/20  W  7-2        at Camp Le Jeune
11/25  L  7-40       at Quantico Marines, Butler Stadium, Washington, D.C.
12/4   L 14-32          Fort Belvoir (H)
```

Photo: Fort Monmouth 1954 football schedule/results (30).

Don Ervin from Tennessee Tech scored a touchdown for Monmouth, which broke a tie near the end of the game. Bob Fry had blocked a Little Creek punt and recovered the ball on the opposing ten yard line; two plays later, Ervin ran it in from the eight yard line to put the game away.

Not only was Fry a talented athlete, he was a service sports and NFL star who was also a humble and good family man.

Rest in Peace, hero.

FORT CARSON SPORTS, 1950s

The Fort Carson, 9th Infantry Division, 1955, yearbook provides a history of the fort's "Treasured Heritage" (31).

Ground had been broken on the site of the new Camp Carson one month post-Pearl Harbor. The property followed along the Rocky Mountains for 16 miles, with varying widths. The total property size was approximately 60,000 acres. Colorado Springs had purchased and sold the property to the Federal Government for $1. The namesake of the facility was renowned frontiersman and later Brigadier General, Kit Carson.

The Army had chosen the site due to its ideal training location, considering both topography and weather. The initial unit based at Carson was the 89th Division. 104,165 soldiers spent time at Camp Carson during WWII. Later, many soldiers left the camp for Korea, but "thousands more poured in for basic training."

Camp Carson officially became a Fort and a permanent installation in August 1954, with the redesignation retroactive to July 1.

Fort Carson played an outsized role in Service Sports in the 1950s, and is an important part of that history. Today, Fort Carson is home to the Fourth Infantry Division and the 10th Special Forces Group (Airborne), in addition to other important units.

1950s CARSON SPORTS EXCELLENCE

The 5 April 1958 *Army Times* edition reported (32) that Fort Carson Mountaineers had finished a strong season in basketball, with a 25-4 win/loss record, and three of those losses were to the mighty Fort Leonard Wood team.

Carson averaged an impressive 95.9 points per game.

Carson stars included guard, Les Roh, and forward, George Altman. Roh was a former Idaho State star, and he averaged 17.3 PPG in the service league. Altman, from Tennessee State, was close behind with 16.3 PPG. Other strong contributors for Carson included Bruce Brothers, Burke Scott, and Jay Jackson.

Going back in time, *Army Times* of 22 December 1956 (33) informed us that Carson basketball lost nine players due to new assignments or release from service. The nine included Dick Marning, Paul Covington, Ray Chess, Evans Tracey, William Johnson, John Funes, Don Vickers, Bob Hill, and Howard Johnson. Coach Don Snyder, however, wasn't "crying the blues," as four newcomers, including Altman, would pick up the slack.

The four newcomers included Altman, Bruce Brothers from Illinois, Jay Jackson from Stanford, and Tom Robinson from Allen University.

Altman was not only a basketball star; he also excelled in baseball at Carson. 4 May 1957 *Army Times* (34) reported that Carson's baseball team had fallen to the Pueblo Dodgers of the Class A Western League, despite George Altman's magnificent performance; "Hitting star" Altman "crashed out a homer, triple and single," giving Altman nine hits in Carson's first three contests.

The 20 July 1957 *Army Times* reported that the Carson nine were a powerful team with outstanding pitching, and Carson would be ready to defend their title in the September 1957 Fifth Army tournament. Carson had run up eleven straight wins with 183 runs and a .442 team batting average - allowing only 27 earned runs.

Carson star Ed Kopacz had 12 hits in 19 at-bats, and worked hard for his .632 batting average; "The 6'3" third baseman belongs to the New York Giants." At the same time, first baseman Altman racked up a .490 hitting average, with 17 RBIs; he led the team in triples, with three.

The 1957 Fort Carson baseball roster included Carlos Ramos, Phil Hirnyk, Jim Balzcci, Gabby Picone, Ace Robinson, J.C. Hartman, Bob Smith, Jack Vandersee, Leon Wagner, Charley Pride, Art Watson, Orval Bowman, Mike Garbeck, John Spiller, Bob Ruck, Willie Kirkland, Jim Applegate, Joe Jordan, Cecil Isaacs, Earl Higgins, John Ramsey, Ed Kopacz, Bill Lee, George Altman, Coach Chris Dubia, and Manager, Capt. Bill Lackey.

Fort Carson was the best team in the Fifth Army in 1957, according to the 21 September 1957 *Army Times* (35), and they won the Fifth Army Crown on the backs of great pitching by Cecil Isaacs and Carlos Ramos.

Carson had been rocked by Fort Leonard Wood in the first game of the tournament, but recovered their poise, defeating Fort Riley 16-1, and then Wood again, twice, 5-4 and 2-0. The Fort Leonard Wood Hilltoppers managed only four hits in the final game while Carson played "errorless" ball.

In the first victory over Wood, pitcher Art Watson started, but was relieved by Charley Pride in the eighth, with two men on and one out; "Pride was greeted by two straight hits, bringing the score to 5-4. Ramos then came in and struck out the next two batters and the side in the ninth to seal the win."

Though Charley Pride was not a starter for Carson, he managed a robust and varied post-service baseball career before he became one of the most famous country singers in history.

Mr. Pride's obituary (36) says that even though he loved music, his lifelong dream was to become a professional baseball player. He certainly ended up being very accomplished in both fields by the time of his passing in 2020 at the age of 86; in the 1970s he was second in record sales, trailing only Elvis Presley, and earned his way into the Country Music Hall of Fame.

Pride had been born in 1934 in Sledge, Mississippi, to a family of sharecroppers. Prior to the Army he pitched for the Memphis Red Sox of the Negro American League, and in 1953 he signed with the Class C farm team of the New York Yankees, the Boise Yankees.

Pride had a keen sense of humor. He and teammate Jesse Mitchell were traded to the Birmingham Black Barons for a team bus; "Jesse and I may have the distinction of being the only players in history to be traded for a used motor vehicle."

Pride kept the dream alive by pitching for several minor league teams, but then he was drafted into the Army in 1956. Following basic training, he was stationed at Fort Carson where he played alongside George Altman and others.

Carson had a strong team that year, and, with Pride, they won the All-Army Sports Championship.

Pride rejoined the Memphis Red Sox upon his completion of Army service, but was hampered by an injured pitching arm. Despite more farm-team work and tryouts, he was unable to make it to the big leagues in baseball, though he succeeded beyond his wildest imagination in music – making the Country Music Hall of Fame in 2000, and cementing his place in history as a musical legend and Great American.

Rest in Peace, hero.

Les Roh's obituary (37) says he had been born in 1933 and that he passed away in 2007. He was a four-year letterman at Idaho State, and graduated in 1956. He still holds the school's all-time basketball scoring record.

Mr. Roh led Idaho State to four consecutive conference championships and four NCAA tournament berths. He was inducted into the Idaho State Hall of Fame and Ring of Honor. He played professional basketball for the Syracuse Nationals and the Caterpillar Cats. The article briefly noted his basketball participation with Fort Carson. He went on to coach and teach following his playing days. Rest in Peace, hero.

George Altman also had an interesting sports trajectory, having transitioned from basketball to professional baseball. A 2019 interview with Douglas Malan of *Black College Nines* sheds some light on his athletics story (38).

Mr. Altman grew up in Goldsboro, North Carolina, and, at 6-foot-4, 200 pounds, was "an imposing figure on the basketball court and baseball fields."

His college, Tennessee State University, didn't initially have a baseball team, so he tried his hand at basketball until a baseball program was added by the college in his junior year. This addition would change the course of his athletic career.

> Mr. Altman became a major league baseball player after college, fashioning a nine-year pro career with the Cubs, Cardinals and Mets as an outfielder and first baseman. He was a three-time All-Star and a career .269 hitter with 101 HRs, 403 RBI, 409 runs scored and 52 stolen bases. He increased those numbers playing professional baseball in Japan until the age of 42.

When the baseball program was established at Tennessee State, they would play against "Army bases" and Negro League teams, including the Birmingham Barons. He was awed to play against strong players like Willie Wells and Doc Dennis, and "we held our own against them."

After graduation he played baseball with the Kansas City Monarchs for coach Buck O'Neil. He made the lineup and ended up signing with the Cubs, but after a year in the minors, "I had to go into military service for a couple years."

Following his military service, he signed a Triple-A contract, and "the rest is history." He played alongside greats like Ron Santo, Lou Brock, Billy Williams, and Ernie Banks. After several years at the professional level, with St. Louis, New York, and Chicago, he went to Japan, where he said things were more relaxed and there was less racial tension.

Following his playing days, he had a successful career in business as a commodity trader.

On 19 March 2023, writer Anthony Castrovince claimed that Altman may have played baseball in more organized leagues than anybody in history (39). He noted the "uniquely diverse" trajectory of Altman's athletic career, having played baseball for the Cubs, Cardinals and Mets; Negro Leagues; Japanese

Pacific League; Army leagues; college ball; and Panamanian and Cuban winter leagues. He once even homered off Sandy Koufax twice in a single game.

Mr. Altman had an amazingly interesting career in sports and business, a great example of the American spirit.

Photo: George Altman baseball card, 1967.

HISTORIC DOUGHBOY STADIUM, FT. BENNING

Photo: Doughboy Stadium, Fort Benning, year unknown, Credit: Anthony J. Martinez (40).

Doughboy Stadium hosted some powerful football teams in front of large numbers of enthusiastic service football fans in the mid-1950s. In 1955, for example, the home team upset the powerful Fort Jackson Eagles in front of a packed house, with 10,000 in attendance (41). By this time, the stadium had already been around for thirty years.

In the game, Jackson's Eagles had struggled for favorable field position and were not able to find their rhythm. Jackson only moved the ball into Benning territory once, in the third quarter, but that would not be their biggest problem of the day – Jackson's quarterback, Hal Ledyard, sustained a broken leg in the first quarter (*details were not provided*). To make matters worse, Jackson subsequently lost two more quarterbacks to injury and was missing their first-string running backs, Tommy Lewis and Neil Worden. Starring for Benning

36

were quarterback Yale Lary (he played both ways, also intercepting a pass on defense), halfback Eddie Crooks, and end, Ernie Stockert.

Yale Lary was the real deal. He was inducted into the Pro Football Hall of Fame in the Class of 1979 based on five All-NFL selections, fifty interceptions, and nine Pro Bowls - all of which occurred in eleven seasons.

"I happened to like the era in which I played. I liked the close knit family atmosphere of the Detroit Lions. There were only 33 players then, and we felt like a family, from the front office down. That aspect of the game has changed and I'm not sure I like it."

Lary was known by fans as a great punter, a breakaway punt returner, and a superb right safety. The Texas A&M alum was clearly multi-talented, and therefore a significant asset for a service team in a time in which players often filled multiple positions in a game.

Second Lion Regular, Lary, Gets Army Call

The champion Detroit Lions learned Thursday that ace defensive halfback Yale Lary will enter the service June 1.

General Manager Nick Kerbawy said Lary received an ROTC commission while a student at Texas A&M and must report for duty as a second lieutenant at Ft. Benning, Ga.

Lary is the second top player lost by Detroit to Uncle Sam since the Lions won their second straight NFL title last December.

Gene Gedman, a freshman offensive halfback from Indiana, was drafted Feb. 24.

Photo: Yale Lary (#28) with the Detroit Lions (43).

Lary was not large in stature, 5-11, 185 pounds, but what he lacked in size he made up for with a big heart and great ability. Author Jack Cavanaugh, in *Giants Among Men*, described Lary as "one of the NFL's most versatile players" (26).

Lary later became a Texas State Legislator and a businessman, and was known for his contributions to sports and public service.

Rest in Peace, hero.

AUTHOR'S 2025 DOUGHBOY STADIUM VISIT

I visited Fort Benning on 25 October 2025, and saw first-hand the classically-designed and iconic Doughboy Stadium, which is situated inside Fort Benning, just south of Columbus, Georgia. The stadium is situated in a quiet neighborhood on the western end of the installation property, not far from the

National Infantry Museum and the Chattahoochee River. It was a perfect fall day.

Upon arriving at Doughboy Stadium in the warm sun, I discovered it was virtually empty, save for one soldier exercising on the track. A family had just arrived, preparing to enjoy some time inside the stadium walking the track which surrounds the field while their children played on the grass.

It wasn't hard to imagine the sights, smells, and sounds of a filled-to-capacity stadium in the 1950s, the crowd buzzing with excitement and anticipation for the big game on a beautiful autumn day, while the announcer's voice over loudspeakers echoed across the surrounding leafy neighborhoods.

The stadium appeared to be well-maintained and had a very distinctive design, using stuccoed arches which connected short towers on the corners. There are bleachers on the north and south sides, and the east side was open. The arched entrance is on the west side.

Doughboy Stadium is not just a stadium, it is a timeless memorial to fallen soldiers of WWI. Construction began in November of 1924, and the stadium was dedicated 17 October 1925.

Figure 242. Fort Benning Doughboy Stadium, 6 Sep 1939 (NARA 342-FH Box 1059 3B-17283).

Photo: Historic Doughboy Stadium, 1939 (44).

A $1.5 million Doughboy "facelift" was completed in 2012, according to the *Ledger-Enquirer* newspaper (45). The remodel had been funded by the Directorate of Family, Morale, Welfare, and Recreation department in anticipation of an upcoming scrimmage game against West Point. The game would have been the first time the traditional Benning/West Point meeting had occurred outside of New York.

"The Doughboys earned a reputation by playing teams from the universities of Florida, Georgia, and Alabama." Benning football was dominant to the extent they finished their season undefeated in 1962.

Stadium upgrades had been purposed to "revive football" at Benning, which had gone without a Post team for several decades, starting in the 1980s, due to a new emphasis on intramural sports.

Upgrade projects included new lighting, speakers, locker room updating, and painting. I'm pleased to report that today's Doughboy Stadium is in fine shape.

Interestingly, the 1926 Doughboys had an assistant coach named Dwight D. Eisenhower, who went on, of course, to become one of the greatest Army generals and a two-time president of the United States.

A 1936 Doughboy yearbook described the facility: "Doughboy Stadium, named in honor of the foot soldier, encircles a football field and track whose suitability are exceeded only by the beauty of the structure itself" (46).

Former Auburn football coach (1981-1992) and Fort Benning ROTC "Doughboy," Pat Dye, wrote on 19 September 2013 of his "Memorable Day at Doughboy Stadium" (47).

Dye said he played service football at Fort Benning in 1963 and 1964 (*though another account says he had led the team to their 1962 undefeated season*). Dye had returned to Benning to be honored as a former Doughboy player, and his thoughts reflected a fondness for his time spent there:

> Doughboy Stadium is a beautiful little facility. It holds about 10,000 folks and there was a big crowd for the event. To be around the Soldiers in their uniforms, the men and women, and honor some of our heroes while I was there made it a special day ... I was fortunate to get the opportunity to talk to the players, coaches, Soldiers, and

Lt. Gen. Robert Brown, who was the commanding officer at Fort Benning …

We won the service championship in 1964 … I was fortunate enough to be named service player of the year (and) met coach (Bear) Bryant …

Playing for the Doughboys is a good memory. I enjoyed my two and a half years in the service. I played football for about four months of the year, and I served in the mechanized infantry … it would make you proud to be an American being around those soldiers and support people on post.

It's notable and remarkable that Fort Benning respected their illustrious past enough to preserve this gem of a stadium which has withstood the test of time in memory of war heroes from days gone by. Modern and historical photos from Fort Benning are included as follows for reference.

Photo: Fort Benning welcome sign, 2025. Author photo ©.

Photo: Doughboy Stadium interior, Fort Benning, 2025. Author photo ©.

Photo: Doughboy Stadium welcome sign, Fort Benning, 2025. Author photo ©.

Photo: Doughboy Stadium overview, Fort Benning, 2025. Author photo ©.

Photo: 2d Lt. Matt Trout running PT, Fort Benning, 2025. Author photo ©.

Figure 31. Fort Benning Interior of New gymnasium at 4th Div area, 2 Nov 1942 (NARA 111-SC Box 24 124389).

Photo: Fort Benning, "New" gymnasium from 1942 (44).

Figure 71. Fort Ber officers' club from Sep 1939 (NARA 3 Box 1059 3B-172£

Photo: Fort Benning officer's club, 1939 (44).

ARMY TIMES ALL-ARMY FOOTBALL POLLS

The *Army Times* All-Army football poll was inaugurated in 1950. Following is discussion of polls from 1954 to 1958, which was post-Korean War Armistice and a very robust time for Service Sports football, especially since more athletes were available to service teams in peacetime. Other athletes entered the service at this time, either through enlistment or draft, sometimes interrupting college or professional sports careers. All of this activity benefitted military Service Sports in the mid-1950s.

The *Army Times* was diligent about the process of selecting players for the All-Army first, second, and sometimes third teams or honorable mentions. Football coaches, sports writers, and sometimes other players and sometimes the public, voted on the players they felt best exemplified the excellence standard of the All-Army designation. Their methodology was transparent, and the polls appear to have been professionally conducted.

If All-Army polls were an accuracy-test of player's abilities and contributions to the sport, it was a remarkable success. Many All-Army picks, no matter first or second team, or even honorable mention, ended up in successful careers in big-time college or professional sports. Many names may already be familiar to you.

Army Times' detailed their approach to selections:

> We hope that voters will not overlook the player who was not a "big name" star in college or pro ball. In the past, several "unknowns" have won All-Army recognition … The important thing, of course, is how good a player is in Army ball.

> The player with the most press clippings is not necessarily the most ball player (sic) in the Army. We hope that the real standouts in Army football, whether they were known for their football activity before they entered the Army or not, will be the … All-Army players (48).

45

USAREUR title clash between the 6th RCT Unicorns and the undefeated 28th Special Troopers ends with Troopers losing the decision and the 1952 title.

1954 *ARMY TIMES* ALL-ARMY FOOTBALL POLL

Army Times' All-Army Football Poll results were announced 11 December 1954 by columnist Tom Scanlon (49). This was the fourth-annual team selected, and the surprise was that a lineman was selected for MVP. Mr. Scanlon said, "It's about time such an honor went to a lineman," as the basic functions of football include blocking and tackling.

The MVP selection, Hal Mitchell, out of Fort Lee, Virginia, was a UCLA alum who had been under pro rights of the New York Giants. Mitchell was in good company, sharing a position on the All-Army First Team with Heisman Trophy winner Billy Vessels, Buck McPhail out of the University of Oklahoma (pro rights with Colts), George Tarasovich out of LSU (pro rights with Steelers), John Michels out of Tennessee (pro rights with Eagles), and others.

Mitchell shared tackle-position First Team honors with Len Deutscher out of Michigan State.

Mitchell was captain of the Fort Lee Travellers, and this was his second year earning the All-Army designation. The 235-pound Mitchell, however, had not been able to overcome the great Ollie Matson the previous year for the MVP designation.

Tarasovich, an end, was described as a good pass receiver and one of Fort Belvoir's fastest linemen, despite weighing 240 pounds. Fort Carson's Dan McBride was highly respected by his opponents as a tough end who scored 12 touchdowns during the season. He set an Iowa receiving record despite his light weight of 185 pounds. Scanlon added that McBride had no plans to play pro football.

Second-teamer Winifred Tillery was described as a four-year letterman at North Carolina who caught 27 passes for 732 yards for the powerful Brooke Medical Center team out of Fort Sam Houston, Texas. Despite his average of twenty yards per catch, he had not yet committed to a pro team.

Also from the Second Team was Stan Wacholz, whose season with the San Francisco 49ers was interrupted by his service obligation. He was considered to be one of the best offensive ends ever to play with Fort Ord, and that is no small feat.

John Michels was referred to as the "hustling guard and co-captain of Fort Eustis Wheels," who starred at Tennessee and played for the Eagles for a year prior to his service (Mr. Michels would go on to become the highly regarded, longest-serving assistant football coach in Minnesota Vikings history).

47

Center Bob Lusk of William and Mary beat out Jim Dooley for starting center at Fort Lee. He was 6' 2" and 210 pounds, and was not assigned to any pro team.

Quarterback selection Jim Powers held the rank of private at Fort Ord, but he was a general on the field. He had been a "three-year man" with Southern Cal and a veteran of four years with the San Francisco 49ers. His passing completion average was 50 percent.

Second Team quarterback Don Engels backed up Tommy O'Connell at Illinois in 1950 and 1951. He put Illinois in the Rose Bowl by defeating Wisconsin with a victory-clinching scoring pass. Engels was a clutch performer for Fort Belvoir and had previously been owned by the Chicago Cardinals, though he was at the time a free agent.

The marvelous Billy Vessels was a First Team halfback, former Oklahoma All-American and Heisman Trophy winner, as previously noted. The "fast and elusive" Vessels scored nine touchdowns in nine games with Fort Sill. He also competently contributed as a passer and defender.

The immensely talented Rick Casares was placed on the Second Team, but only because he had been competing with such a worthy opponent as Coleman "Buck" McPhail for the spot. To this day, Casares is *still* the number four all-time Chicago Bears rusher, with superstar Walter Payton being number one. Casares is on the all-time list ahead of such luminaries as Gale Sayers, Bronko Nagurski, and Bobby Douglass.

Casares was All-State, All-Southern, and All-American out of Tampa, Florida. Not only was he a star in football, but he also excelled in basketball at the University of Florida, supporting his wide-ranging athletic prowess.

The All-Army Selection Group included coaches of Army post teams, including Brooke Medical Center, Fort Ord, Fort Lewis, Fort Carson, Fort Eustice, Fort Leonard Wood, Fort Devens, Fort Hood, Fort Meade, Fort Monmouth, Fort Sill, Fort Jackson, Fort Lee, and Fort Belvoir.

Various sports writers including Tom Scanlon and thirty-two coaches from regimental leagues contributed to selections. The regimental leagues were based out of Fort Campbell, Fort Bragg, Fort Riley, Fort Dix, and Fort Benning.

Rick Casares, invaluable to the Bears, is not only tough, but very speedy. He can go at top speed indefinitely

Photo: Army All-Star and Chicago Bear, Rick Casares, 1958 (14).

The 1954 All-Army football selections were as follows:

1954 FIRST TEAM

- ✓ End, **Dan McBride**, Fort Carson, College: Iowa, 6' 1", 185 lbs, Age 23, Hometown: Burlington, Iowa.
- ✓ End, **George Tarasovich**, Fort Belvoir, College: LSU, Pro Rights: Steelers, 6' 4", 240 lbs, Age 24, Hometown: Bridgeport, Connecticut.
- ✓ Tackle, **Hal Mitchell**, Fort Lee, College: UCLA, Pro Rights: Giants, 6' 1", 235 lbs, Hometown: Lawndale, California.
- ✓ Tackle, **Len Deutscher**, Fort Lewis, College: Michigan State, 6' 4", 245 lbs, Age 24, Hometown: Michigan City, Indiana.
- ✓ Guard, **Rudy Feldman**, Fort Hood, College: UCLA, 6' 0", 198 lbs, Age: 22, Hometown: Palo Alto, California.

49

- ✓ Guard, **John Michels**, Fort Eustis, College: Tennessee, Pro Rights: Eagles, 5' 11", 200 lbs, Age: 23, Hometown: Philadelphia, Pennsylvania.
- ✓ Center, **Bob Lusk**, Fort Lee, College: William and Mary, 6' 0", 210 lbs, Age: 22, Hometown: Williamson, West Virginia.
- ✓ Quarterback, **Jim Powers**, Fort Ord, College: USC, Pro Rights: 49ers, 6' 0", 195 lbs, Age: 26, Hometown: Beverly Hills, California.
- ✓ Halfback, **Billy Vessels**, Fort Sill, College: Oklahoma, Pro Rights: Edmunton (sic), 6' 0", 195 lbs, Age: 22, Hometown: Cleveland, Ohio.
- ✓ Halfback, **Bobby Haner**, Fort Belvoir, College: Villanova, Pro Rights: Redskins, 5' 10", 195 lbs, Age: 23, Hometown: Philadelphia, Pennsylvania.
- ✓ Fullback, **Buck McPhail**, Fort Sill, College: Oklahoma, Pro Rights: Colts, 6' 0", 200 lbs, Age: 22, Hometown: Oklahoma City, Oklahoma.

1954 SECOND TEAM

- ✓ End, **Winifred Tillery**, Brooke Medical, College: NC State College, 6' 0", 180 lbs, Age: 21, Hometown: Morehead City, North Carolina.
- ✓ End, **Stan Wacholz**, Fort Ord, College: San Jose State, Pro Rights: 49ers, 6' 2", 207 lbs, Age: 22, Hometown: San Jose, California.
- ✓ Tackle, **Frank Monti**, Fort Carson, College: University of San Francisco, 6' 2", 225 lbs, Age: 22, Hometown: Minersville, Pennsylvania.
- ✓ Tackle, **Bob (Tiny) Goss**, Brooke Medical, College: SMU, Pro Rights: Browns, 6' 5", 260 lbs, Age 21, Hometown: Dallas, Texas.
- ✓ Guard, **Joe Martone**, Fort Monmouth, College: Tennessee, 5' 11", 240 lbs, Age: 26, Hometown: Glen Cove, New York.
- ✓ Guard, **Joe Ramona**, Fort Sill, College: Santa Clara, Pro Rights: Giants, 6' 0", 210 lbs, Age 24, San Jose, California.
- ✓ Center, **Jimmy Johnson**, Fort Jackson, College: Georgia Tech, 5' 11", 190, Age: 23, Hometown: Knoxville, Tennessee.
- ✓ Quarterback, **Don Engels**, Fort Belvoir, College: Illinois, 6' 2", 192 lbs, Age: 23, Hometown: Chicago, Illinois.
- ✓ Halfback, **Leo Miles**, Fort Lee, College: Virginia State, Pro Rights: Giants, 6' 1", 204 lbs, Age 23, Hometown: Washington, D.C.

50

- ✓ Halfback, **Billy Sanders**, Brooke Medical, College: Southwest Texas, 5' 8", 165 lbs, Age: 24, Hometown: Hillsboro, Texas.
- ✓ Fullback, **Rick Casares**, Fort Jackson, College: University of Florida, Pro Rights: Bears, 6' 2", 220 lbs, Age: 22, Hometown: Tampa, Florida.

Commentary on selected players:

From PFC Larry Cahn, *Fort Ord Panorama*:

Jim Powers – *"Master of offensive strategy. The players know that whatever the opposing defense sets for them they will have to stop something different. Powers has driven foes crazy with his play calling."*

From Cpl. Sy Roseman, Sports Publicist, Belvoir:

Bob Haner – *"Haner's ability knows no ends. He never rests, does everything, and has been a wonderful asset to his teammates. One of the club's leading ground-gainers, fine extra point and field goal kicker. Makes an excellent pass receiver and does all the punting. To add, he's the best defensive back on the Engineers."*

From Sgt. Bill Hogan, Sports Publicity, Carson:

Ed Soergel (Third team) – *"For the first half of the Sill game Nov. 7, before he was injured, Soergel was by far the standout player on the field, overshadowing Vessels, McPhail, and others better known nationally. The 1953 All-Army quarterback is having the most brilliant year of his career. He's completed about 68 percent of his passes and rates as the best defensive back on the club. With him, the attack generates a potent scoring punch. Without him, the club takes on a lackluster which is surprising in view of the talent at hand."*

The outstanding George Tarasovic (alternately spelled by the Army as Tarasovich) was remembered by the *York Daily Record* on 7 November 2019 (50): "For as tough and intimidating he was on a football field, George Tarasovic was fun-loving, kind and generous off it."

His toughness was on display in a time in football where rules were more relaxed, "and only the most resilient survived." Tarasovic was known for being rough with running backs in a rough-man's game. He spent thirteen years with the Pittsburgh Steelers introducing himself to runners in a manner that they wouldn't forget. There's a reason the 6' 4", 240-pound Tarasovic was on the All-Army First Team.

LSU star Tarasovich was the 18th overall pick, second round of the 1952 NFL draft by the Steelers. Overall, he completed fifteen seasons in professional football, though his time had been interrupted in 1954 and 1955 due to military service.

Tarasovic was nicknamed by his teammates the "Mad Russian." A former Giants running back said that Tarasovic was "one of the toughest SOBs I ever played against."

Tarasovic had a late start in football, though his exceptional skills, size, and quickness caught the eye of college scouts. He spent a year at Boston college, but ended up at LSU, where he blossomed into an All-American and Southeast Conference All-Star at middle linebacker.

The reverse of his Steelers football card (year not given) reads:

> George is one of those men with unlimited physical potential. Right now he's probably the most destructive man on the Steeler defensive line. Through his seven-year career with the pros they've had trouble finding the right niche for him. He played several seasons as a linebacker. He's now at home on the defensive flank, with speed, size and savvy. His brother Phil was a star tackle at Yale.

Upon retirement from football, Tarasovic remained active in his community and in helping people.

Rest in Peace, hero.

Photo: George Tarasovic, Pittsburgh Steelers football card.

1955 *ARMY TIMES* ALL-ARMY
FOOTBALL POLL

Army Times All-Army Poll 1955 was published 17 December 1955 (51).
1955 was the last year the selections were split into First, Second, and Third
teams; in 1956, they instead combined all selections into one team of
twenty-two, and in later years into two "platoons."

The All-Army football selection process was a robust system of merit-based selection for the best-of-the-best in the Continental United States (CONUS), Far East Command (FEC), and European Command (USAREUR). Reliable input and recommendations were procured from Service Sports coaches, sports writers, and in some cases, *Army Times* readers.

Time proved the credibility of those chosen as All-Army; many, if not all, went on to make significant contributions in the form of college football careers, professional football careers, coaching careers, or in various fields of business.

Many of the men chosen had already been well known in the football world, but others not so much. Many had college experience, some had professional football experience, some had neither (though this was rare); what they all shared was natural athletic ability and a drive to succeed.

Humility was their hallmark. Some men indicated genuine surprise at having been chosen for the All-Star team. And, as evidenced by many of their obituaries, few made a big deal about their remarkable success in Army sports to their loved ones. In fact, it appears that very few

family members were even aware of the extent of their football participation on overseas or domestic military posts.

Highlighting these men meets the purpose of this book – to fill historical gaps in knowledge and to raise awareness of the efforts of heroes past.

An article accompanying the poll results, "Buck McPhail MVP On 1955 All-Army," appeared on the front page of the 17 December 1955 *Army Times* issue. The 6'0", 200-pound Oklahoma star had had a "great season" with Fort Sill, in one case notably running up 142 yards against the strong Fort Ord Warriors defense. McPhail was the "second most popular *Army Times* All-Army MVP winner since the poll was inaugurated in 1951 (second only to the great Ollie Matson)," prompting Ord coach Bill Abbey to say that McPhail was one of the hardest-hitting backs he had seen.

The five All-Star repeat choices included McPhail, George Tarasovich, John Michels, Joe Ramona, and Jimmy Powers.

The 1955 *Army Times* All-Army football selections were as follows:

1955 FIRST TEAM

Position	Name	Team	College
End	George Tarasovich	Fort Belvoir	LSU
End	Dan Sekanovich	12th Inf. (Europe)	Tennessee
Tackle	Bill Quinlan	Fort Carson	Mich. State
Tackle	Gerald Perry	Fort Ord	California
Guard	John Michels	Fort Eustis	Tennessee
Guard	Joe Ramona	Fort Sill	Santa Clara
Center	Jim Schrader	86th Inf. (Europe)	Notre Dame
QB	Cotton Davidson	Fort Bliss	Baylor
HB	Paul Cameron	Fort Ord	UCLA
HB	Harry Spears	9th Divarty (Europe)	Florida
FB	Buck McPhail*	Fort Sill	Oklahoma

*MVP

1955 SECOND TEAM

End	Flavious Smith	Fort Knox	Tenn. Poly
End	Ron Miller	Fort Ord	USC
Tackle	Jack Shanafelt	24th Div. (Korea)	Penn
Tackle	Donald Early	4th Div. ST (Europe)	So. Carolina
Guard	John Hammock	Fort Jackson	Florida
Guard	Ray Correll	Fort Benning	Kentucky
Center	Dick Tamburo	Fort Hood	Mich. State

QB	Jim Powers	Fort Ord	USC
HB	Don Barton	Fort Knox	Texas
HB	Tony Curcillo	Fort Carson	Ohio State
FB	Don Robinson	2d Inf. (Europe)	California

1955 THIRD TEAM

End	Jim Ladd	Fort Sill	n/a
End	Floyd Sagely	Fort Sill	n/a
Tackle	Gerald Hart	Fort Bliss	n/a
Tackle	Bob Fleck	Fort Monmouth	n/a
Guard	Joe Branch	Brooke Med. Ctr.	n/a
Guard	Ray Howard	Fort Hood	n/a
Center	Bert Clark	Fort Sill	n/a
QB	Max Schmidt	11th Inf. (Europe)	n/a
HB	Billy Wells	Fort Belvoir	n/a
HB	Jim Ellis	SACOM	n/a
FB	Harold Han	27th Inf. (Hawaii)	n/a

Selected "Who's Who" 1955 All-Army summaries published in *Army Times*:

> **DAN SEKANOVICH** – Played four years at the University of Tennessee, 1950-1953. In '54 was with the Montreal Allouettes as first string end. Expects to return to Montreal when he is released from the Army in November 1956.

> **GEORGE TARASOVICH** – Winner of All-Southern conference honors at LSU in 1952, PFC Tarasovich played in the All-Star game and the Blue-Grey contest before joining the Pittsburgh Steelers. A defensive star with the Belvoir Engineers, he also led the team in pass receiving with 34 catches good for 335 yards. The 6-3, 245-pounder turned in one of his greatest games this year against Fort Sill when he caught five passes for 58 yards. He plans to return to the Steelers following his discharge. Also made All-Army first team last year. Age 25.

> **BILL QUINLAN** – The Cleveland Browns picked Quinlan as their third draft choice this month and have already signed the 235-pound 6-3 Carson star. His coach at Carson, 2d Lt. Jerry Clark, predicts Bill will make the grade with the Browns as a defensive end. "He's one of the finest linemen I've ever seen in a football

56

uniform, bar none." Was a member of Michigan State's 1953 Rose Bowl team that defeated UCLA.

GERALD PERRY – Starred with the University of California and then went on to the Detroit Lions. Tough and fast for a 6-4, 240-pounder. Did most of Ord's extra point kicking off. Against the Los Angeles Rams in an exhibition game this year, he played 56 minutes and was one of the best lineman on the field. A private, 24 years old. From Los Angeles, Calif.

JOHN MICHELS – An All-Army first team selection last year, 2d Lt. Michels was again outstanding for the Eustis Wheels on offense and defense this year. Eustis coach Bob Frala called Michels "the most outstanding player at any position that I have seen in service ball this year." A high school star in Philadelphia, Michels went on to win All-Southern Conference honors with the University of Tennessee in 1951 and 1952. Played a year of pro ball with the Philadelphia Eagles. Stands 5-11, 210 pounds, 23 years old.

JOE RAMONA – Earned All-Pacific Coast honors with Santa Clara before playing year of pro ball with the New York Giants. Won All-Army honors last year and proved even more popular with voters this season. Aggressive and rugged … Sill players call him the "greatest guard in football." Stands 6 feet, weighs 200.

JAMES SCHRADER – All-American at Notre Dame in 1953 now under contract to the Washington Redskins … His coach, 1st Lt. Leaton Cofield, calls Schrader "one of the greatest centers and linebackers ever to play Army football. I rate him better than Clayton Tonnemaker …" Was second draft choice of the Redskins … Stands 6-3, weighs 230.

FRANCIS (COTTON) DAVIDSON – Played college ball at Baylor from 1950-54 and was named to several All-American squads. Played pro ball with the Baltimore Colts last year. In game against LA Rams completed seven straight passes in final minutes to set up TD that beat Rams 21-20.

FRANCIS DAVIDSON Quarterback 6'1" 185 Baylor
"Cotton" was the Colts' number one draft choice in 1954 after leading the Southwest Conference in passing and ranking 11th in the nation as a college senior. As a pro freshman he completed 28 of 63 aerials for 309 yeards, including seven straight strikes that enabled the Colts to nip the Rams in the final seconds, 22-21. Gifted with a powerful throwing arm, he fires bullets. He spent the 1955-56 seasons in the Army, being named All-Army quarterback in '55. Last year he returned to do all of the Colts' punting. He's from Gatesville, Texas. Born: November 30, 1931.

PAUL CAMERON – One of the most popular choices in the All-Army poll this year. A vicious runner and great competitor. Consensus All-American with UCLA in 1954, he went on to win pro rookie honors of the year for his defensive work with the Pittsburgh Steelers. Extremely fast for a 200-pounder.

COLEMAN (BUCK) McPHAIL – Fort Sill's leading scorer this year with 72 points. Starred offensively and defensively ... made All-Army team last year ... will probably be back with the Baltimore Colts next year. Played with the Colts in 1953 after winning All-American honors with Oklahoma in 1952. Stands six feet, 205 pounds, 25 years old ... Won "Most Valuable Player" election in All-Army poll.

RON MILLER – Jimmy Powers' main passing target all year at Ord. Real good hands and can hold the ball if it is near him at all. Of the independents with the Warriors (Ord) while playing the San Francisco 49ers, Ron was the only one they wanted. He finally signed with the Los Angeles Rams although he has a year left at Southern Cal where he was an All-Coast selection in 1952. Stands 6-4, weighs 210.

JACK SHANAFELT – 24th Div. Korea. While at the University of Pennsylvania, Lt. Shanafelt was twice named lineman of the week in national polls and made *Look's* All-American team in 1953. A member of the All-Far East team which meets the Far East Marine All-Stars in the Torii Bowl in Tokyo Dec. 17.

58

RAY CORRELL – His team lost only one game, to Shaw AFB, and beat post teams such as Fort Jackson, Keesler AFB and Eglin AFB, as well as winning Benning league title. Former University of Kentucky All-American. Played in East-West and Senior Bowl in 1953. On All-Time Cotton Bowl team 1951. All-Time Kentucky team and All-Time Southeast Conference team in 1955 ... Stands 6-2, weighs 230.

JIMMY POWERS – Also All-Army last year. Good passer ... will pass you to death or run the same spot 15 times if he finds a weakness ... Strictly a pro and plays like one. Was All-Coast in 1946 and 1947 while with Southern Cal and played defensive ball for the 49ers from 1950-1953.

TONY CURCILLO – Curcillo proved a popular choice with All-Army voters ... Former Ohio State star, he is fast for 205-pounder, stands 6-2, 24 years old, and belongs to the Chicago Cardinals.

DON BARTON – A sensation in the Fort Knox loop this year. Scored 114 points for undefeated ARTC Black Falcons and made unnumerable sensational runs. Starred for University of Texas from 1951-53. Owned by the Green Bay Packers.

10,000-plus fans witnessed Belvoir win the Conch Bowl game, 32-13, in Key West, Florida on 10 December 1955, according to an article in the same edition. Oddly enough, the brief article does not say who their opponent was. However, the overflow crowd saw a lot of action, including from Billy Wells, former Michigan State All-American and Washington Redskin, and from end George Tarasovich who scored the opening touchdown on a short pass from QB Joe Huske. Alternate QB Art DeCarlo also tossed a scoring pass to end Kent Peters to add to the total.

The 17 December 1955 *Army Times* edition also discussed the loss of Brooke Medical Center football player, Frank Eidom, who perished in an automobile accident in October. Despite the incident, he received many votes for All-Army honors, and Brooke sports reporter Bob Bolling considered him the MVP; "Frank played the hardest of any man I've ever seen. He was the best runner and leading scorer on the Brooke team."

ART DE CARLO   Halfback   6'2"   196   Georgia
Signed as a free agent during the 1957 grind after being released
by Washington, Art saw considerable service in the Colts' defensive
backfield. He had originally been selected on the sixth round of the
1953 draft by the Chicago Bears, who traded him to Pittsburgh.
After spending 1954 and '55 in the Army, De Carlo was swapped
to the Redskins, for whom he played defensive halfback in 1956.
In college he toiled at five different positions, including offensive
end. He was voted the Most Valuable Defensive Player in the 1952
Blue-Gray tilt. He makes his home in Baltimore. Born: March
23, 1931.

The Oklahoman reported 8 March 2005 the passing (52) of All-Army MVP,
Coleman "Buck" McPhail, in Costa Mesa, California. McPhail attended the
University of Oklahoma from 1949-1952, and was voted All-American in
1952; "He and Billy Vessels were the first two running backs in collegiate
history to gain 1,000 yards each, while on the same team, in the same season
(1952)." He went on to play for the Baltimore Colts in the NFL, with which
he spent two years.

McPhail was an XO with the 598th Field Artillery Battalion at Ft. Sill from
1954-56, during which time he was named Army football MVP in 1955.
Subsequent to his playing days, he coached football at University of
California, Berkeley, helping the Golden Bears earn a trip to the Rose Bowl.
He also coached at Illinois, which time included an Illinois victorious Rose
Bowl appearance in 1964. After coaching, McPhail moved on to a
successful career in the business world.

He was survived by his wife, Carol Ann, of 52 years.

Rest in Peace, hero.

1956 *ARMY TIMES* ALL-ARMY FOOTBALL POLL

Army Times All-Army Poll 1956 results were published 15 December 1956 (53). There was a chart (below) labeled *Army Times* All-Army 1956, and an additional article titled, "Vinnie Drake Named MVP On 1956 All-Army Team."

This year they combined the First and Second Teams to make a single, larger team, though there is also an Honorable Mention roster.

Army Times All-Army 1956

Pos.	Rank	Name	Team	College	Pro	Age	Hgt.	Wgt.	Hometown
E	PFC	JIM GREER	CCB, 3d Armd, Europe	Eliz. City, N.C.	Browns	25	6-3	195	Huntington, W. Va.
E	1st Lt.	GILMER SPRING	Fort Eustis, Va.	Texas	Edmonton	24	6-2	210	Apple Spring, Tex.
E	SP3	KEN HALL	Fort Bliss, Tex.	No. Texas State	49ers	24	6-1	206	Dallas, Tex.
E	SP3	JERRY JANES	Fort Hood, Tex.	LSU	(None)	21	6-5	235	Mooringsport, Ohio
T	1st Lt.	BILL RAYFIELD	Fort Bliss, Tex.	Hampton Inst.	Browns	25	6-0	230	Baltimore, Md.
T	2d Lt.	JOE MEHALIC	I Corps, Korea	Virginia	Eagles	25	6-3	225	Boonton, N.J.
T	Lt.	JACKSON BRUMFIELD	Fort Sill, Okla.	Miss. Southern	49ers	25	6-0	225	Franklinton, La.
T	PFC	DICK SHIPLEY	Fort Jackson, S. C.	Maryland	(None)	23	5-10	240	Frederick, Md.
G	2d Lt.	DALE HAUPT	Fort Benning, Ga.	Wyoming	(None)	27	6-0	220	Manitowoc, Wis.
G	SFC	JAY HAMPTON	504th AIR, Ft. Bragg	(None)	(None)	32	5-9	180	War, W. Va.
G	1st Lt.	RON HOFFMANN	SACom, (Europe)	St. Lawrence	(None)	24	5-9	190	Farmingdale, N.Y.
G	Pvt.	LARRY HARTSHORN	Camp Zama, Japan	Kansas State	Cards	23	6-0	230	Eldorado, Kans.
C	Pvt.	DICK SZYMANSKI	13th Inf., Europe	Notre Dame	Colts	23	6-3	235	Toledo, Ohio
C	Lt.	FRED RODY	Fort Sill, Okla.	Mich. State	(None)	24	6-2	215	Flint, Mich.
QB	2d Lt.	VINCENT DRAKE	CCB, 3d Armd, Europe	Fordham	Winnepeg	25	6-2	210	Ansonia, Conn.
QB	Pvt.	CHARLIE MALOY	Fort Dix, N.J.	Holy Cross	(None)	24	6-3	180	Rochester, N.Y.
HB	Pvt.	MALCOLM HAMMACK	Fort Ord, Calif.	Florida	Cards	23	6-1	210	Roscoe, Tex.
HB	Pvt.	SAM BROWN	Fort Ord, Calif.	UCLA	(None)	23	5-10	185	Oakland, Calif.
HB	PFC	DAVE ROGERS	3d Div., Ft. Benning	Indiana	(None)	22	6-0	210	Warren, Ohio
HB	. . .	BOB JUDD	NACom, Europe	Xavier, Ohio	(None)	. .	5-9	185	Peoria, Ill.
FB	PFC	TOMMY DAVIS	1st Cav., Tokyo	LSU	(None)	22	6-0	205	Shreveport, La.
FB	1st Lt.	EARL BECHTEL	Fort Hood, Tex.	Ohio State	(None)	26	6-2	208	Bellville, Ohio

Honorable Mention

ENDS — Jim Ladd (Fort Sill), Lou Sawchik (Fort Benning), Tom Pepsin (13th Inf., Europe), Russell Dennis (Fort Dix). **TACKLES** — Sherm Plunkett (Fort Dix), Tom Gulan (NACom), Marion Minker (32d Inf., Korea), Ed Gossage (17th Inf., Korea), Bob Ledbetter (Fort Hood). **GUARDS** — Bob Scarborough (Fort Belvoir), Claude Roach (Fort Sill), John Powell (Fort Hood), Willie Beamon (86th Inf., Europe), Joe DeLoca (Fort Ord). **CENTER** — Tom Adkins (Fort Monmouth). **QUARTERBACKS** — Paul Larson (Fort Ord), Bill Bradshaw (40th AAA, Japan), Tom Yewcic (Fort Polk), Charles Brackens (13th Inf., Europe), Pete Ghirin (Fort Eustis), Joe Clark (4th Div., Fort Lewis). **HALFBACKS** — Charles Stanley (35th FA Gp., Europe), Carl Hollowell (Fort Richardson, Alaska), Don DeFeudis (86th Inf., Europe), Mal Williams (504th AIR, Fort Bragg), John Matsock, (Fort Sill), Mel Smith (38th Inf., Fort Lewis), Vince Caleandro (Fort Devens). **FULLBACKS** — Frank Purnell (Brooke Medical Center), Chuck Lawson (Fort Riley Non-Division Special Troops), Mitchell Ware (Neurent, 518th Signal Gp., Europe).

The 1956 *Army Times* All-Army football selections were as follows (single group):

NAME	POS.	TEAM	COLLEGE	PRO
Jim Greer	End	CCB, 3d Armd, Europe	Eliz. City, N.C.	Browns
Gilmer Spring	End	Fort Eustis, Va.	Texas	Edmonton
Ken Hall	End	Fort Bliss, Tex.	No. Texas State	49ers
Jerry Janes	End	Fort Hood Tex.	LSU	n/a

Bill Rayfield	Tackle.	Fort Bliss, Tex.	Hampton Inst.	Browns
Joe Mehalic	Tackle	I Corps, Korea	Virginia	Eagles
Jackson Brumfield	Tackle	Fort Sill, Okla.	Miss. Southern	49ers
Dick Shipley	Tackle	Fort Jackson, S.C.	Maryland	n/a
Dale Haupt	Guard	Fort Benning, Ga.	Wyoming	n/a
Jay Hampton	Guard	504th AIR, Ft. Bragg	n/a	n/a
Ron Hoffman	Guard	SACom, Europe	St. Lawrence	n/a
Larry Hartshorn	Guard	Camp Zama, Japan	Kansas State	Cards
Dick Szymanski	Center	13th Inf., Europe	Notre Dame	Colts
Fred Rody	Center	Fort Sill, Okla.	Mich. State	n/a
Vincent Drake	QB	CCB, 3d Armd., Europe	Fordham	Winnipeg
Charlie Maloy	QB	Fort Dix, N.J.	Holy Cross	n/a
Malcolm Hammack	HB	Fort Ord, Ca.	Florida	Cards
Sam Brown	HB	Fort Ord, Ca.	UCLA	n/a
Dave Rogers	HB	3d Div., Ft. Benning	Indiana	n/a
Bob Judd	HB	NACom, Europe	Xavier, Ohio	n/a
Tommy Davis	FB	1st Cav., Tokyo	LSU	n/a
Earl Bechtel	FB	Fort Hood, Tex.	Ohio State	n/a

DICK SHIPLEY   Guard   5'10"   245   Maryland
A late entry into the Colt fold as a free agent, Dick will probably be tested at an offensive line post. He was once the property of the New York Giants, who nabbed him after he had graduated from Maryland in 1955. He called defensive signals for the Terps. His most recent grid action was at Fort Jackson (S. C.), where he played two years while in the Army. He's a resident of Frederick, Md. Born: March 11, 1933.

The accompanying article said that Europe quarterback Vinnie Drake "stole the show" along with four other European players. Drake, out of Fordham (1953), and described as a "balding second lieutenant," was voted MVP All-Army. The Far East Command contributed three men to the list, including Tommy Davis, who had been a strong contender for MVP honors.

A biography of Larry Hartshorn (54) says that he had been an NFL offensive guard for the Chicago Cardinals in 1955 and 1957 (before and after his military service). He also played Canadian football with the Calgary Stampeders in 1958. All other selected players were from stateside; twenty-two total were chosen.

Fort Ord and other large Post teams contributed the most players; Fort Ord, rated the nation's top Service team, contributed two players to the All-Army squad: Malcolm Hammack and Sam "First Down" Brown.

Selected "Who's Who" 1956 All-Army summaries published in *Army Times*:

VINNIE DRAKE – Was USAREUR's total offense leader with 902 yards. Led passers with 871 yards on 46 completions in 83 attempts and was responsible for 12 TD's during Northern League games. In all games (9), Drake completed 70 of 130 passes for 1607 yards and 19 TD's, 11 of these TD passes going to Jim Greer, also All-Army.

JIM GREER – Caught 35 passes for 1103 yards. In Northern League games tied NACom's Bob Judd with 41 points for league lead. Made honorable mention Little All-American with Elizabeth City, N.C. College in 1954. Also fine basketball player.

GILMER SPRING – Served as assistant coach for Eustis this year and co-captain of team last year. While at Texas U., was third team All-American on both AP and UP polls. Property of Washington Redskins but played for Edmonton Eskimos in Canada in 1954.

JERRY JANES – Exceptionally fast for a big man. Also punts and consistently kicks-off over goal line. Missed three games because of injury early in season but was key man in Hood's important win over Fort Sill. Tough on defense and good pass receiver. Played year at LSU and has three years of college eligibility remaining.

KEN HALL – Popular with coaches in All-Army poll. Was little All-American at North Texas State and played in College All-Star game in 1954. Outstanding receiver for Green Bay Packers before entering Army, but now belongs to 49ers and expects to play with them after discharge in February.

BILL RAYFIELD – Played four years at Hampton Institute and is signed by Cleveland Browns but his Army category was recently extended to indefinite. Popular on and off the field and was voted most valuable player for Bliss last year. A favorite of Fourth Army coaches.

JACKSON BRUMFIELD – Star at Mississippi Southern before turning pro with San Francisco 49ers. A standout for Sill for two seasons. Did most of the kicking off. Big and rugged.

63

LARRY HARTSHORN – Plays out of Camp Zama, Japan. College ball with Kansas State, pro ball with Chicago Cardinals. Consistently good performer, on Far East Army all-star team.

DICK SZYMANSKI – Won All-American honors at Notre Dame before turning in fine job for Baltimore Colts in a year. Heavy favorite with European coaches in All-Army poll.

DICK SZYMANSKI   Center   6'3"   230   Notre Dame
After making an auspicious debut with the Colts as an offensive center in 1955, Dick entered the Army. He returned to pro action midway through last season and was cast in a linebacking role. Rid of his service rust, he should regain his place as one of the league's standout linemen in 1958, regardless of whether he aids the attack or defense. He played every second of offense for the West team in the 1956 Pro Bowl. At N.D., he was hailed by Navy coach Eddie Erdelatz as "one of the finest linebackers we have ever been called upon to face." A four-year varsity performer for the Fighting Irish, Dick injured his spleen in the 1954 Penn game and underwent emergency surgery. He's from Toledo, Ohio. Born: November 7, 1932.

CHARLIE MALOY – After starring at Holy Cross, turned down pro offers to enter law school. Was backfield coach at Boston University 1953-54. Won many honors in college ranging from All-New England, All-East, All-American. Fine passer, cool and clever field general. Without Maloy, Dix offense would have been nil.

MALCOLM HAMMACK – Won All-American honors at University of Florida before playing one year with Chicago Cards. Averaged 8.8 yards per carry for Ord. Ord Coach Don Coryell says of his play this year, "Very good punter, passer, blocker, pass receiver, and rugged offensive back. Has excellent team spirit and is an inspiration to his teammates."

SAM BROWN – All-American at UCLA last year. Averaged 7.8 yards per carry this season. Exceptional pass receiver and punter, good passer, and good defensive back as well as a very fast and tricky runner who brings fans to their feet. Also baseball player and is under contract to Los Angeles in the Coast League.

DAVE ROGERS – Played two years with the University of Indiana where he still has a year of eligibility left. Gets out of the Army this week. Scored nine TDs for 3d Div. team and made many long runs. San Francisco 49ers and L.A. Rams have their eyes on him and he wants to play pro ball. Led Indiana in scoring in 1953 with five TDs. Re-entering Indiana in February. Lt. Richard Munson, backfield coach for the School Brigade team at Bragg calls Dave "one of the greatest football players I have ever seen."

Photo: LSU's Tommy Davis football card. Fullback, kicker. 6'0", Wt. 204.

TOMMY DAVIS – Two years at LSU. Voted top player in 1955 New Year's Day Rice Bowl All-Star game. On Far East All-Army team again this year, In All-Japan Conference was high scorer with 11 TDs, 16 conversions and four field goals, to lead the Bulldogs to the championship. Also good defensive back. Very popular with coaches in the All-Army poll.

Selected All-Army player biographical backgrounds:

Mr. Hartshorn was born in 1933 in Oil Hill, Kansas, and was an excellent high school athlete, earning All-State honors in football in 1950. He played baseball and football for Kansas State. The article said that his NFL participation was interrupted when he was drafted into the Army, whereupon he was sent to Camp Zama, Japan.

Mr. Hartshorn's football skills were immediately recognized in Japan, and his single season in the AFFE leagues led to his All-Army election. Following his service and his relatively brief professional football career, he served the community by coaching football and wrestling. He passed away on 19 September 2007.

Rest in Peace, hero.

Charlie Maloy's obituary (55) is a source of detailed information regarding his sports career and life. Mr. Maloy was a retired judge, having been born in and had worked in the Rochester, New York area. He was a "standout 3-sport athlete," and was heavily recruited for college ball. He chose Holy Cross, where he earned All-American, 3x All-New England, and many other honors while quarterbacking the Crusaders, ultimately leading to being drafted by the New York Giants in 1953. However, another draft, to the Army, took precedence, and he "was assigned to play football for an Army team that competed with other branches." Once he completed his military service, he decided to go to law school in lieu of playing professional football. He had a successful career as a judge, was a devout Catholic and solid member of the community, and had a loving wife and family.

Rest in Peace, hero.

Photo: Brigadier General D'Orsa, Commanding General, Berlin Command, presents SFC Crook a wrist watch for being selected as a member of the All-Army football team. [NARA] NAID: 315834122 RG: 111 Records for the Office of the Chief Signal Officer, Series: Photographs of American Military Activities

1957 *ARMY TIMES* ALL-ARMY FOOTBALL POLL

The 1957 *Army Times* All-Army selections were loaded with athletic talent, including major-college and professional football stars - names like Forrest Gregg and Roosevelt "Rosey" Grier, and others, played alongside lesser-known, but very talented Army soldiers. There was even a future state governor on the roster!

Fob James, an Auburn University All-American, who would later become a two-time Alabama governor, was named All-Army MVP for 1957. *Army Times* of 21 December 1957 reported that James had been presented with a wristwatch by renowned *Army Times* sports editor, Tom Scanlon, in the office of Brig. Gen. R. G. MacDonnell, post CG (56) - "James, a modest, soft-spoken man, said it was a day he would remember the rest of his life."

The previous week, James had received a silver trophy at Fort Belvoir in recognition of his MVP accomplishment. Present at the ceremony were Comdr. (Ret.) John G. Urquhart, MSgt. Nelson Peterson, and Brig. Gen. R.G. MacDonnell.

James was no stranger to success, having starred at Alabama Polytechnic University (Auburn) prior to Army Service; his numbers in 1955 were impressive (57), and helped Auburn to a twelve-game win streak as of mid-October 1955:

		RUSHING			
	Runs	Yards	L	Net	Avg.
James, lh	62	528	29	499	8.0
Childress, fb	71	292	2	290	4.1
Shell, rh	18	116	1	115	6.4
Walsh, fb	13	122	0	112	8.6
Adams, lh	8	42	0	42	5.3
Cook, qb	10	52	11	42	4.1
Hoppe, rh	8	35	0	35	4.4
Tubbs, qb	28	65	38	27	0.9
Burbank, qb	8	28	6	22	2.7
AUBURN	234	1326	87	1239	5.3
OPPONENTS	190	616	189	427	2.2

"Fob James is the most outstanding halfback I have coached in service ball. Played 60 minutes all year long, was the team's leading scorer and best defensive back on the squad." – Sam Puterbaugh, Head Coach, Fort Belvoir Engineers.

"Fob James of Belvoir is the best back (Fort) Dix has seen in '57 and the only one who could slither through the 'Seven Slabs of Steel' with any success. Speedy, shifty, he runs hard and has fine savvy. An excellent defender as well." – PFC Jim O'Toole, Sports Editor, *Fort Dix Post*.

Photo: Congratulations to All-Army MVP and future two-time Alabama governor, Fob James, 1957 (58).

Joining Fob James on the "First Platoon" All-Army selection list was fellow Alabamian, Bob Luna, playing out of Fort Hood, Texas. Luna was a member of Auburn's rival football powerhouse, the University of Alabama, from 1951-54, per his obituary (59). Luna was a talented all-around athlete and played both football and baseball for Alabama, earning a Paul "Bear" Bryant

69

award in the process. He was inducted into the Alabama Football Hall of Fame.

ALABAMA

1952 STARTING OFFENSE
Back Row: Bobby Marlow, Tommy Lewis, Clell Hobson (15), Bobby Luna.
Front Row: Hyrle Ivy, Jack Smalley, Fred Mims, O.E. Phillips, Jerry Watford, Van Marcus, Joe Curtis.

Photo: Courtesy Brad Green, Curator, Paul W. Bryant Museum, Tuscaloosa, Alabama.

Luna's athletic skills and drive earned him not only All-Army football honors, but later earned him a place with professional NFL teams, such as the Pittsburgh Steelers and San Francisco 49ers.

Bob Luna passed away on 14 March 2008 in Franklin, Tennessee.

Rest in Peace, hero.

The 7 December 1957 *Army Times* newspaper (60) introduced the *Army Times* All-Army football selections for 1957 with a headline reading: "'Fob' James All-Army MVP."

James, a star halfback with the Fort Belvoir Engineers, was the top vote-getter in the seventh annual All-Army football poll. A close second in the poll was quarterback Charlie Brackens of the Ulm Vicksburgers (13th Inf.) in Europe.

70

Undefeated Fort Dix supplied four players to the All-Army team, which for this year would be broken down into two platoons, first and second, and a "3d Team."

1957 FIRST PLATOON

Position	Name	Team	College	Pro
End	Jim Hanifan	Schweinfurt (Europe)	California	Toronto
End	Bill McKenna	Fort Monmouth, N.J.	Brandeis	Calgary
Tackle	Ed Fouch	Fort Sill, Okla.	So. Calif.	Rams-Toronto
Tackle	Sherm Plunkett	Fort Dix, N.J	Md. State	Colts
Guard	Forrest Gregg	Fort Carson, Colorado	SMU	Packers
Guard	John McMullan	Fort Dix, N.J	Notre Dame	Giants
Center	Bob Pellegrini	Fort Knox, Ky.	Maryland	Eagles
Back	Charlie Brackins	Ulm (Europe)	Prairie View	Packers
Back	Bob Luna	Fort Hood, Tex.	Alabama	49ers
Back	Forrest James	Fort Belvoir, Va.	Auburn	Montreal
Back	Sam Brown	37th Inf. (Europe)	UCLA	n/a

1957 SECOND PLATOON

Position	Name	Team	College	Pro
End	Andy Nacrelli	Brooke Medical, Tex.	Fordham	Eagles
End	Don Holleder	21st Inf. (Hawaii)	West Point	n/a
Tackle	Roosevelt Grier	Fort Dix, N.J	Penn State	Giants
Tackle	Willie Davis	Fort Carson, Colo.	Grambling, La.	Browns
Guard	Fred Thurston	Brooke Medical, Tex.	Valparaiso	Eagles
Guard	Jim Markelonis	Antilles (Puerto Rico)	Tennessee	n/a
Center	Phil Stewart	Ft. Richardson, Alaska	Tulane	n/a
Back	Jerry Johnson	Fort Hood, Tex.	Texas Tech	Edmunton*
Back	Don Mitchell	Tokyo Bulldogs	VPI	n/a
Back	Leon Riley	Fort Dix, N.J	Detroit	Eagles
Back	Charlie Evans	15th Inf., Ft. Benning	Miss. State	n/a

*sic

1957 THIRD TEAM

Name	Team
Howie Schnellenberger, end	Fort Knox, Ky.
Robert Costa, end	47th Inf., Fort Lewis, Wash.
Ted Edling, tackle	Schweinfurt (Europe)
Jack Kelder, tackle	EASCOM (Korea)
John Mellakas, guard	Fort Dix, N.J.
Ron Marciniak, guard	Fort Bliss, Tex.
Ed Kleist, center	EASCOM (Korea)
Geno Cappoletti, back	Fort Sill, Okla.
Charlie Sumner, back	Fort Lee, Va.
Charles Stanley, back	VII Corps (Europe)
Dick Blakely, back	1st Cav. Divarty (Korea)

Selected quotes from Army football coaches and sports writers:

"*Jerry Johnson is the most outstanding football player in the Fourth Army area and the best split-T quarterback I have ever seen. Hood is primarily a passing team and Johnson has completed 41 out of 82 for 50 percent and 900 yards. Johnson's greatest asset is his ability to analyze the situation.*"

- **Lt. Wayne H. Etheridge, Head Coach, Fort Hood Tankers.**

"*Andy Nacrelli is very fast, runs patterns to perfection and is as elusive as any back on the field when he gets the ball. Every opponent we meet will put two men on him almost every time he comes down the field on a passing situation.*"

- **2d Lt. Ed Bradford, Head Coach, Brooke Medical Center Comets.**

"*Bill McKenna's receptions have totaled over half of our passing yardage this year including three of our touchdowns. He is not only a great receiver but also one of the main sparks in our ground attack because of his superb blocking ... he is a credit to the game, his coaches, and the Army.*"

- **Vincent O'Connell, Head Coach, Fort Monmouth Signaleers.**

"*Jim Hanifan, leading pass receiver in the nation in 1954, has carried my team through its third undefeated regular USAREUR league season. He is, in my estimation, the most outstanding end in Army and college ball today.*"

- **Capt. Leaton C. Cofield, Head Coach, Schweinfurt Crusaders.**

"*This man (Don Mitchel [sic]), is the best all-around back I have seen in the Army, He has played 60 minutes for the past four games. At this writing, after five games, he has the most points in the Far East with 66 for five games ... He is fast, powerful, and an above average back on defense.*"

- **1st Lt. Robert S. Antkowiak, Head Coach, Camp Tokyo Bulldogs.**

ARMY TIMES All-Army football team PFC Fred (Fuzzy) Thurston (center) and SP3 Andy Nacrelli receive Lord Elgin watches from Maj. Gen. William E. Shambora, CG of Brooke Army Medical Center at Fort Sam Houston, Tex. Thurston, guard and linebacker for the Brooke Comets, will play pro ball with the Chicago Bears. Nacrelli, an end, is a Philadelphia Eagles draft choice.

"Julius Blakeney has led my team to six straight victories and ... is averaging 16 yards per carry, outstanding in anyone's league."

1st Lt. Gene Hanson, Head Coach, Divarty Redlegs, 3d Div., Fort Benning.

"In picking Ed Fouch as most valuable player, I'm taking into account not only his play on the field, but also his work with our younger, less experienced linemen ... he has done more than was expected of him."

- SP3 Jack Brannan, Sports Editor, *Fort Sill Cannoneer.*

"The most outstanding player in the Eighth Army Conference was Bill Stokes, quarterback of 1st Cav. Divarty. His passing and brilliant ball

handling led his team to a second place finish, behind the EASCOM Loggers. Before entering the Army, he played with Alabama State."

- **PFC Gerald A. Schmidt, Sports Editor, *Cavalier*, 1st Cav. Div., Korea.**

Army Times All-Army 1957

1st Platoon

		Player	Team	College	Pro	Age	Hgt.	Wgt.	Hometown
E	PFC	JIM HANIFAN	Schweinfurt (Europe)	California	Toronto	24	6-3	205	Cohina, Calif.
E	Pvt.	BILL McKENNA	Fort Monmouth, N.J.	Brandeis	Calgary	24	6-3	210	Salem, Mass.
T	PFC	ED FOUCH	Fort Sill, Okla.	So. Calif.	Rams-Toronto	24	6-3	233	Santa Ana, Calif.
T	PFC	SHEEM PLUNKETT	Fort Dix, N.J.	Md. State	Colts	24	6-4	265	Okla. City, Okla.
G	PFC	FORREST GREGG	Fort Carson, Colo.	SMU	Packers	23	6-3	235	Sulphur Springs, Tex.
G	PFC	JOHN McMULLAN	Fort Dix, N.J.	Notre Dame	Giants	24	5-11	235	South Bend, Ind.
C	PFC	RON PELLEGRINI	Fort Knox, Ky.	Maryland	Eagles	23	6-3	223	Waterboro, Pa.
B	PFC	CHARLIE BRACKINS	Ulm (Europe)	Prairie View A&M	Packers	25	6-3	205	Dallas, Tex.
B	SP2	BOB LUNA	Fort Hood, Tex.	Alabama	49ers	22	6-0	187	Huntsville, Ala.
B	2d Lt.	FORREST JAMES*	Fort Belvoir, Va.	Auburn	Montreal	23	5-10	170	Lanett, Ala.
B	PFC	SAM BROWN	87th Inf. (Europe)	UCLA	(None)	25	5-10	185	McClymond, Calif.

*—Most Valuable Player

2d Platoon

Pos.	Rank	Player	Team	College	Pro	Age	Hgt.	Wgt.	Hometown
E	SP3	ANDY NACRELLI	Brooke Medical, Tex.	Fordham	Eagles	24	6-1	195	Chester, Pa.
E	2d Lt.	DON HOLLEDER	21st Inf. (Hawaii)	West Point	(None)	23	6-2	187	Webster, N.Y.
T	PFC	ROOSEVELT GRIER	Fort Dix, N.J.	Penn State	Giants	25	6-5	290	Elizabeth, N.J.
T	PFC	WILLIE DAVIS	Fort Carson, Colo.	Grambling, La.	Browns	23	6-2	240	Texarkana, Tex.
G	PFC	FRED THURSTON	Brooke Medical, Tex.	Valparaiso	Eagles	23	6-0	245	Altoon, Wis.
G	PFC	JIM MARKELONIS	Antilles (Puerto Rico)	Tennessee	(None)	28	5-8	220	Niagara Falls, N.Y.
C	PFC	PHIL STEWART	Ft. Richardson, Alaska	Tulane	(None)	21	6-0	195	Baton Rouge, La.
Ba.	SP3	JERRY JOHNSON	Fort Hood, Tex.	Texas Tech	Edmonton	23	5-10	175	Lubbock, Tex.
B	PFC	DON MITCHELL	Tokyo Bulldogs	VPI	(None)		5-10	185	Emporia, Va.
B	Pvt.	LEON RILEY	Fort Dix, N.J.	Detroit	Eagles	24	6-0	195	Schenectady, N.Y.
B	Cpl	CHARLIE EVANS	13th Inf., Ft. Benning	Miss. State	(None)	25	5-9	195	Perkingston, Miss.

3d Team

Pos.	Player	Team
E	HOWIE SCHNELLENBERGER	Fort Knox, Ky.
E	ROBERT COSTA	47th Inf., Fort Lewis, Wash.
T	TED EDLING	Schweinfurt (Europe)
T	JACK KELDER	EASCOM (Korea)
G	JOHN MELLAKAS	Fort Dix, N.J.
G	RON MARCINIAK	Fort Bliss, Tex.
C	ED KLEIST	EASCOM (Korea)
B	GENO CAPPOLETTI	Fort Sill, Okla.
B	CHARLIE SUMNER	Fort Lee, Va.
B	CHARLES STANLEY	VII Corps (Europe)
B	DICK BLAKELY	1st Cav. Divarty (Korea)

Honorable Mention

ENDS
Huey Hunter (Fort Hood, Tex.), Dean Meeks (11th Abn. Divarty Sp. Tps., Europe), Art McGee (Orleans, France), Charles Hardy (Bamberg, Germany), Emerson Dickie (Fort Dix, N.J.), Walt Cabral (Fort Carson, Colo.), John Lewis (Fort Knox, Ky.), Pete Mari (SACom, Europe), Henry Poniatowski (Fort Myer, Va.).

TACKLES
Alvie (Boots) Edits, (Brooke Medical, Tex.), Ted Wisniewski (Fort Belvoir, Va.), Preston Dills (27th Inf., Hawaii), Clyde Roebuck (562d Inf., Fort Campbell Ky.), Vince West (26th Inf., Korea), Dennis Harvey (Fort Richardson, Alaska), Phil Assmus (Fort Lee, Va.).

GUARDS
Ken Cummer (Schweinfurt, Germany), Dom Pica and Dick Stapp (Fort Belvoir, Va.), Charles Gibbons (Fort Hood, Tex.), Jim Pothop (SACom, Europe), Bill Schmidt (504th Inf., Fort Bragg, N.C.), Alfred Khuni (15th Inf., Fort Benning, Ga.), Jim Hughes (47th Inf., Fort Lewis, Wash.), Melvin Clanton (Orleans, France).

CENTERS
John Talam (Brooke Medical, Tex.), Dick Kackmeister (Fort Hood, Tex.), Jimmie Timms (WACom, Europe), Bill Evans (4th Divarty, Fort Lewis, Wash.).

BACKS
Lee Morris (187th Rakkasans, Fort Campbell, Ky.), Hugh Pewin (121st Signal—1st Eng. Falcons, Fort Riley, Kans.), Bill Fleischmann (Fort Carson, Colo.), Gayle Dick (EASCOM, Korea), Loris Nussbaum (Fort Eustis, Va.), Bill Stokes (1st Cav. Divarty, Korea), George Robinson (Camp Zama, Japan), Julius Blakeney (3d Divarty, Fort Lewis, Wash.), Ed Esteban (350th Inf., Fort Lewis, Wash.), Arlie Slayton (505d Abn. Inf., Fort Campbell, Ky.), Larry Graham (Schweinfurt, Germany), Ed Crook (Berlin Bears, Germany), Gene Campbell (4th Divarty, Fort Lewis, Wash.), Frank Greliardi (EASCOM, Korea), Elzie Tillery (Fort Dix, N.J.), Jamie Caleb and John Johnson (Bremerhaven, Europe), Rubin Saage (Fort Bliss, Tex.), Lemmel Harkey (Fort Sill, Okla.), Abe Woodson and Alex Litmea (Fort Leonard Wood, Mo.), Bobby Hilton (Ladd Army Base, Alaska), Dick Beard (8th AAA, Europe), Bob Lance (Brooke Medical, Tex.), Clarence Lamb (Fort Myer, Va.), Don Comstock (Fort Carson, Colo.), Frank Tamburello (Fort Belvoir, Va.), Joseph Paglieli (Fort Knox, Ky.).

CHARLIE BRACKINS
Ulm Quarterback
MVP Runner-Up

FORREST (BOB) JAMES
Belvoir Halfback
Most Valuable Player

All-Army First Platoon selection, Forrest Gregg, had an illustrious football career in both playing professional football and coaching it. Gregg's Pro Football Hall of Fame entry says he was born on 18 October 1933 in Birthright, Texas. He was inducted into the Pro Football Hall of Fame on 30 July 1977, along with other class members, Frank Gifford, Gale Sayers, Bart Starr, and Bill Willis.

Gregg's professional career spanned 15 seasons, 193 games. He had been a second-round draft pick in 1956 by the Green Bay Packers.

Furthermore, his Hall of Fame biography said he had been "one of the best to play his position in the history of the game." He starred at Southern Methodist prior to his having been drafted into the NFL. At 6'4", 249 pounds, Gregg was considered somewhat undersized for his position by NFL standards, but he worked hard on finessing and outthinking his opponents, obviously to great success. He was an "iron man," having missed only one start in an eleven-year span.

FORREST GREGG
Tackle — Southern Methodist University
Height 6'4", Weight 230. Born in Birthright, Texas, October 18, 1933

Second year in professional football   Packers 2nd draft choice in 1956   Can play offensive or defensive tackle as well as defensive end   For two straight years, 1954 and 1955, was named to All-Southwest Conference team   Played in East-West Shrine game and the Hula Bowl in Hawaii   Was captain of the SMU grid team in 1955   In service the last two years   He joins former SMU star Bill Forester on the Green Bay roster   Attended Sulphur Springs, Texas High School and played football, baseball and participated in track   Residence: Dallas, Texas.

Gregg was a nine-time Pro Bowl selection, and was named to the NFL's All-Decade Team of the 1960s. He won three Super Bowl rings, between his time with the Packers and the Cowboys. Gregg later coached in the NFL from 1969 to 1987, leading the Browns, Packers, and Bengals.

Rest in Peace, hero.

Second Platoon All-Army selection at the tackle position, Roosevelt "Rosey" Grier, was listed as 6'5", 290 pounds; easily one of the physically largest players in Service football, back in the days when the average lineman would have been a couple inches shorter and 40 or 50 pounds lighter. Grier played out of Fort Dix, and had played at Penn State before moving on to a very productive NFL career.

In his autobiography, *Rosey, An Autobiography, The Gentle Giant* (61), he dedicated a chapter to his time in the Army. To start with, he wasn't pleased at having been drafted in peacetime during his second year in the NFL, though he strongly believed in his duty to serve his country.

He had to report to the Army within days of the Los Angeles Pro Bowl, and he decided to adopt a positive attitude about his non-voluntary service. Ironically, his Eastern Conference Pro Bowl team would include Ollie Matson and Yale Lary - Army stars, both. Grier's Army draft sparked a lot of calls from reporters, curious about the All-Pro member of the world champion Giants entering the Army.

He said he felt better about being a pro athlete entering the Army when he saw how many other professional athletes were joining him, among them: Alvin Clinkscale, Sherman Plunkett, Cy Hugo Green, Sandy Koufax, and Don Drysdale.

He was soon introduced to being a draftee stationed at Fort Dix. He had been given no special treatment either way, as far as he could tell, although given his size they initially had trouble outfitting him in an Army uniform.

> The rigors of military life – getting up at five o'clock in the morning, getting lots of exercise, learning how to make a bed the Army way ... were not disagreeable to me. Besides, I liked the plentiful food.

Grier was appointed acting platoon sergeant, in which he demanded the best from himself and his men. He befriended a fellow G.I. named Wally Choice, who also loved athletics and was a basketball player from Indiana (Choice played for Indiana University and later with the Eastern Professional Basketball League).

Grier noted that he had the opportunity to play football "with an excellent group of athletes at Fort Dix" after basic training. Not only were they excellent athletes, but they were also undefeated, earning a place in an inter-service bowl game (Satellite Bowl) in Cocoa Beach, Florida in December

1957. Unfortunately, according to Grier, the men stayed up too late the night before the game and were not able to give their best, losing to Carson (*Ed.* – *see 4 January 1958 game summary*).

Ultimately, Grier was released from duty six months early; his Army service was eighteen months total, after which he went straight to the Giant's training camp in Bear Mountain, New York (*Note: Under assistant coach, Tom Landry*). At the camp, Charlie Conerly was across the hall, and Frank Gifford and Kyle Rote were nearby.

Ironically, the Giants' season-opening opponent in 1958 was the Chicago Cardinals, with the great Service Sports veteran Ollie Matson.

> "The man to stop in this game," Coach Landry told us, "is their running back, Ollie Matson. He's fast and he's good. If he gets the ball and starts to run, you'll have to work hard to catch him."

Grier, of course, knew about Matson and his skillset. The game plan worked, and the Giants beat the Cardinals 37-7.

It wasn't long before Grier faced a tough opponent, Norm Van Brocklin, with Philadelphia. Van Brocklin got the best of the Giants in that game, and rolled up 238 yards passing and two touchdowns for the win.

Grier's legend was summarized in 2025, Grier's 93rd year, by Brock Vierra on *si.com* (62), noting that he is one of the select few NFL alums who have lived into their 90s. At the time, Grier was the oldest living NFL player.

Not only was Grier a literal mountain of a man, but he also "lived a life appropriate for his stature."

The Penn State All-American designation and 1955 NFL draft accomplishments were supplemented by Grier having also been a two-time track and field All-American. He was one of the four legendary Los Angeles Rams' "Fearsome Foursome," along with Merlin Olson, Deacon Jones, and Lamar Lundy.

Grier earned three All-Pro honors and two Pro Bowl selections before he retired in 1967. The high-profile portion of his life, however, had just begun.

Photo: Grier quarterback-sack (61).

As an actor, Grier made almost 70 television appearances, but he may have been more well-known for being on U.S. Senator Robert Kennedy's bodyguard team. Grier had been guarding Kennedy's wife, Ethel, at the time Kennedy was shot by Sirhan Sirhan, whom Grier helped subdue following the shooting.

Grier was a minister, author, and a motivational speaker who spoke at the 1984 Republican National Convention. Grier had an unsuccessful run for governor of California in 2018.

"One of the greatest gentlemen of football, Rosey Grier continues to define what it means to be a living legend."

Thank you for your service, hero.

Selected "Who's Who" 1957 All-Army summaries published in *Army Times*:

> **CHARLEY BRACKINS** – Quarterback, close second in votes for MVP. Was leading scorer in Europe's Southern Conference. He gained 268 passing yards and 314 rushing yards. Formerly starred for Prairie View A&M, Tex., and also played professionally with the Green Bay Packers in 1955. Was ALL-USAREUR last year.

SAM (FIRST DOWN) BROWN – The only holdover from the *Army Times* 1956 All-Army squad. Sam was a star halfback for the 87th Inf. Conquerors in Europe. Won All-Army honors last year with Fort Ord. He was a 1954 UCLA All-American. A "fast and tricky" runner.

JERRY JOHNSON – Fort Hood quarterback passed for more than 1000 yards this year. Former Texas Tech star 1951-55. Was named most outstanding athlete in the Fourth Army in 1956.

DON MITCHELL – Averaged 10 yards per game for the Tokyo Bulldogs. Formerly starred for VPI.

JIM HANIFAN – An end who was a former California All-American in 1954 and starred for the USAREUR championship team, Schweinfurt Crusaders (86th Inf.).

DON HOLLEDER – "Famed All-American from West Point" who played quarterback and end for 21st Inf. Team from Hawaii. Drafted by the Philadelphia Eagles.

BOB PELLEGRINI – Player/coach at Fort Knox, and was nationally known. Pellegrini was a two-time All-American at Maryland, and was named outstanding player at 1956 College All-Star game.

PHIL STEWART – Fort Richardson (Alaska) Pioneers lineman was named Alaska MVP. Played for Tulane and Alabama; left Alabama for military service. Had offer from Cleveland Browns.

SHERM PLUNKETT – Fort Dix lineman who played with fellow All-Army Rosey Grier at Fort Dix. Played college football with Maryland State College.

ED FAUCH – Played tackle for University of Southern California in 1954, and played in the Rose Bowl in 1955. Was named All-Fourth Army team the previous year.

JIM MARKELONIS – Played college football at Tennessee, seeing action in the 1951 and 1953 Cotton Bowls, and in the Sugar Bowl in 1952.

1958 *ARMY TIMES* ALL-ARMY FOOTBALL POLL

The 13 December 1958 *Army Times* (63) published results for the 1958 All-Army poll - "Korea's Estrada All-Army MVP."

"Division-level Army football came to Korea for the first time this season, and left a major impression upon the eighth annual *Army Times* All-Army football poll."

PFC Rudy Estrada, a talented back in the Korea Conference, was awarded Most Valuable Player honors based on input from coaches and sports writers. Estrada played with the Korea Area Command Loggers, which also put four other conference players in the poll results, second team.

200 Army coaches and sports writers had been polled, selecting, among others, four first team honorees who had played Army football for 3-6 years. This year's first team is notable for having the fewest pro athletes among the team selections. Only Curry Juneau (Browns) and John Lewis (Colts) had professional football ties, but all except two (Thires Pickett and Charlie Barkman) had college playing experience.

Despite the lack of prior formal experience, Sgt. Barkman had six years of Army playing time, and through capable coaching he was able to excel at guard position for Fort Campbell. Barkman had also spent time with the 187th Rakkasans in Japan.

Thires Pickett brought five prior years' experience with Army football, and managed to "outplay big-name college linemen" this year.

First-teamer Eddie Crook helped his Berlin Bears to an undefeated season in the Europe's Northern Conference. Crook was a multi-talented athlete, having been a past All-Army light-middleweight boxing champ at Fort Benning.

The MVP runner-up was Curry Juneau of Brooke Army Medical Center.

Estrada had been a former star with New Mexico A&M, and was a "triple-threat" for the Loggers, including as defensive back, halfback and quarterback. Estrada's coach, Sam Puterbaugh, said that Estrada "can play offensive back for any pro team in the states."

Estrada was the unanimous choice for All-Army voters from Korea.

1958 FIRST TEAM

Position	Name	Team	College	Hometown
End	Curry Juneau	Brooke Medical.	Miss. Southern	New Orleans, La.
End	John Lewis	Fort Meade	Mich. State	Fremont, Ohio
Tackle	William Kerr	Brooke Medical	Kent State	Warren, Ohio
Tackle	Thires Pickett	Fort Campbell	n/a	Twinsburg, Ohio
Guard	Phil Canton	Fort Hood	West Va.	Uniontown, Pa.
Guard	Charlie Barkman	Fort Campbell	n/a	New Kingston
Center	Jim Mense	Fort Riley	Notre Dame	Hamilton, Ohio
Back	Rudy Estrada	Korea Area Cmd.	New Mx A&M	Las Cruces, NM
Back	Earl Cato	Fort Belvoir	Vanderbilt	Hartsville, Tenn.
Back	Eddie Crook	Berlin Bears	West Va.	Detroit, Mich.
Back	Eddie Vincent	Fort Carson	Iowa	Los Angeles, Ca.

1958 SECOND TEAM

Position	Name	Team
End	Dick Price	Aschaffenburg (Europe)
End	Terrell Hunter	Korea Area Command
Tackle	Carl Larpenter	Fort Carson
Tackle	Larry Price	35th Inf., 25th Div, (Hawaii)
Guard	Vince Scorzone	Korea Area Command
Guard	Gary Nunnelee	7th Div. (Korea)
Center	Joe Ryan	Fort Dix
Back	Dick Allison	Sandhofen (Europe)
Back	Jack Stephans	Fort Dix
Back	Travis Buggs	1st Cav. Div (Korea)
Back	Lee Hermsen	Fort Belvoir

PHIL CANTON
Hood Guard

CHARLIE BARKMAN
Campbell Guard

THIRES PICKETT
Campbell Tackle

JIM MENSE
Riley Center

Selected quotes from Army football coaches and sports writers:

"*Earl Cato* *was our best back last year but received a broken arm in the third game and was out for the rest of the season. Without a doubt, he's the best in service football. I sincerely believe that Cato has displayed as much ... ability (as) Fob James (All-Army MVP last year).*"

- **MSgt. Nelson L. Peterson, Head Coach, Fort Belvoir Engineers.**

"*Pickett* *is the best tackle I've seen this year. His superior performances have figured in every win ... he's the toughest player I've seen all season.*"

- **CWO Theodore J. Dexter, Head Coach, Fort Campbell Screaming Eagles.**

"*Lt.* *John Bredice* *was one of the finer ends in the pro league in 1956 with the Philadelphia Eagles ... he proved to be the key player (quarterback) on the team. He completed 49 passes in 75 attempts for 819 yards and five touchdowns.*"

- **1st Lt. R. W. Hoerning, Coach, Fort Benning, Ga.**

"*Pickett* *was exceptionally outstanding on both offense and defense and definitely a team player. He whipped every tackle he faced this year.*"

- **SP5 Ken Lord, Sports Reporter, Fort Campbell, Ky.**

"*While playing for a winless club,* *Dick Price* *was the outstanding pass receiver in USAREUR. He has the finest hands I've seen on an end in years. He is as good a pass receiver, if not better than West Point's All-American Don Holleder.*"

- **1st Lt. John H. Stevenson, Coach, Aschaffenburg Cubs.**

Selected "Who's Who" 1958 All-Army summaries published in *Army Times*:

CURRY JUNEAU – Had been Brooke's top man for versatility – defense or offense, end or linebacker. At Mississippi Southern the previous year won third team All-American honors on the AP squad ... was captain of Mississippi Southern in his senior year.

JOHN (THUNDER) LEWIS – Averaged 70 yards per game for Fort Meade during the year. Accounted for more than half the team's total passing yardage. Played at Michigan State and for the Vancouver Lions (CFL), after which he was with the Baltimore Colts. Was named All-American and All-Big Ten, and later earned honorable mention with the All-Army team while with the Fort Knox Tankers.

TERRELL HUNTER – Standout for the Korea Area Command Loggers on offense and defense. He edged out All-Korea Conference Howard Williams of the 7th Division for second team All-Army honors.

HEADQUARTERS 7th INFANTRY DIVISION
OFFICE OF THE COMMANDING GENERAL
APO SAN FRANCISCO 96207

BILL KERR – Anchored the strong Brooke line during the 1958 season. The 260-pounder was All-Mid-American twice and All-Ohio twice while at Kent State.

CARL LARPENTER – University of Texas scholarship athlete, with his schooling interrupted by Army service. Will return to Texas upon completion of Army tour next month. Was a standout all year for the Carson Mountaineers, at 6-1, 220 pounds.

VINCE SCARZONE – Top lineman in the All-Korea Conference, as voted by league coaches; he was especially outstanding as linebacker.

GERY NUNNELEE – Center position for the 7th Division Bayonets in the All-Korea Conference, but earned All-Army spot as guard due to receiving many more (voting) points than any

83

guard. Played varsity ball for three years at the University of Washington. A unanimous choice on the All-Korea Conference team.

JIM MENSE – Led the 26th Inf. to Fort Riley regimental league championship. Fort Riley was the only team to defeat Brooke Medical Center this season. Played brilliantly as offensive center and defense middle linebacker. All-American honorable mention at Notre Dame; drafted by Green Bay Packers, but intends to instead return to his accounting job at Avco Corp. in Cincinnati.

JOE RYAN – Played college ball at Villanova, and was drafted by the Chicago Bears. Fort Dix coach, Jim Ward, called Ryan "the steadiest, most spirited and best all-around player on the club." 6-2, 230 pounds, from Staten Island, New York.

EDDIE VINCENT – Selected to All-Big Ten teams for three state years while starring at Iowa. Was All-Big Ten rushing champ in 1954. Played in 1956 College All-Star game. Played six games with the Los Angeles Rams before being drafted into the Army. "Extremely fast."

JACK STEPHANS – Six feet, 193 pounds. "Main cog in Fort Dix attack, completing 91 of 175 passes (52 percent) for 1045 yards." Graduated Holy Cross and was drafted by the Steelers, but passed up the NFL to compete in Canada for the Toronto Argonauts. Was to be discharged in 1959, and hoped to enter the NFL.

TRAVIS BUGGS – Star halfback for the championship 1st Cav. Div. Cavaliers, was unanimous selection by coaches on the All-Korea Conference team. One of the most elusive backs in the league.

LEE HERMSEN – Played for Marquette University and the Green Bay Packers. A 5-11, 185-pound second lieutenant from Green Bay.

North Iowa Today reported (65) that Eddie Vincent was born 23 June 1934, and grew up in Steubenville, Ohio, but later, along with Cal Jones and Frank Gilliam, became "part of the 'Steubenville Trio' which made their way from

Ohio to Iowa to play football." Vincent earned first-team All-Big Ten honors in 1955 and was second-team in 1954.

Photo: Jack Stephans, Holy Cross 1955. College of the Holy Cross, "Purple Patcher 1955". Purple Patcher Yearbook (64).

The Los Angeles Rams drafted Vincent, but his career was cut short due to injuries. Vincent earned his bachelor's degree from California State University, Los Angeles, and worked thirty-five years as a probation officer. He was elected mayor of Inglewood, Calif. in 1983, where he spent thirteen years. He was also elected to the state assembly and senate in the late 1990s and early 2000s. Mr. Vincent passed away on 31 August 2012.

Rest in Peace, hero.

Lee Hermsen was a graduate of Green Bay West High School (66). He "was a standout and lettered in football, track and basketball and won a state championship in track." He participated in ROTC and starred in football at Marquette University. He was drafted by the Chicago Bears in 1957, but was soon traded to the Green Bay Packers (*no records on his pro playing status were located*).

Mr. Hermsen graduated Marquette University in 1958 and was commissioned as a 2nd Lieutenant in the U.S. Army, later promoted to 1st Lieutenant. He continued to follow his beloved Green Bay Packers throughout his life, and served his church and community.

Rest in Peace, hero.

CONUS SERVICE SPORTS 1952-1958

This section describes sports events and activity pertaining to the CONUS U.S. Military Service Sports program, which operated under the umbrella of military Special Services. Entries were taken from military documentation, contemporaneous newspaper articles, and archival documentation.

This section is intended not to be a narrative as much as it is a record and history through chronological documentation, though there is some accompanying commentary. I also expanded athletic reports by researching and providing background information on some of the athletes, particularly those whose pre- and post- service accomplishments were notable.

You will notice some apparent gaps in time and information. This is not oversight, but simply a product of incomplete archival records. In actuality a very small percentage of records were kept and archived over many decades (National Archives II, Maryland, claims only 3% or less of all records were kept/archived), and those that *were* kept were often housed in scattered locations, databases, and facilities. What you will see in this section has been pieced together from many different sources.

RYCOM SERVICE CLUB AT FORT BUCKNER

1952

Legendary Miami Dolphins coach Don Shula worked out for the Camp Polk Armadillos, Louisiana, football team in 1952 during his time in the National Guard, according to the 30 August 1952 *Army Times* (67). At the time, the former John Carroll University star, who had once rushed for 125 yards against a strong Syracuse team, was a roster defensive back for the Cleveland Browns along with Carroll teammate Carl Taseff. The *Times* reported that workouts were in anticipation of the upcoming Thanksgiving Turkey Bowl in New Orleans, in which Polk was to meet the Keesler Air Force Tarpons.

Photo: Don Shula, Fort Polk, 1952, Wikimedia Commons.

The 22 November *Army Times* reported that the New Orleans Turkey Bowl game between Polk and Keesler had been canceled; reason not given. However, Polk was to instead host Keesler at Camp Polk for the first annual Pine Bowl Classic, and the game would be broadcast on radio. There would also be a halftime performance and appearances from "many well-known stars and celebrities." (*Ed. note - The results of the Pine Bowl game were unable to be located in archived records*).

It was felt the 1952 Polk team had improved over the 1951 team under new coach, Capt. James Underwood; the squad was "loaded with former college stars." Working out with the team were: All-American Vic Janowicz and Ray Hamilton from Ohio State; Carl Taseff and Don Shula from the Cleveland Browns; Ohio State football captain, Karl Kaplanoff; and All-Army legend Andy Hillhouse from Texas A&M.

Coach Underwood was pleased with the quality of players trying out and felt that service ball veterans would give the collegians a serious challenge for starting positions.

Stars and Stripes newspaper (68) recognized that All-American, pro, and other football talent can and did come from small college backgrounds (and U.S. Military Service teams!):

> The pros found out long ago that there is a lot of ignored football talent, publicity-wise, out there in the high grass and the tall timber.
>
> Frank Catski of the Browns, an all-league center, is from Marshall College, which, for your information, is in Huntington, W. Va. Deacon Dan Towler of Los Angeles, the leading ball carrier of 1952, came from Washington and Jefferson. Don Shula, defensive whiz of the Baltimore Colts, played at John Carroll.

The 15 August 1951 *Stars and Stripes* quoted Shula on the quality of pro football training, particularly with the Browns: "I knew the Browns had a great pass defense; now I know why. Why, I even had to learn a little boxer's shuffle to be able to move backwards and keep my eye on the ball."

Sports Illustrated/CNN's Don Shula timeline (69) says that Shula's National Guard unit had been activated in January of 1952 and was deactivated in November of 1952, at which time Shula returned to Cleveland directly from Camp Polk. The next day he signed a $5500 contract with the Browns.

Don Shula went on to coach some of the greatest NFL teams ever assembled at Miami, which included stars such as Bob Griese, Larry Csonka, Jim Langer, Nick Buoniconti, Paul Warfield, Mercury Morris, Jim Kiick, Dan Marino, the "Killer Bees" (Bob Baumhower, Bob Brudzinski, Lyle Blackwood, Glenn Blackwood, Doug Betters, Kim Bokamper), and more.

A memoriam for Don Shula from the Miami Dolphins (70), dated 4 May 2020, says that Shula was the "winningest coach in the history of the National Football League," and that his perfect season in 1972 "stands alone in the 100-year history of the league." He took teams to the Super Bowl six times, winning two (1972, 1973) with the Dolphins.

Don Shula was a compassionate man, giving his time and talents to various charities.

The memoriam was silent on his time and football experience in the Army, as many were, but the purpose of this book is to fill those information gaps to the greatest extent possible.

Rest in Peace, hero.

Photo: Don Shula, John Carroll, ca. 1951

Another sports star, this time in baseball, Johnny Antonelli, served his country with the Army in 1951 and 1952. While serving with the Military District of Washington, he also used his fine athletic skills for the Colonials baseball team, according to the 30 August 1952 *Stars and Stripes* (71).

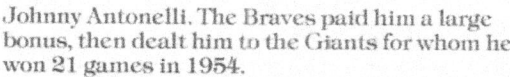

Johnny Antonelli. The Braves paid him a large bonus, then dealt him to the Giants for whom he won 21 games in 1954.

Photo: Johnny Antonelli (72)

Boston Braves "Bonus Beauty" pitcher Antonelli missed three Major League baseball seasons due to his military commitment; however, he hadn't lost his touch, fortunately. *Stars and Stripes* reported Antonelli's Colonials meeting the mighty Brooke Army Medical Center Comets of San Antonio in the quarterfinals of the National Baseball Congress tournament. Brooke was the defending champion team, was favored to win, and was looking to repeat.

Antonelli would be the starting pitcher for the undefeated Colonials, which had already won two tournament games. Brooke was also undefeated, but only one team would leave with their perfect record intact.

Brooke brought out the big guns to defend their title, including ex-New York Yankee third baseman, Bobby Brown, and former St. Louis Browns players Owen Friend, Dick Kokos, Bob Turley, and Rocky Ippolito.

Brooke's probable starter would be Bob Turley of the Texas League's San Antonio Missions and later of the St. Louis Browns.

Not all was roses in the world of Service Sports; the 30 August 1952 *Army Times* also reported the Fort Eustis head coach, Al Vandeweghe (no apparent relation to basketball star Kiki - I checked!), was caught recruiting baseball players into the Army with promises of "a good deal" - play on an Army baseball team and get a good assignment.

These quid pro quo deals were in violation of Army policy, per a Second Army spokesman. Vandeweghe (civilian) was fired for sending letters on Eustis Special Services letterhead, explaining that if a party was drafted, he took his chances, but if he enlisted he could see the mentioned benefits.

The article noted that Vandeweghe had come to Fort Eustis from William and Mary, from which he had been "released" due to "mysterious circumstances" (possible grade fixing). Vandeweghe was a former star football player and coach at William and Mary.

In other 30 August news, New York Giant rookie pitcher, Alex Konikowski, said, "pitching service baseball can be a big help." Konikowski had entered Army basic training in 1952 and was assigned to the Fifth Infantry Division and would pitch for the 2d Regiment.

In an early-September National Baseball Congress tournament Service baseball matchup, former Washington Senator pitcher Bob Ross of Fort Ord would meet former St. Louis Cardinal pitcher Tom Poholsky of the Military District of Washington in a Saturday night matchup, which promised to be hotly contested per the 31 August 1952 *Pacific Stars and Stripes* (73).

The three-game program would also include Fort Dix against Brooke Army Medical Center, and Camp Atterbury (Ind. 31st Dixie Division) against the Fort Leonard Wood Hilltoppers.

The Washington Colonials were 5-0, and looking to keep their unbeaten record intact, and Fort Ord was close behind at 4-1. The Colonials featured "Boston Braves bonus ace" Johnny Antonelli, who in the previous game had denied former New York Yankee Bobby Brown any hits.

Photo: Jerry Coleman, USMC Sports Hall of Famer and New York Yankee, ca. 1950s (72). Lt. Col. Coleman was the only Major League Baseball player to see combat in two wars. WWII postponed his baseball start and the Korean War interrupted his baseball career (74). Marine pilot Coleman played on eight Yankee pennant teams. Rest in Peace, hero.

San Diego's Navy football team matched up well earlier in the year against the Southern Cal Trojans in front of 40,137 fans (75); though Southern Cal won 20-7, the Navy acquitted themselves well statistically. Unforced errors, however (fumbles), hurt Navy's chances in the game. *Stars and Stripes* of 12 October 1952 (76) reviewed the Trojan's win at San Diego, giving Southern

Cal's defense the credit, while noting that their offence had been lacking in performance.

San Diego was given credit for achieving the closest score to Southern Cal in defeat, having "dominated the offense," despite only one scoring drive. Navy ran up 212 rushing yards and 133 passing yards, though an interception and fumbles prevented further scoring. In contrast, Southern Cal accomplished only 79 yards running and 19 yards passing, though it was enough for the win.

Stars and Stripes reported (77) from San Rafael, CA, on 25 October 1952 (78) that a televised game between Alaska's Elmendorf Air Base and Hamilton Field would take place. The Elmendorf Rockets were a "hot team from a cold country," and during the season they outscored their opponents 160-13.

Elmendorf player/coach Jack Bailey was an Arkansas University fullback teamed up with "speedy little halfback" Ernie Barron to work offense for the Rockets. Hamilton's running game, on the other hand, featured Texas University star Byron Gillory, returning following an illness. The Saturday game from Hamilton Field would be televised coast-to-coast.

Army Times columnist Tom Scanlon wrote on 29 November 1952 that the top service football teams were to meet in the Poinsettia Bowl in San Diego's Balboa Stadium on 20 December (79). The Poinsettia Bowl was considered to be the Armed Forces championship football game. The matchup would be between the Army or Air Force against San Diego's Naval Training Center or San Diego's Marine Corps Recruit Depo. The San Diego teams would meet in the Red Feather Bowl to determine the Navy or Marine representation.

Army or Air Force representation for the Poinsettia Bowl had not yet been determined. The article noted that, for an unknown reason, "the game was not officially sanctioned by the Defense Department's interservice sports program," and so the decision as to which team would play would be made at the Command level.

The Williamson team-strength rating service, which included Service Sports teams, was found to be flawed, and therefore determining the best Army or Air Force team would be challenging (Bolling AFB's number one rating was reasonable, but some other high-rated teams did not perform up to the rating, and other teams like Breckenridge were rated too low). Top contenders for the

Command decision were Camp Breckenridge, Bolling AFB, Fort Eustis, Fort Leonard Wood, or Scott AFB.

Army Times anticipated the crowd count at the Poinsettia Bowl would likely be the highest Service Sports football game attendee number of the season. The article pointed out that the game would not be a true Armed Forces championship, as Far East teams like the powerful Camp Drake Bulldogs were not considered (Scanlon made a comparison to the Rose Bowl, which purported to be the national championship, but which was just one of multiple bowl games).

Importantly, Scanlon went on to note, "The game will ... do much toward focusing nationwide attention upon the fine football played by service teams, too often overlooked in the nation's press," stating also that the better service teams were stronger than many college teams which received much more attention.

29 November 1952 *Army Times* discussed the arriving basketball season, noting there was a new Monmouth coach, "Mule" Haas, who would guide the Signaleers in competition against powerful service teams, including Quantico Marines, Indiantown Gap, Bainbridge Naval. Fort Meade, Fort Dix, Camp Kilmer, and McGuire AFB.

The Monmouth team would consist of 15-18 players on the roster, and several, such as Burrell Shields, Hardy Williams, Al Snyder, and Joe Schwartz, had college experience. Shields played basketball with John Carroll, but was also a member of football's Cleveland Browns. Monmouth would miss the contributions of Jim (Lum) Edwards, who transferred to Breckinridge. Edwards was a scoring machine, having put up 840 points over four seasons, with a 20 PPG average.

Even more impressive on the scoring front was M/Sgt. Arnie Melloy, who racked up 1715 points in four seasons. Melloy was not originally expected to return for the '52/'53 season, as his service obligation expired, but he "signed up for another hitch."

The *Army Times* reported on 27 December 1952 (80) that a single major Army football team in the United States remained undefeated – the Camp Breckinridge Eagles (Kentucky), having won nine in a row. Their impressive

All-Army Candidates In Action

LARRY COUTRE and SAMMY REYNOLDS, two of the leading contenders for halfback posts on the ARMY TIMES All-Army team, are caught showing their stuff in recent games. In top photo, Coutre (24) of Camp Breckinridge is hot-footing it around end against Indiantown Gap for 15 yards and a touchdown. In bottom photo, Reynolds of Fort Eustis is about to meet up with some Fort Lee Travellers. The three Lee players, from left, are Rudy Andabaker, Don Green and Hal Seidenberg. Block on Green and Seidenberg is being thrown by Wheel defensive end Earl Holmes. That's Joe Palumbo (58) at left and another Eustis guard, Elwood Raborg, on the ground at lower right corner. Breck topped the Gap, 34-27. Eustis took Lee, 33-0.

Photo: All-Army team in action, 1952 Army Times (81).

consistency put them in the New Year's Day Salad Bowl in Phoenix, facing San Diego Naval Training Center for honors.

In the same edition, Camp Roberts' 7th Armored Divarty basketball team had a surprise victory against Fort Leonard Wood in the All-Army tournament in Fort Sam Houston, Texas, taking the win, 56-50. There was outstanding play by Frank Kuzara, who scored 78 points over four games; the next highest was Charles Steagall with 47 points.

The command championship teams included First Army out of Fort Dix, Second Army out of Fort Eustis, Third Army out of Fort Bragg, Fourth Army out of Fort Sill, Fifth Army out of Fort Leonard Wood, and Fort Belvoir. Notable players were Third Army MVP Carl Braun from Fort Bragg, Sixth Army MVP John Wilson, Fifth Army MVP Rich Evans out of Camp Carson, MVP Fifth Army Carl Meinhold, Second Army MVP Ben McNeil, 61-point scorer, Dick Schnittker, and others.

1953

Photo: USCGA Jones Field, New London, CT, 1953, [NARA] RG 26, Records of the U.S. Coast Guard.

Army Times of 3 January 1953 (82) highlighted the "outstanding product" of Service basketball, Jackie "Jack" Turner, a former Western Kentucky

Hilltopper and then a Brooke Army Medical Center Comet. The 6' 4", 170 lb. Turner was said to be "one of the greatest cagers to wear the maroon and white." He was the leading scorer for the Comets, having racked up 158 points in nine games with a scoring average of 17.5 per game.

Turner arrived at Brooke at the end of the 1951-52 season as a three-year letterman with Western Kentucky. He contributed significantly to the Hilltoppers' success in his two seasons, leading his team to 22/28 wins in 1950 and to 23/28 wins in 1951.

Turner helped the Comets get over the loss of playmakers Jose Palafox, Bill Tom, and Herb Hoskins.

Peach Basket Society (83) recognized Turner's talent:

> A basketball star out of Bedford, Indiana, Jack Turner would go on to Western Kentucky. Turner served in the military following his junior year and returned to Western in 1953 and helped lead them to a 29-3 record. He was drafted by the New York Knicks in the first round of the 1954 NBA draft and would play 65 games for the Knicks.

Turner's obituary says he lived from 29 June 1930 to 5 October 2014 (84). He had been a professional basketball player for the Knicks and was a veteran of the U.S. Army. He was a member of the American Legion Gillen Post #33, a member of the NBA Retired Players Assoc., and a former Kentucky Colonel. He was survived by his wife, Delores.

Rest in Peace, hero.

Also in the 3 January 1953 edition was an account of the Camp Breckinridge Screaming Eagles' ninth consecutive win, 48-0, over the Ohio Valley Conference college All-Star team on Christmas Day. *Army Times* All-Army player and Notre Dame star Larry Coutre found the end zone twice for the Eagles, matching the performance of quarterback Bob Kilfoyle, who accounted for two scoring throws to help solidify the margin of victory.

Defensively, Eagles' "defensive half" Jim Moyer intercepted a Chuck Porter pass and took it 70 yards for the score. Other notable performers included the Breckinridge "mighty backfield" of Bernie Stephens, Ron Clark, and Coutre, all together accounting for 307 rushing yards. The undermanned collegians "yielded in the face of superior manpower" from the undefeated Eagles.

The article noted that despite San Diego's loss to Bolling AFB in the Poinsettia Bowl, their team remained one of the best in the country, and the contest was a good test of comparative strengths.

Dates of 1953 All-Army championship tournaments were announced: Basketball, Second Army, would be April 7-11, Track and Field, Third Army, would be June 12-13. And baseball teams were now eligible to compete in an All-Army tournament.

> Regimental, group, or comparable combined unit teams representing not more than 5000 men will be eligible for the All-Army basketball tournament.

> Squads representing major commands in All-Army championships will be limited to the following number of men, including team officials: boxing: 13, basketball 12, baseball 18, … track and field 15.

> In 1952 there were three All-Army tournaments, for basketball, boxing, and track and field.

Well, the Salad Bowl results were in, reported the 10 January 1953 issue of *Army Times*, and it wasn't good for the Breckinridge elevens, who were trounced by San Diego, 81-20. 14,000 fans witnessed Breckinridge struggle against the heavier linemen of the San Diego Bluejackets. "After rolling over team after team this year for an impressive undefeated season, the Eagles had the misfortune to meet the San Diego Naval Training Center club in the Salad Bowl."

Strong performers for San Diego included fullback Dale Atkeson, who drew first blood on a one-yard carry. Don Elbart blocked an Eagles punt, enabling George Musacco to bring the football in from the six for a score.

San Diego's quarterback, Wilbur Robertson, connected with Bucky Curtis for a twenty-four-yard touchdown. Odie Posey followed with an eighty-yard run for another score. Breckinridge's Bernie Stephens was first to score for the team with a ten-yard run. A "Best Player of the Game" trophy was awarded to Bluejacket tackle, Dave Parrish.

99

The same issue of *Army Times* attempted to determine the "strongest 11" in 1952, but said "since most of the strongest teams did not play one another, it's no easy problem." The Camp Drake Bulldogs (Far East), undefeated, were loaded with talented former college and pro players, including Clayton Tonnemeyer, two time All-American and Green Bay Packer All-Pro from Minnesota; Jack Stroud, All-American from Tennessee; Bill Austin at guard, former New York Giant; tackle Verdese Carter; halfback Bill Van Heuit; halfback Lynn Chewning; guard Rodney Rust; halfback Mike Maccioli; tackle John Hock; linebacker Pete St. Clair; and halfback Buster Humphreys.

Given previously undefeated Camp Breckinridge's defeat in the Salad Bowl, the stateside best-team choice was not clear, though Fort Eustis, Camp Lejeune, and Bolling ranked high. Other top teams included Brooke Medical, Fort Leonard Wood, Fort Ord, and Forts Lee, Belvoir, and Jackson.

The top basketball team in the Subway Service Basketball League was the Fort Jay Blues, allowing only a stingy 48.3 points per game. Players were Ed Kavulski, Romeo McCormick, Bob Anderson, Lim Wall, Don Leva, Walt Dockerill, Julie (?) Golubow, Jack Leinger, George Grabinski, Larry Haas, Ed Baucom, Elie Cayce, and Seward Ogden.

The 10 January 1953 issue continued with basketball coverage, noting that 6' 5", 205 lb, Bob "Wheels" Wheeler led Camp Roberts to the All-Army basketball title in 1952, and there was hope that feat would be repeated. Wheeler had played with the University of Idaho prior to the Army, where he earned All-League honors.

The "Sports in Brief" section reported that Willie Mays played two years with the Fort Eustis post baseball team, and Giants manager Leo Durocher said he'd give five players for Willie Mays of the Army. It was also reported that that the 1952 All-Army selection and Brooke Medical star had signed to play with the New York Giants following his service obligation.

The 17 January 1953 *Army Times* reported (85) on Fort Belvoir basketball's great success, with three of the best teams in the East succumbing to Belvoir's strength, that is, until they met the Quantico Marines.

Quantico ruined Belvoir's near-perfect season, limiting their win streak to eleven. The Marines forced Belvoir's record on the season to 11-2, with both losses having been to Quantico (proving Quantico's consistency).

U.S. Marine, Paul Arizin, the "famous pro of the Philadelphia Warriors," was one of the notable big men in basketball, having come up through the ranks at Villanova where he became collegiate basketball player of the year in 1950 (86). Sgt. Paul Arizin served as a U.S. Marine from 1952-1954, which was sandwiched between two NBA stints. Pre-Marines, Arizin earned NBA Rookie of the Year, and post-Marines he earned multiple All-Star honors in each of his ten seasons as a 6' 4" NBA player. Arizin is in the Naismith Memorial Basketball Hall of Fame and the Philadelphia Sports Hall of Fame. He is also listed as one of the 50 Greatest Players in NBA History.

Basketball Network reported that Arizin walked away from his professional career when the Warriors moved to San Francisco in 1962. Arizin was only 33, already having numerous NBA seasons under his belt. Arizin's friend, Frank Blatcher, explained, "He was a regular guy who went to Mass every day, so he decided that it was better for him to stay in Philly and be near his family/friends."

Paul Arizin went on to a career selling computers for IBM. He passed away on 12 December 2006 in Springfield, Pennsylvania.

Rest in Peace, hero.

Service team causing trouble for top college team:

Tom Scanlon's 19 September 1953 *Army Times* column asks, "You think Army football teams aren't tough? Well, don't talk to Jim Tatum …" (87).

Scanlon said that the highly-rated University of Maryland team scrimmaged Fort Belvoir, and the scrimmage "Wasn't for fun, but for blood. This wasn't a workout, this was for real … Tatum was seeing red as he found his first-stringers being mauled by Belvoir's team. Score – which will certainly not be released by Maryland University – was 15-6. Tatum had his first-stringers playing almost all of the game and he was so mad about the outcome that he wouldn't talk to anyone after the game."

Belvoir's Hank Lauricella, Tennessee All-American, fired off an 80 yard run thanks to space created by Belvoir's line, assisted in large part by another Tennessee All-American and previous All-Army player, Bill Pearman. Bob Haner excelled at fullback, and linebacker George Morris of Georgia Tech was outstanding. Belvoir put Maryland first-string tackle Bob Morgan into the hospital, and Lynn Beightol and Tom Sleep were injured.

Photo: Paul Arizin, Philadelphia Warriors, 1950s, courtesy ballerblogger/Flickr.

Maryland had a great team, but on this day it was the Belvoir eleven who shone a little brighter.

The 16 November 1953 *Stars and Stripes* featured a college football-score summary, which by itself was standard for the time. However, the interesting part is that Service Sports were integrated into the game results, with no separate delineation from the NCAA teams. This tells us that Service Sports football teams in many cases were on par with NCAA football teams in quality of play. This makes sense, because, particularly at that time, U.S.

Military Service Sports teams were loaded with college and sometimes pro talent.

COLLEGE FOOTBALL

East

Pitt 40, N.C. St. 6
New Hampshire 7, Springfield 6
Thiel 52, Allegheny 6
Westminster 13, Slippery Rock 6
Geneva 22, Clarion Tchrs. 7
Edinboro Tchrs. 33, Brockport 6
Drexel 20, Swarthmore 6
Johns Hopkins 13, Dickinson 12
Moravian 34, Wagner 19
American Int'l 39, Adelphi 6
Penn Military 7, Albright 0
Haverford 22, Susquehanna 13
W. Chester 20, Bloomsburg 7
New Haven 7, Brandeis 6
Union 27, Hamilton 0
Norwich 40, RPI 20
Franklin & Marshall 19, Muhlenberg 7
Juniata 21, Ursinus 6
Cleveland 23, San Francisco 21
Pittsburgh 14, New York 10
Philadelphia 45, Baltimore 14
Buffalo 20, O. Northern 0
Bridgeport 25, Wilkes 14
Boston Coll. 33, Detroit 20

South

Kentucky St. 32, Knoxville 6
Hampden-Sydney 28, Randolph-Macon 12
Emory & Henry 34, W.Va. Tech 14
Fla. Normal 58, Savannah St. 0
Bethune-Cookman 26, Xavier 6
McMurray 21, Howard Payne 6
Lebanon Valley 32, W. Maryland 20
Morgan St. 26, Hampton Inst. 14
Sewanee 21, Southwestern 0
Bolling AFD 27, Camp Lejune 23
Fayeteville 13, St. Paul Poly 6
Va. Union 15, Maryland St. 7
E. Kentucky 20, Louisville 13
Dillard 26, Tuskegee 8
Winston-Salem 16, Elizabeth City 12
Carson-Newman 26, Howard 14
Morristown 38, Livingston 18
Catawba 18, Guilford 0
Middle Tenn. St. 34, E. Tenn. St. 28
Miss. Southern 30, La. Tech 0
Tampa 26, Ark. Tech 20

Midwest

Case 47, Wash. & Jeff. 25

Denison 27, Oberlin 20
Miami (O.) 20, Dayton 7
Wheaton 33, Milliken 6
Detroit 14, Green Bay 7
Chicago 27, Washington 24
Washburn 27, Springfield (Mo.) 7
Quincy 39, Navy Pier 13
Ft. Hays St. 39, Kan. Wesleyan 0
Albion 27, Adrian 7
Cent. Mich. 33, Mich Normal 33
Valparaiso 14, Wayne 14
Idaho St. 34, Nevada U. 13
Wooster 54, Hiram 7
Ill. Normal 20, E. Ill. 0
W. (Ill.) 27, N. Ill 0
Kent St. 40, W. Michigan 0
W. Reserve 21, Butler 20
Ohio Wesleyan 34, Wittenberg 7
Mount Union 28, Muskingum 23
St. Ambrose 19, Bradley 12
John Carroll 36, Toledo 7
Wilmington 26, Marietta 7
Heidelberg 26, Akron 0
N. Dakota 18, S. Dakota 14

Southwest

Sam Houston St. 25, Stephen F. Austin 14
N. Tex. St. 38, W. Tex. St. 6
Texas Tech 49, Tulsa 7
Southern U. 70, Wiley 13
Hardin Simmons 39, New Mex. A&M 0
E. Tex. St. 40, SW Tex. St. 19
Trinity 62, Midwestern U. 7
Texas W. 28, Arizona 20
Ariz. St. (Tempe) 26, Brigham Young 18
Ark. St. 14, Tenn Tech 7
Coll. of Ozarks 14, Ark. St. Tchrs. 13

West

Moffett Field 32, Long Beach Islanders 20
Cent. Wash. 23, W. Wash. 12
Ft. Ord 35, San Diego NATS 7
Teas A&I 19, Austin Coll. 13
San Diego Marines 14, San Diego St. 7
Fresno St. 9, Pepperdine 2
Los Angeles 24, Chicago 24

Pacific Stars & Stripes

In his 19 December 1953 *Army Times* column, "Second Guess" (88), Tom Scanlon commented on Service football powers Fort Ord and Fort Jackson:

While Notre Dame and Maryland fans continue to argue (and if anyone is interested, my money would have been on Notre Dame if these two teams had met), isn't it too bad that Fort Jackson isn't able to meet Fort Ord in service football? Jackson football fans think Beattie Feathers had the best service team in the country this year, Ord or no Ord, and an Ord-Jackson game would certainly stop a lot of argument. Too bad Ord doesn't meet Jackson in the Salad Bowl on New Year's Day instead of Great Lakes Navy, a club Ord shouldn't have too much trouble with.

The same edition also reported a Fort Belvoir basketball loss to Fort Dix at Belvoir, 109-66, a game in which Duke All-American Dick Groat put 28 points on the board, and the great Don Byrd added 16 for the decisive win. Belvoir had been victorious in 12 of the previous 14 games.

Belvoir's only losses were to the Dix All-Stars and to Western Kentucky (the score of 92-83 shows the service team had been very competitive with the major college team). Dix stars included Bob Reiss from Columbia, Andy McGowan from Manhattan, Ron MacGildray from St. Johns, and Dick Duckett.

It was noted that Bryd never played college ball, though in a game against Bainbridge he held All-American and pro ball player, Ernie Beck (Philadelphia Warriors), to 13 points while contributing 21 points for Dix. Scanlon described him as "one of the most graceful basketball players around."

Also of note is Belvoir's game against the third-ranked team in the country, Duquesne, in which Belvoir came within 2 points of matching Duquesne's score (72-70). This was a game in which Groat scored 25 points.

The 19 December 1953 edition (22) reviewed the upcoming Ord versus Quantico Poinsettia Bowl football game from San Diego, saying that the Ord Warriors were poised to "whip" the All-Marine champs. Quantico had beaten Camp Pendleton for the All-Marine title the previous weekend, 21-14, despite former Notre Dame halfback John Petitbon having been on the Quantico injury list. Ord was the top ranked service team in the nation.

1954

In 1954, America was just past the "Forgotten War" in Korea, and many active-duty veterans were available for Service Sports in the Continental United States, as well as overseas. It was a strong period of time for sports in general; 1954, for example, saw the once-thought-unattainable sub 4-minute running mile fall due to the efforts of history maker, England's Roger Bannister.

1954 was also a time of "football oddity" at the Cotton Bowl, in which Tommy Lewis of Alabama "lost his head" when seeing Dickie Moegle of Rice running toward the end zone; Lewis, who was not in the game at the time, but rather on the sidelines, rushed onto the field and tackled Moegle, resulting in Rice being awarded the touchdown and defeating Alabama, 28-6.

Service Sports were coming on strong in 1954, now that the Korean War had been put on permanent hold. Historical records show that Service Sports programs ramped up in the 1950s, to the extent that tens of thousands of fans would see football, basketball, baseball and other sports competitions on the U.S. mainland and overseas. The sports were popular and widely appreciated.

Internet Archive posted a game program from the 1954 All-Army basketball tournament, including rosters (89). The tournament site was Fort Lewis, Washington, and the tournament dates were 5-9 April 1954.

Participants included USARPAC, Western Command, Sixth Army, Military District of Washington (Fort Belvoir), First Army (Camp Kilmer), Fifth Army (Fort Leonard), Third Army (Camp Gordon), Fourth Army (Camp Chaffee).

Nearly all of the players listed, with the well-known exception of the indomitable Don Byrd, had college experience. Rosters read like a list of who's who in basketball, including Byrd, Dick Groat, Bob Wheeler (drafted by NBA, but that draft was trumped by the Army's draft), Don Solinski (captain of St. Bonaventure University basketball team), Win Wilfong (1957 NBA draft first-rounder; Atlanta Hawks), Jerry Pease (Southern Cal), and others.

The Missouri Sports Hall of Fame inducted Win Wilfong in 1989, noting his prior teams included the University of Missouri, University of Memphis, and St. Louis Hawks (90).

Alfred Winfred "Win" Wilfong was born 18 March 1933 and died 18 May 1985. He was a Missouri native who played for the University of Missouri from 1951-1953, and with the University of Memphis (ostensibly after his military service) 1955-1957.

Mr. Wilfong played professionally for four years, including with the St. Louis Hawks, Cincinnati Royals, and Kansas City Steers, amassing 1826 career points. The Memphis Men's Basketball site (91) says that Wilfong is 29th on Memphis' all-time scoring list. He "could do everything from score to rebound, from pass the ball to defend." In his two-year tenure at Memphis, he averaged 21.5 PPG and 12.3 RPG. He exceeded 30 points in a game eleven times.

Wilfong led the Tigers to the NIT tournament in Madison Square Garden when that tournament was the most prestigious one, and, despite their one-point loss in the championship game to Bradley, Wilfong put up 31 points and was named tournament MVP. He was later designated All-American in 1957.

He was a "true American, small town hero" who died of cancer too early - age 52.

Rest in Peace, hero.

ALL·ARMY

1954
BASKETBALL
TOURNAMENT

5 - 9 APRIL ★ FORT LEWIS, WASHINGTON

1300 hrs
USARPAC vs Western Comand

USARPAC "Hawaii"

NAME	NUMBER	POSITION	HEIGHT	SCHOOL
Loui, Edward	7	F	5'7"	Univ. of Hawaii
Tomita, Itsuo	6	F	5'8"	Farrington HS. Honolulu
Schenk, Richard	77	F	6'2"	Baldwin Wallace Col.
Roos, Robert	9	C	6'3"	Univ. of Hawaii
Taguma, George	8	G	5'10"	Farrington H., Honolulu
Vaickus, Alex	90	C	6'5"	St Marys Col.
Song Thaddeus	5	G	5'11"	St. Louis H., Honolulu
Maguire, John	70	F	6'1"	Roosevelt H., Honolulu
Bento, Harry	66	G	6'3"	Univ. of Hawaii
Love, David	88	G	6'1"	Columbia Univ.
St Leger, John	99	F	6'3"	Univ. of Richmond

WESTERN COMAND "Rhinos"

McDowell, J.	30	F	6'4"	Southeastern Louisiana
Klabunde, J.	11	F	6'1"	Marquette
Stroup, C.	42	F	6'4"	Penn State
Stanley, J.	34	F	6'	Oneonta State
Lozier, D.	24	F	6'	Manchester College
Hoard, W.	31	C	6'4"	Dayton
McMaster, H.	53	C	6'6"	Michigan State
Brown, J.	20	G	5'11"	Contra Costa College
Kammerer, T.	44	G	6'2"	St Thomas
Bollinger, D.	22	G	5'8"	Southern Illinois Univ.
Mook, J.	33	G	6'	Ohio State
King, P.	55	G	6'1"	Ball State

1500 hrs
Sixth Army vs Military District of Washington

SIXTH-ARMY "Fort Ord"

Dunn, Charley	11	G	6'1"	Marquette Univ.
Albeck, Stan	12	G	5'11"	Bradley Univ.
Thiessen, Jack	13	G	5'11"	Whitworth College
Sullivan, Virgil	14	F	6'2"	Pepperdine College
Pounds, Bobby	15	G	6'2"	UCLA
Johnson, Andy	16	F	6'4"	Portland Univ.
Freeman, Bill	17	F	6'5"	Whitworth College
Duggan, Kevin	18	F	6'4"	San Francisco St Col.
Wheeler, Bob	19	C	6'5"	Univ. of Idaho
Peterson, Bob	20	F	6'5"	Oregon Univ.
Pease, Jerry	21	C	6'6"	USC

MDW "Fort Belvoir"

Great, Dick	10	F	5'11"	Duke
Lansaw, Paul	11	F	6'2"	Cornell-Kentucky
Don Byrd	3	C	6'3"	High School
Solinsky, Don	5	G	5'11"	St. Bonaventure
Donnelly, Bud	4	G	5'11"	La Salle
Ellis, Crystal	20	F	6'4"	Bowling Green
Iehle, Fred	14	F	6'3"	La Salle
Diddle, Ed	25	G	6'2"	W. Kentucky
Daly, Dick	15	G	6'	St Francis of Brlyn
Langas, Bob	22	C	6'4"	Wayne Univ.

First Army vs Fifth Army

FIRST-ARMY "Camp Kilmer"

Lienhard	14	F	6'4"	Univ. of Kansas
Taylor	6	G	6'	Long Island Univ.
Soemens	16	F	6'6"	New York Univ.
McCullough	17	C	6'6"	Loyola of Balt.
Bagley	11	G	6'3"	St. Marys
Kennedy	15	F	6'3"	Iona
Cannon	7	G	6'2"	Univ. of San Francisco
Clark	10	G	6'3"	St. Peters College
Quates	13	F	6'4"	Alabama State
Christensen	3	G	5'9"	McPhersón Kans.
Holmes	9	C	6'4"	Cleveland Ohio

FIFTH-ARMY "Fort Leonard"

Benny Purcell	10	G	5'9"	Murray State Col. (Ky)
Harlan Tolle	11	G	5'10"	Morehead St. Col. (Ky)
Jim Kilpatrick	12	G	6'	Texas Christian Univ
Richard Reinking	14	F	6'3"	Stetson Univ.(Fla)
Mel Mills	15	F-G	6'1"	Kansas State
Richard Baumgartner	20	G	6'	Indiana University
Frank Glover	21	F	6'2"	Morris Brown Col.(Ga)
Win Wilfong	13-22	F	6'2"	University of Missouri
Robert McGhee	25	F	6'3"	Kansas State Col.
Calvin Burnett	31	C	6'5"	St. Ambrose Col (Ia)
Jim Justesen	32	C	6'4"	University of Wisconsin

Coach Joe Newton

Third Army VS Winner of 1300 hrs. game

THIRD-ARMY "Camp Gordon"

Bob Smith	34	F	6'4"	Lincoln College
Ed Carpenter	33	F	6'4"	Wisconsin University
Eric Domroise	24	F	6'4"	Valpariso
Jim O'Brien	23	F	6'1"	Canisius
Cardy Gomma	27	F	6'1"	Muhlenberg
Bill Edwards	36	C	6'5"	St. Bonaventures
John French	35	C	6'7"	La Salle
Dick Koffenburger	25	G	6'1"	Maryland University
Roger Davies	31	G	6'3"	St. Bonaventures
Bill McMahon	28	G	6'1"	St. Johns
Jim Warington	29	C	6'1"	La Salle

Forth Army VS Winner of 1300 hrs game

FORTH-ARMY "Camp Chaffee"

Buck, Phillip	33	G	5'11"	Indiana University
Dochrman, Will	41	F	6'4"	Valparaiso
League, Bailey	39	F	6'	Indiana Central Col
Luttrull, John	31	G	5'11"	Millikin University
Mase, J.C.	40	C	6'6"	Southwest Texas St.
Montgomery, Dale	34	C	6'3"	Wyoming University
Moore, Gerard	32	G	5'10"	Washburn University
Shackleford, Warren	37	G	6'	Tulsa University
Spitz, Donald	38	C	6'4"	Valparaiso
Stalker, Edgar	35	F	6'2"	Upper Iowa University
Stickles, Charles	30	F	6'2"	Hastings University
Womnck, Frank	36	G	5'10"	Texas University

Coach Lt. Col. Milton Acuff

109

The 9 January 1954 *Army Times* reported (92) that the top ranked Ord Warriors crushed Great Lakes in football's Salad Bowl in Phoenix, 67-12, in front of 10,000 fans on New Year's Day. *Army Times* All-Army MVP, Ollie Matson, was named the most outstanding player of the game by sportswriters. He scored three touchdowns to seal the victory for Ord. Great Lakes was led by Texas Tech star quarterback, Junior Arterburn, who brought the Navy to a temporary lead with a scoring pass to Gene Schroeder. Don Heinrich and Jackie Price quarterbacked for Ord, combining for 201 passing yards.

The 20 January 1954 *Stars and Stripes* reported that the New York Giants had signed two service football stars to pro contracts, Ken McAfee of the Quantico Marines and Cliff Livingston of the Fort Ord Warriors (93). Giants coach Jim Lee Howell said that both signees would fit in with the Giants' plans to rebuild their team into a top NFL contender. Livingston would again join Don Heinrich, who was also a Giants signee. Notably, both men had played in the recent Poinsettia Bowl, which ended with Ord's victory over the Marines in San Diego for the service championship.

The 3 April 1954 *Army Times* was loaded with Army basketball playoff news and updates (94). Nine Command Championship teams gathered at Fort Lewis, Washington, for the Fifth Annual All-Army basketball tournament, which would run from 5-9 April. The winning team would move on to the Inter-Service championship tournament at Great Lakes, IL, 14-15 April.

The Inter-Service defending champion was the Navy team from Los Alamitos, Calif.

> Among the nationally famous stars in the All-Army event are the O'Brien twins of Aberdeen Proving Ground, Fort Ord's Andy Johnson, Belvoir's Dick Groat, and Kilmer's Herman Taylor.

The defending All-Army champion, and the current favorite team to win, was the Fort Belvoir Engineers, a team which featured the great Dick Groat and the sensational Don Byrd (who had starred for Fort Leonard Wood the previous year).

There was no tournament in 1951 due to the Korean War, but somehow they were able to hold the tournament in 1952 (war still going), in which the Sixth Army's Camp Roberts won.

All participating teams earned their spot by way of command tournaments.

Other teams participating were Camp Chaffee (Fourth Army), WACom Rhinos (European Command), and USARPAC Musketeers (Hawaii).

Other stars to look out for included Kilmer's Herman Taylor, NYU's Mel Seeman, St. Mary's Bill Bagley, Aberdeen's All-American Johnnie O'Brien, Univ. of San Francisco's Don King and his twin, Eddie King.

Fort Leonard Wood, MO, was described as the "odds on" favorite in the 5th Army basketball finals. A Hilltoppers win would make it four championships in a row. Wood would meet the winner of Fort Benjamin Harrison v. Hqs. Fifth Army in the finals.

Hqs. had defeated Fort Carson's 31st Dixie Division in an exciting come-from-behind win, 67-62, on the stellar play of DePaul All-American, Nick Kladis, among others. Kladis put 23 points on the board, with sixteen of those points coming in the second half. Following closely was teammate Joe

Erskine with nineteen. Erskine, Kladis and Bill Thompson contributed to four consecutive baskets to pull ahead of Carson, which, despite the efforts of Ted Greiner and others, fell short in the end.

Fifth Army tournaments stars up to that point included Carson's Little Johnny Woods and Entee Shine out of Notre Dame (who was also an All-Army football selection from the previous year), and also Dick Reinking, who scored 10 points against Fort Harrison to help propel Wood into the finals.

Also reported was Camp Gordon's Ramblers having won the Third Army championship with a close win over the Camp Rucker Vikings, described as "an electrifying photo-finish."

> Jim O'Brien carved himself a niche in Third Army immortality during the final game of the tournament, staged last weekend at Gordon's Sports Arena. The clock had run out in the overtime period with the Ramblers trailing … O'Brien had taken a desperation jump shot but was fouled. O'Brien toed the free throw line and rippled the nets with the tying and winning points.

The clutch win, helped by O'Brien's twenty-seven points and timely free throw makes, would send Gordon to the All-Army tournament at Fort Lewis.

The same edition reported that Fort Ord's Jerry Pease scored 44 points to propel Ord to a Sixth Army title. Ord defeated Fort Lewis 94-80 in the finals.

Ord had initially trailed Lewis 45-40, but changed their strategy by placing 6-6 Pease close to the basket where Lewis did not have the size to stop him from scoring. Pease had been a four-year letterman at USC.

Lewis star and Stanford alum, Ed Tucker, put 27 points on the board, but it wasn't enough to stave off defeat from the hot Ord team. Other point contributors to Ord's win included Andy Johnson (18), Bob Pounds (15), Bob Peterson (5), Charles Dunn (5), and others. Eric Roberts (Washington State) from Lewis contributed 20 points to their losing effort.

A ballot of coaches, managers, and sports writers named Bill Reigel (Duke University) of Rucker and Jim O'Brien (Canisius) to the All-Tournament team, along with O'Neil Weaver (Midwestern Univ.) of Rucker, Gene Smith (Xavier) of Jackson, and Neil Gordon (Furman).

112

The 7 April 1954 *Hope Star* (Arkansas) reported that 6'8" cage star, Junius Kellogg, was in critical condition following a car wreck, along with four other professional basketball players who received less-serious injuries (95). The former Manhattan College star was a "Harlem Globetrotter" at the time.

His doctors believed his chance for recovery was poor.

Mr. Kellogg's legacy is his honesty, having tipped off police to his being asked to shave points in college basketball in 1951; "An investigation revealed that several college players were involved in fixing games."

Mr. Kellogg was inducted into the Virginia Sports Hall of Fame (96), which noted that he had exposed the national college basketball gambling scandal. Kellogg had been drafted into the Army in 1945 and was named "Army Area Outstanding Athlete of the Year" in 1948 (basketball and football). He was also the first African-American player at Manhattan.

When Kellogg turned down $1000 to shave points, it led to discovery of cheating by 32 players of seven "national powers," who had collectively "fixed" 86 games between 1947 and 1950.

The Hall of Fame article clarified the horrific results of his car accident – he was paralyzed, but Kellogg was still able to stay involved in the sport he loved, basketball, in which he eventually coached in the National Wheelchair Basketball Assoc.

"In August of 1998, Kellogg passed away, but he will always be remembered as a national hero and one of Virginia's finest athletes."

Rest in Peace, hero.

The 10 April 1954 *Stars and Stripes* reported (97) that Camp Chaffee decisively beat Camp Gordon 91-70, earning a spot in the finals, while remaining unbeaten. Chaffee star Gerard Moore of Washburn University put up 24 points to seal the win.

The previous day, Fort Belvoir won twice in dominating fashion, first - against Fort Leonard Wood, 87-66, and second - against Rhine General Depot, 89-74.

Fort Ord stayed alive in the tournament with a 92-87 victory over Aberdeen Proving Grounds despite Aberdeen's scoring machine, Johnny O'Brien,

Seattle University All-American, tossing up 41 points. The winner of the Ord-Belvoir game would meet Camp Gordon to determine Chaffee's finals opponent.

The 11 April 1954 *Stars and Stripes* (98) said that Ord earned the remaining finals spot with a victory over Gordon, 78-68, and would face Fort Chaffee on the 11th for the championship title.

Ord relied on Southern Cal star, Jerry Pease, for 23 points, but his high-scoring effort was slightly outdone by Camp Gordon's Jim O'Brien, who scored 27 points in their losing effort. The article said that Fort Ord faced an "uphill battle" against Chaffee, who "waltzed unbeaten into the finals of the double-elimination tournament." Since it is a double-elimination tournament and Ord had lost one, if Ord won, a second game would have to be played to determine the champion.

Finally, the 12 April 1954 *Stars and Stripes* reported (99) that Chaffee topped Ord, 87-79, for the All-Army basketball championship title. Chaffee point-producers included Chuck Buckles, former Hastings College star, and Gerard Moore from Washburn – each producing 22 points. The article further pointed out that the Air Force championship had also concluded in Cocoa, Florida, in which undefeated Sheppard AFB beat rival Andrews AFB of Maryland. The Air Force tournament drew teams from all over the world, including from Germany, Alaska, and Newfoundland. Sheppard had eliminated Scott AFB, Keesler AFB, and Warren AFB to reach to the final game.

In basketball news, the 24 April 1954 *Army Times* (100) said "Championship Army Team Loses In Inter-Service." The Camp Chaffee-based All-Army champions unexpectedly lost two games, one to Great Lakes Navy (90-84), and one to the Quantico Marines (89-80) in the "world wide Interservice tournament" in Great Lakes, Illinois.

Following the All-Star losses, Air Force easily dispatched the Great Lakes Blue Jackets, 91-66, for the title. Prior to the tournament Chaffee had been undefeated for 13 games. "The Arkansas Cinderella club was the only team in the All-Army tourney without an All-American or a big name player in its lineup."

Chaffee trailed Quantico closely until Chaffee star J. C. Maze fouled out. Stars for the Marines included Paul Arizin and Richie Regan. Chaffee floor leaders included Chuck Stickles, Gerald Moore, and Phil Buck.

Dick Knostman for Andrews AFB took control in the championship game, putting 21 points on the board. Knostman and Duane Enochs controlled the boards for Air Force.

Paul Arizin was named tournament's MVP.

In baseball news, "Army Ball Helped Mays, Says Former Teammate," according to *Army Times* of 7 August 1954 (101). SFC Clarence Wilson of the 87th Infantry Regiment said, "I played left field for Fort Eustis last season. The Army was wasting a man. They didn't need me. Willie Mays played center."

Wilson made clear his admiration for one of the greatest, if not the greatest, baseball players of the decade.

Wilson's experience as an Army ballplayer was impressive, but perhaps not quite as impressive as his Silver Star honor. Despite his heroics, Wilson was in awe of Mays, saying that he was "one of the greatest guys I ever met." Willie was the fastest player he had seen go after a ball, and "baseball was his life; it's all he talks about."

Wilson felt that service ball really helped Mays. When Mays was with Eustis, he was practicing hitting into right field and also pulling his long balls down the left field line; "I watched him spread his stance and concentrate his power. He hit .540 with us and most of the pitchers we faced were major leaguers."

The 14 August 1954 *Army Times* reported (102), "Ollie Matson Stars Against the Rams" (*See also: "Fort Ord Meets the Los Angeles Rams, 1955," section*).

Army Times All-Army MVP, Ollie Matson, "Streaked through the entire Los Angeles Rams twice as the Ord Warriors dropped an exhibition game to the pros, 34-14." Two of Matson's incredible feats, scoring from 92 yards and 74 yards, resulted in the only touchdowns obtained by Ord in front of 12,889 fans in Los Angeles. This game followed an earlier-in-the-week game against the San Francisco 49ers, in which Ord fell 42-14.

Ollie Matson, Chicago Cardinals, 1955.

Photo: Ollie Matson, 1955, Chicago Cardinals; formerly of the
Fort Ord Warriors, California (25).

The Warriors were All-Service champions in 1953, and though some top players expected imminent reassignments, the team was expected to remain strong.

The same edition reported that Fort Meade's football schedule for the season would include Norfolk NAS, Cape May, New Castle AFB, Atlantic City NAS, USNES, Howard U., Ft. Monmouth, Severn River NAS, and Chemical Center. Also, Fort Bliss's new coach, Paul Mueller, formerly of the

Philadelphia Eagles would take control of the team, preparing to meet Camp Carson, Fort Sill, San Diego Naval Training Center and Fort Hood. The schedule also included the powerful Brooke Army Medical Center.

Also in the 14 August edition, it was reported that 1953's *Army Times* All-Army top vote getter from Europe, Tom Dickerson, was picked up by the Washington Redskins at the quarterback position. Dickerson starred for the 28th Div. Special Troops USAREUR champion team.

Columnist Tom Scanlon in the 21 August 1954 *Army Times* opined on Roger Bannister's "Mile of the Century," in which Bannister broke four minutes while coming from behind to pass John Landy and finish in 3:58.8 (*Author note: The official time was 3:59.4*). Scanlon quoted Fort Lewis track coach Frank McBride as saying, "I think Bannister has run the top race of his career and will never run another like it." Bannister was helped by pacing from previous world record holder Landy, and would not likely have such an opportunity in the future.

As it turns out, Bannister did not repeat his sub-four-minute mile without Landy – later in 1954, he beat Landy again in the mile by .8 seconds, 3:58.8 to 3:59.6 (103). Landy blamed his loss on having looked back to his left just as Bannister passed him on the right. Landy's post-race response was a quote for the ages: "While Lot's wife was turned into a pillar of salt for looking back, I am probably the only one ever turned into Bronze for looking back." But Landy had the last laugh – he broke Bannister's record on 21 June 1954.

It was All-Army baseball time at Fort Carson, Colorado, according to the 18 September 1954 *Army Times* (104). The All-Army tournament opened with Fort Lee "rocking the defending All-Army champs," Fort Belvoir, 14-7.

Starring for Fort Lee was Wes Covington, who smashed two long home runs, while Lee's "Ace right-hander," Warren Rutledge, notched a 26th straight win in the books.

Coming on strong in hitting for Belvoir was second baseman Jack Ryan, who gained three hits in four at-bats. Los Angeles Dodgers pitcher, Don Shaffer, the Belvoir starter, was rocked by Lee for nine hits and eight runs in five innings.

Covington, who had a future with the Milwaukee Braves, was Lee's top hitter all year, having come from the Minneapolis Millers into the Army.

In other action, Al Anasitch, a Fort Leonard Wood outfielder, was rotated into the starting lineup due to starter Whitey Herzog's discharge from service. Detroit Tiger rookie, Bill Black, went the distance for Wood; he had yet to lose a game in service competition. Wood outscored Dix for the win, 3-2. The losing pitcher was Boston Red Sox "Bonus Baby," Dick Brodkowski. Baltimore Orioles' Steve Molinari put one of Black's fastballs over the right field wall to assist the Dix scoring attack.

"Dix got its other run in the 6th when Chicago Cub bonus catcher Dick Tindall singled ... Andy McGowan across with two out."

All-Army tournament favorite, Fort Ord, drew a first-round bye.

The tournament would move from Carson's Kit Carson Stadium to Memorial Field in Colorado Springs for the championship game ... The winner of the All-Army tournament would represent the Army in the inter-service championships ... to be hosted by Carson, Sept. 23-24.

"Among the major league players participating on the command championship teams participating in the All-Army tournament this year are Harry Chiti of Lee, Joe Landrum and Faye Throneberry of Jackson, Dick Groat of Belvoir, and Darryl Spencer of Fort Sill."

The 18 September edition also reported that "Fort Wood Mops Up in 5th Army Tournament." Fort Leonard Wood earned a spot in the All-Army baseball tournament at Fort Carson by soundly defeating Fort Riley, 14-4. Riley had beaten Carson, one of the favorites, earlier in the week, 4-1.

Wood third baseman, Dick Gray, "owned by the Dodgers," hit a decisive home run to left field to end the game on a ten-run rule at 14-4. Ken Reitmeier, who had been slowed by injury turned out to be the winning pitcher for Wood; he pitched four innings, giving up five hits and three runs.

Wood first baseman Chuck Weiss also contributed a big home run to center field, clearing the 390-foot distance. Los Angeles Dodgers third baseman Ray Mladovich returned the favor, hitting a homer for Riley in the fifth, on his way to being named the tournament MVP. More pro talent in the tournament included Yankee farmhand Jim DePalo, Cardinal John Willingham, and Philadelphia's Ron Hammett.

Wood contributed four members to the Fifth Army All-Star team: outfielder Whitey Herzog, second-baseman Bob McKee, outfielder Pete Vitale and pitcher Bill Black.

FORT SILL'S JOE MORGAN is one of the many good-looking major league prospects to be seen in the All-Army tournament at Fort Carson, Colo., this week. Morgan starred at third base and at bat in the Fourth Army tournament and was named the tournament's Most Valuable Player. He is 22 years old and is owned by the Milwaukee Braves. He will report to Jacksonville of the Sally League when his Army career is over.

Photo: 18 Sept 1954 Army Times.

The Fifth Army Tournament All-Star team included:

119

- ✓ Joe Liebsch, Fitzsimons, first base
- ✓ Bob McKee, Wood, second base
- ✓ Wally Fassier, Riley, short stop
- ✓ Ray Mladovich, Riley, third base (MVP)
- ✓ Lennie Green, Carson, center field
- ✓ Pete Vitale, Wood, right field
- ✓ Bill Dudding, 5th Hqs, catcher
- ✓ Zach Monroe, Carson, pitcher
- ✓ Art Murray, Riley, pitcher
- ✓ Bill Black, Wood, pitcher

Notably not on this list was Fort Carson's Billy Martin, a Yankee baseball star in real life, who, according to *Army Times*, "played errorless ball throughout the tournament."

Whitey Herzog was player/manager for Fort Leonard Wood's baseball team, and not only was Herzog a powerful force in the Army, he went on to become one of the best known major league managers in baseball history.

According to the *New York Times* (105), Herzog "Won three pennants and a World Series as the St. Louis skipper, promoting what was called 'Whiteyball,' combining speed, defense, and pitching." These major accomplishments were in the 1980s, which was several decades after he had first been signed on as a player by the New York Yankees in 1949, but Herzog acknowledged, "Baseball has been good to me since I quit trying to play it."

Herzog never made it out of the Yankees minor league system as a player, though the time spent in camps was valuable for developing his baseball skillset; he learned immensely from renowned manager Casey Stengel. And though Herzog never made the top echelon of baseball as a player, he did manage a playing career spanning eight seasons with four American League teams.

Herzog appeared in 634 major league games with a career batting average of .257.

Herzog's career-calling was as baseball manager, and he embraced that side of the game with a passion. He leveraged "Whiteyball" to dominate in ballparks that had "fast artificial turf and spacious outfields, first at Royals

Stadium in Kansas City and then at Busch Stadium in St. Louis." His system culminated in a World Series title in 1982.

Baseball's Hall of Fame accepted Herzog's entry in 2009.

Hall of Fame shortstop Ozzie Smith said that Herzog was focused on game fundamentals, and always made sure his teams were well-prepared. He had great rapport with his players.

Whitey Herzog passed away on 15 April 2024.

Rest in Peace, hero.

In other 18 September 1954 news, *Army Times* reported that Fort Hood football crushed Paul Quinn College 34-6 in their 1954 football opener in front of 13,000 fans. Stars for Hood included Jessie Jones, who scored from the one yard line, and Deloyd Reed who scored from 35 yards. Later, back Aaron Dixon put more points on the board with a fourteen-yard running touchdown. Former Hood player Walt Napier helped Quinn to their only points with an interception of Hood QB Jim Rhinehart's pass for a touchdown.

Pro Football Archives (106) says that Napier played for Paul Quinn College from 1954-1957. He then played with the Dallas Texans of the AFL in 1960 and 1961, as a 6-4, 275-pound defensive tackle.

More football news from 18 December: Fort Leonard Wood suffered a decisive 41-6 loss to Great Lakes Navy in front of a stadium-capacity 6000 fans. Former Chicago Bear and All-Navy end, Gene Schroeder, drew first blood with a pass-catch-and-score barely three minutes into the game. Purdue star Bernie Flowers added two touchdowns for Great Lakes to help put the game out of reach for the beleaguered Wood squad.

In the "Army Football Roundup," we learn that Carson would face a "star-studded" Navy team, which included Tony Curcillo, Ohio State; Art Hyde, Harvard All-East selection; Charley Chambers, SMU tackle; and Verle Scott, All-Big Seven center out of the University of Nebraska.

Army Times of 2 October 1954 (107) announced that All-Army champion Fort Ord won the 1954 All-Service baseball championship by defeating Norfolk Naval Air Station's All-Navy team, 5-3, in Colorado Springs in front of 3000 fans at Memorial Stadium.

Ord's winning pitcher was Reeve (Bud) Watkins of the Sacramento Solons; Watkins also managed three hits to bookend teammate Jimmy Landis' contributions of a triple and the game-winning home run.

Ord was Sixth Army champion before going on to win the All-Army title, same location, two weeks prior. Ord's 7-1 victory over the San Diego Marines earned their place in the championship game. The winning pitcher was Ord's Jim Russell, formerly of the Kansas City Blues.

Landis, owned by the Chicago White Sox, was named MVP of the tournament. The tournament All-Star team was:

- ✓ First base, John Jaciuk, Norfolk Navy
- ✓ Second base, Jim Moore, Fort Ord
- ✓ Third base, Will Johnson, Warren AFB
- ✓ Shortstop, Bob Lillis, Fort Ord
- ✓ Left field, Bob Hoeft, Norfolk Navy
- ✓ Center field, Jim Landis, Fort Ord
- ✓ Right field, Jack Steinagel, Fort Ord
- ✓ Catcher, Bob Roselli, Fort Ord
- ✓ Pitcher, Jim Russell, Fort Ord
- ✓ Pitcher, Bill Dufour, Norfolk Navy
- ✓ Pitcher, Bud Watkins, Fort Ord

In football, Fort Carson beat Fort Bliss 32-0 in front of an overflow crowd of 6500 enthusiastic fans at Fort Carson, according to the 2 October *Army Times*. Carson scored three running and two passing touchdowns, while they held Bliss to 95 rushing yards. Carson stars contributing to the win were Ed Soergel, Dan McBride, and halfback Carl Smith. Bill Jackson took over as Carson QB in the fourth quarter and promptly hit Len Vandehey for a touchdown pass to seal the win.

CHUCK HOLLOWAY OF FORT ORD AND UCLA

Chuck Holloway was an interesting player with the mighty Fort Ord Warriors (and also with the legendary UCLA Bruins), particularly because there is a personal account of some of his time spent at Fort Ord relative to Army life and Army football. His name also appeared in several publications during the early and mid-50s, including *Army Times*, *Star Presidian*, and the special football analysis magazine, *Stanley Woodward's Football 1957*.

The 30 July 1954 edition of the *Star Presidian* (108) announced that the 1953 All-Service football champion, Fort Ord Warriors, would meet the Los Angeles Rams in their opening game of the season in Long Beach. The Ord lineup was to include "well-known Army and collegiate gridders" - Holloway, Ed Henke, Dave Mann, Gene Mitchen, Ollie Matson, and Bob Peviani, among others; however, they would be without "rugged guard" Pat Cannamela, who had broken his ankle in a recent scrimmage.

The 2 October 1954 *Army Times* reported from Fort Ord (109) that Ord had walloped Windbreaker AC of San Francisco, 46-0, which includes an 89-yard pass play from Jim Powers to Holloway, who ended up with two pass-reception touchdowns in the game. A week later, again according to *Army Times*, Holloway made big plays to help propel Ord to a 48-14 win over the Camp Pendleton Marines at Fort Ord; "Shifty Ord halfback Holloway provided the longest run of the day as he gathered in a Marine kickoff in the first quarter and galloped down the sideline 90 yards for a touchdown," in the first quarter. He struck again in the third quarter, beating the Pendleton defenders for a 71-yard touchdown reception.

An online publication titled *Chuck Holloway Chronicles* (110) included an interview of Mr. Holloway pertaining, in part, to his time in the Army.

Mr. Holloway was born in Detroit, Michigan, in the midst of the Great Depression, and migrated to California in 1950, ultimately enrolling at UCLA in 1952 where he worked part-time jobs to help pay for school. He was also in the ROTC program, but when he dropped out of ROTC to concentrate on his studies he was immediately drafted into the Army, though he said, "getting drafted was good for me. If I had not been drafted I probably would have flunked out of UCLA and probably never finished college."

He was assigned to Fort Ord, California (which has since been decommissioned as an installation) for basic training. He had been a private in rank, earning $72.00 monthly, most of which he sent home to his family. He said that he was trying to avoid having to go to war in Korea, so he tried out for the boxing team and the track team, among other things. He had mixed success in boxing, so he focused on track.

Ord's "unofficial track coach," and the person who recruited Holloway, was former Olympian and UCLA athlete, George Brown. Brown was the top long jumper in the world at the time, and he taught Mr. Holloway the art of jumping. Under Brown's tutelage, Holloway long-jumped 24'-8 ¼", a personal best.

Holloway said Fort Ord "had very good athletic teams," noting that Ord's track team had competed against Stanford and Arizona State. They also won the Sixth Army, All-Army, and Inter-Service track championships. Mr. Holloway won the low hurdles in those competitions in 1953 and 1954. He placed fifth in an AAU tournament in St. Louis in 1953.

Holloway wanted to try out for football once the track season wrapped up, enticed in part by the high quality of Ord's football team. He said there were nine former professional players and many good college players on the team, including Ollie Matson and Dave Mann, whom he called "two of the best offensive players in the United States (*Author note: Matson's prowess is well-detailed in other parts of this book; Dave Mann was drafted by the Chicago Cardinals in 1954*)."

Once he made the team, the schedule included practice in the morning, and then they would have the rest of the day to themselves, including the ability to go on and off base with a pass.

Holloway spent his first Ord football season with the second string, but made first string his second year, in which Ord went on to win the All-Army and Inter-Service football championships. In 1953, Ord played the L.A. Rams and the San Francisco 49ers, losing to both, but at the same time showing great competitiveness.

Cal's Joe Kapp spoils pass aimed at UCLA's Holloway.

Photo: UCLA's Chuck Holloway, in white, goes up for a pass (111).

Holloway said he had a good game against the Rams at Long Beach Stadium, and there were UCLA coaches watching which led to his football scholarship offer from the Bruins.

In his second year with Ord, Holloway was placed at the wide receiver position, where he would frequently discuss his passing routes with quarterback Jim Powers, formerly with USC and the pro 49ers. Powers would ask him if he could beat the defensive back, and Holloway's typical response was that he could, without even faking. And then he would do it.

Not only had UCLA been scouting the team, but Arizona and Arizona State also showed up to scout and recruit, and Arizona State made an offer to teammate Gene Mitchum.

Mr. Holloway was discharged in February of 1955, wherein he went straight to UCLA where he had a football scholarship waiting for him. He tried to be excused from football's spring practice so he could focus on track, but he ended up having to do both, which he felt made it difficult for him to excel in track. His 1955 UCLA football team was ranked fifth in the country, and in 1956 they played Michigan State in the Rose Bowl.

He graduated UCLA in 1957 with a Bachelor of Science degree, and went on to play football in the CFL for the Calgary Stampede.

Thank you for your service, Mr. Holloway.

The 6 November 1954 *Army Times* (112) reported the Carson-Sill game would feature All-Army quarterback versus All-Army quarterback. Penrose Stadium in Colorado Springs was to be the meeting site for Carson's Ed Soergel, first team All-Army, and Sill's Dan Page, All-Army second team.

Soergel had many large-school scholarship offers, but chose Eastern Illinois College, "where he went on to become one of the school's all-time players." Soergel was later drafted by the Cleveland Browns, but, like some others of this generation he chose instead to enter the Canadian Football League with the Toronto Argonauts. Page, on the other hand, played for a "proven football power," University of Texas, prior to entering the Army.

The 13 November 1954 *Army Times* discussed the great Ollie Matson, "Times' All-Army '53 MVP Pro Ball's Best in '54." Matson had continued to impress in an apparently smooth transition from service ball to the pros; he had been well-prepared for the next level.

Matson had been named All-Army MVP based on his excellent play for the Fort Ord Warriors and he was "the hottest article in the National Professional Football League" until he was injured (concussion) while playing against the Philadelphia Eagles the past weekend. Matson played both ways, offense and defense, for Fort Ord, and later did the same for the professional Chicago

Cardinals. His exploits included a 9_-yard kickoff return for a score in a 17-14 upset over the Steelers.

Washington Redskin coach, Joe Kuharich, who had coached Matson at the University of San Francisco, said Matson was "the best all-around football player I've ever seen. No one can match his speed."

Another sensational back was lauded in this same edition; Oklahoma University's All-American, Merrill Green, who had "sparked the great 1952 and 1953 Sooner teams with his clutch running and won the 1953 Oklahoma-Colorado game with a last minute scoring sprint." At Fort Sill, coach Fred C. Smith had been trying Green at quarterback – a testament to his versatility and athleticism. Green would be on hand to fill in should All-Army selection Dan Page get injured. In the meantime, he had distinguished company in the backfield – college All-Americans and later All-Army selections Billy Vessels and Buck McPhail.

Speaking of Fort Sill, the same *Army Times* edition reported that Sill had "walloped" Carson, 40-16 in front of 9200 fans in Colorado Springs; both were considered two of the strongest Service teams in the nation, and Sill was riding a six-game winning streak coming into the game.

In the game, All-Army quarterback Ed Soergel drew first blood, scoring on a run from the one, but Sill quickly returned the favor, using the mighty combination of Oklahoma stars Vessels and McPhail to lead the way. Carson's next and last touchdown score would come by way of the Soergel to Dan McBride passing combination, set up by the capable running of Ohio State's Tony Curcillo.

Sill used two platoons in the second half, and "completely dominated the game." Merrill Green scored twice in the fourth quarter to put the game away for Sill.

Proceeds from the game went to the Combined Charities Fund Drive at Carson.

The 27 November 1954 *Army Times* reported that the Carson v. Sill football match raised $8500 for charity. It was also reported that a "new gadget" became available – a football line marking machine, which allowed straight lines to be applied faster.

It is a safe bet that a Major General would appreciate straight lines. The same *Army Times* edition discussed the Director of Football at Fort Hood, Major General Tom "Trap" Trapnell of the Fourth Armored Division.

Gen. Trapnell had been a West Point football star in the 1920s; though six feet tall and only 160 pounds, he delivered "pounding runs, vicious blocks, and booming punts." He was thought to be one of the toughest players ever to wear the cadet jersey.

"He's the kind that would always come through for you," said West Point coach Earl Blaik. Trapnell was a tailback in the single wing formation and he played "halfback" on defense. He earned spots on All-American teams and was admitted into Army football's Hall of Fame.

At Fort Hood, Gen. Trapnell was encouraging to players, who highly respected his history which included valor in battle which earned him a Distinguished Service Cross.

'TRAP' TRAPNELL

From Football Star To Major General

By JOHN MASHEK

FORT HOOD, Tex.—Those who recall the West Point teams of 1924, '25 and '26 will remember the name Tom (Trap) Trapnell. He is now Maj. Gen. Thomas J. H. Trapnell, CG of the 4th Armd Div.

Though packing a slender 160 pounds on a six foot frame, Trap, as he was nicknamed, was one of the toughest competitors to ever don a Cadet jersey.

Photo: Army Times, 27 November 1954.

General Trapnell was so tough that he survived into the next century, passing away at age 99 in February of 2002. A *Los Angeles Times* obituary said that he had been a Bataan Death March survivor in WWII and was even an advisor in both the Korean and the Vietnam Wars. At the end of WWII, the strong, athletic Trapnell was down to one hundred pounds due to nutrition deprivation. He retired in 1962 as commander of the 3rd U.S. Army.

Thank you for your service, Gen. Trapnell.

Speaking of Fort Hood, the 27 November 1954 *Army Times* also reported Fort Hood's football victory over Brooke Army Medical Center 20-13 at Leonard Wood Field. At the game's conclusion, the Hood Tankers stood at 8-2 for the season, with the Brooke Comets close behind at 7-3. Contributing to victory were Tanker runners Whitney Armstrong, Duncan McCauley, and Jim Rinehart. The Comets were led by passer Ray Gonsalves, Christ Shaw, Winifred Tillery, and Billy Sanders. The crowd numbered five thousand for the game in Fort Sam Houston, Texas.

In other 27 November 1954 sports news, *Army Times* said the Armed Forces All-Star basketball team would send its best players to the March Pan American Games in Mexico City. All-Star team coach Norm Pilgrim from Sheppard AFB had been an All-American at Oklahoma A&M and was a veteran of All-Air Force basketball tournament finals.

Fort Leonard Wood coach Jerry Loeber had top talent, and "could field a team which could hold its own in any service competition." Bob Melton was a 26-year-old cage star and Harlem Globetrotter William (Bob) Leonard was a former Hoosier and college All-Star. Both men were still in training, but hoped to be eligible to play prior to tournament time. Leonard planned on a basketball career with the Baltimore Bullets following his military service.

More football news in the 27 November 1954 edition: PFC Roy Garland was described as a speedy 5-10, 170-pound halfback who scored ten touchdowns in nine games. Coach Robert Cook said that Garland was "the top broken field runner … in Army football." Garland hoped to perform for UCLA the following year, as he had connections to the Los Angeles area. He said he would not mind playing with Ollie Matson again, as they had shared a backfield at Fort Ord.

Camp Hanford QB

PFC AL KIRKLAND, who played with Southern California in the 1952 Rose Bowl, is now quarterbacking the Camp Hanford, Wash., Atomeers. Kirkland doubles as backfield coach.

Photo: Camp Hanford's quarterback, Al Kirkland, 1954, Army Times.

The 4 December 1954 version of *Army Times* (113) sports news discussed Bolling Air Force handing the great Fort Belvoir team their first defeat of the season in front of 10,000 spectators, 48-27. Belvoir's Pullen Field was bombarded with rain and wind, but the fans stuck it out and, despite their team's loss, were rewarded with an exciting, high scoring game.

Bolling's Tommy O'Connell, the former Cleveland Browns and Illinois star, was too much for the Belvoir defense, throwing six touchdown passes and scoring one on his own.

Bolling took the Eastern military title and earned a trip to the Poinsettia Bowl in San Diego. Bolling finished the season at 9-0-1, with Belvoir at 6-1-1.

Contributing significantly for the Belvoir Engineers were Don Engels, Jerry Lodge, Dave Suminski (fumble recovery), and George Tarasovich. Bolling players Charlie Jones and Bob Schneidenback also put points on the board to help push the Generals to victory.

Dave Suminski is honored in the Wisconsin Badgers Hall of Fame; inducted 2001 (114). He was raised in Ashland, Wisconsin, and played offensive and defensive tackle for the Badgers 1950-1952. His honors included All-Big Ten, AP All-American, and Wisconsin Badgers MVP. He was drafted by the Washington Redskins in 1953, then played and coached at Fort Belvoir, VA, 1954-1955. He was on the Armed Forces All-Star team 1954-1955 [*The Forgotten Athletes of the American Forces Far East* (11) shows that he was voted onto the AFPS All-Service First Team]. His pro career included time with the Chicago Cardinals, Hamilton Tiger Cats, and the Canadien Gray Cup team.

Rest in Peace, hero.

Tommy O'Connell's obituary (115) says that he had been a professional football player 1953, 1956-1957, 1960-1961; "He played at the quarterback position in the National and American Football Leagues with the Chicago Bears, Cleveland Browns and Buffalo Bills." He had been a high school star in Chicago and then played college ball with Notre Dame, and then with Illinois where he contributed to an undefeated season in 1951 and a number one ranking. The 1952 season ended with a Rose Bowl victory over Stanford, 40-7. Following football he became a businessman whose son, Mike, became a longtime player in the NHL.

Rest in Peace, hero.

Another heavyweight football team fell on the same day; Fort Ord took a loss from San Diego's PhibPac Invaders, 35-21, in a game termed as an Army-Navy grid classic, noting that the Warriors held a statistical edge, but not the win. In other action, Fort Riley All-Stars defeated Carson 41-20 in front of six thousand fans, perhaps in part due to Carson's loss of All-Army quarterback, Ed Soergel. Riley quarterback Charlie Harding was the workhorse for the day, connecting with Dan McBride for multiple touchdowns and entering the end zone for his own score to seal the win. Harding had been under contract with the Detroit Lions at the time, and proved his mettle.

Other Riley contributors included second string quarterback Ed McCauley, halfback Vernell Ross, and fullback Ace Groomes.

The 4 December 1954 edition of the *Army Times* was heavy on football news, but also discussed basketball's Fort Jackson, S.C., cage team showing "great promise." Jackson's strength came from four returnees from the previous season, including high-scoring Neil Gordon, a 6'6" former Furman University star, Don Cox from South Carolina, and brothers Tom and Bill Scott out of Lambath College and Western Kentucky, respectively.

The Jackson team only had one player with no college experience, Steve Benya. Jackson had lost Gene Smith to professional basketball, but Gordon would take his place as one of the team's future pros, having already signed with the New York Knickerbockers.

Army Times on 25 December 1954 (116) named eight Army basketball "aces" who would get All-Star team tryouts. The eight Aces were:

- ✓ 2d Lt. **Frank Guisness**, Fort Lee, Va., University of Washington's second highest all-time scoring leader.
- ✓ 2d Lt. **Cecil (Pete) Silas**, Fort McClellan, a star with Georgia Tech and the nationally famous Phillips Oilers, Silas holds Tech's all-time scoring mark with 1084 in three years.
- ✓ PFC **Robert Peterson**, Fort Ord, Calif., All-Coast at the University of Oregon.
- ✓ 2d Lt. **Robert Speight**, Fort Bliss, Tex., North Carolina State star.
- ✓ PFC **Will Wilfong**, Fort Leonard Wood, Big Seven All-Conference choice at the University of Missouri two years ago as a sophomore.
- ✓ Pvt. **Walter Walowac**, Fort Knox, Ky., Marshall College star.
- ✓ PFC **Jack Williams**, Eielson AFB, Alaska, Wake Forest star.
- ✓ Pvt. **Don Byrd**, Fort Belvoir, Va.; an outstanding player for Fort Leonard Wood, Mo., and Belvoir the past two years.

The players were to report to Wright-Patterson AFB, Ohio, to practice for the Armed Forces all-star team. All had been college stars except for Mr. Byrd.

The Wright-Patterson practices/drills would result in fifteen selections for the Armed Forces All-Star team. They would also have a session with a selected AAU team for the right to compete at the Mexico City Pan American Games in March of 1955.

The selection of Byrd, though with no college experience, "will come as no surprise to those who have seen him perform on a basketball court." He was a high school star in Cleveland, but proved himself over the past couple of years in Army basketball, while competing against established stars such as Paul Arizin, Maurice "The Magnificent" Stokes, Ernie Beck, Art Spoelstra and Dick Knostman. He was said to raise the level of his game while competing against the better-known players.

Another "Ace," Guisness, was no stranger an elite level of play, having set many scoring records while with the University of Washington; "He likes to use a driving hook shot which is almost impossible to guard against."

Ten Air Force players selected for All-Star team tryouts included three men who played on the 1952 Olympic team: Bob Kenney and Dean Kelley, both of whom played at Kansas and then with Andrews AFB, as well as Kerwin Englehart from Yokata AB in Japan. Rounding out the Air Force selections were:

- ✓ Bill McCullum, Lockbourne AFB
- ✓ Bob Williams, Sheppard AFB
- ✓ Billy Hogue, Sheppard AFB
- ✓ Gil Roark, Warren AFB
- ✓ Barry Porter, Kirtland AFB
- ✓ John Clune, Dover AFB
- ✓ Earl Redwine, Walker AFB
- ✓ John Wilson, East Illinois State College
- ✓ Gil Reich, Lake Charles AFB
- ✓ Dick Estergard, Furstenfeldbruch AB, Germany

Coaching duties were assigned to Lt. Norm Pilgrim of Sheppard AFB, a former All-American at Texas A&M.

The same *Army Times* edition reported Fort Sill's defeat of Bolling AFB in the Poinsettia Bowl in front of 10,000 fans, giving Sill the national Service Sports football title, replacing last year's Army Service champion Fort Ord.

"Sill's powerful line and running game proved too much for the Generals." All-Army honoree and Heisman Trophy winner, Billy Vessels, dominated both on offense and defense, including having snared four interceptions. Sill's Merrill Green ran seventy-three yards for a score, and 1953 All-Army quarterback and former Texas star, Dan Page, ran sixty-six yards for another score to contribute to Sill's victory.

Photo: 5th Infantry Division. Original not labeled; possibly Fort Indiantown Gap, Pennsylvania, 1951-53. Author private collection ©.

"A fine Sill line bottled up Bolling quarterback Tommy O'Connell, the passing wizard who won *Air Force Times*' Most Valuable Player award this year."

It was noted that Fort Ord would meet Fort Hood in the Shrimp Bowl in Galveston, Texas on January 2nd. Ord's only loss was to San Diego Navy's PhibPac, and the previous Sunday Ord crushed the semi-pro California All-Stars 52-0 in the Lettuce Bowl game.

Sparks Sill

BILLY VESSELS, two-time All-American and Heismann Memorial trophy winner from Oklahoma University, is now starring for the Fort Sill Cannoneers. Against Sheppard AFB, Vessels led Sill to a 38-8 victory as he scored two touchdowns and set up a field goal with a long run. Vessels is completing his basic officers course at Sill.

Photo: Billy Vessels, Army Times (116).

All-Army fullback Buck McPhail contributed ninety-seven yards on seventeen carries, and O'Connell was 14 of 22 for passing. This was Sill's twelfth win in a row.

Also reported on page 25 was humble Hal Mitchell's response to his having been selected as the MVP of the *Army Times* All-Army football team: "This certainly comes as a surprise and an honor to me. I was just hoping to make the team again." Mitchell was the first lineman to be selected All-Army MVP, and considered the selection as his "top thrill in football."

While Fort Ord football had been edged out by Fort Sill in 1954, Ord's basketball team, the previous year's Sixth Army champions, was looking strong; they were believed to be the prime contender to be 1955 Service champion. The Warriors would retain Univ. of San Francisco and former pro forward Don Lofgren, but they feared losing the services of Bob Peterson should he earn a spot on the Armed Forces All-Star team. The 6' 5" Lofgren and 6' 6" Peterson had been scoring workhorses for the Warriors, contributing double-digit numbers for victories.

Also, to no one's surprise, former All-Army star, Ollie Matson, now with the Chicago Cardinals, was named *Sporting News* All-Pro, per a team announcement.

Army Times of 23 October 1954 (117) reported that post basketball teams would be limited to thirty games on their schedule, and would likely need to make a revision to be within compliance. An Army DA Circular revised guidelines to restrict basketball to thirty games for the season, and baseball to fifty regular season games. These limitations did not apply to post-season play. For comparison, post basketball teams normally would schedule approximately 50 games in a season.

Fort Meade, for example, had already scheduled 50 games and would need to make an adjustment.

The new ruling also addressed travel distance concerns by restricting opponents only to other teams from their command. The exception would be an adjacent command with a round trip distance of less than 500 miles. Commanding generals were free to make exemptions from these guidelines.

Whether or not football would similarly face certain restrictions was not yet known. The current football schedules were not subject to the new rules. The point of the rules was to encourage more participation in "lower-level sports activity" and to decrease emphasis on spectator sports.

The same *Army Times* edition reported the "Strong Carson Line Makes Split-T Gel." Carson was said to be one of the many teams around the country to employ the "flashiest offense in football today," the Split-T, which had been developed by Don Faurot, Jim Tatum, and Bud Wilkinson in 1943 for the "powerful Iowa Pre-Flight Seahawks."

Fort Carson was considered to have a strong and agile enough line which would benefit the system; lineman doing their jobs well was considered integral to the system.

The system was given credit for Carson's strong start to the season. Coach 2d Lt. Chet Lukawski had been a former standout guard for Kentucky's Paul "Bear" Bryant when the team was regularly qualifying for bowl games.

All-Big Seven Nebraska center, Verl Scott, was singled out for praise, and was considered the anchor of the Carson Mountaineer line, which averaged 207 pounds from end to end. Other contributing stars included Tulane's Mike Housepian, Bradley's Bill Zimmer, San Francisco U.'s Francis Monti, and William and Mary's 230-pounder, Tom Horner.

Iowa's Dan McBride was "one of the most pleasant surprises of the season," with his excellent blocking and pass receiving.

Carson' strength was their depth, and they were going to be hard to beat.

The 23 October 1954 edition also reviewed the Fort Carson vs. semi-pro Dallas Hornets matchup, in which Carson destroyed the pros 34-0 in front of 2300 fans; "Carson led 28-0 by halftime and completely dominated the game."

Carson was led by quarterback Ed Soergel and by halfback Carl Smith, who took over as quarterback later in the game. Earlier in the action, Smith was on the receiving end of a touchdown pass from Soergel, and Ohio State's Dan McBride was the recipient of another touchdown pass. Smith also ran one in in the fourth quarter to seal the win. Dallas's 138 yards gained paled in comparison to Carson's 408 yards. Also starring for Carson were Bill Jackson and Van Vendehey.

Carson service sports clearly operated at a high level in the mid-1950s and it holds an honored place in the legacy of 1950s military athletics.

Photo: Dallas Hornets semi-pro football team members picking up equipment. Subjects not identified. WBAP-TV (Television station : Fort Worth, Tex.). [News Clip: Semi-pros form team at Dallas], video, October 7, 1954; (https://texashistory.unt.edu/ark:/67531/metadc1820827/: accessed October 16, 2025), University of North Texas Libraries, The Portal to Texas History, https://texashistory.unt.edu; crediting UNT Libraries Special Collections

THE MIXED LEGACIES OF JOHN A. KAISER ("FATHER SEVEN OXEN") AND RAY MALAVASI

The 16 October 1954 *Army Times* (118) discussed Pvt. John A Kaiser of Fort Dix, who was an Army physical training (PT) paradox, scoring a remarkable 459 out of 500 on the Army PT test. The "Minnesota farm boy" registered the maximum sit-ups, pull-ups, and squat jumps, missing a perfect score only due to a 50-second 300 yard dash time.

Kaiser, of Btry. B, 724th FA Bn, had overcome rheumatic fever just seven years earlier. The 6'2", 170-pound trainee attended St. John's University (Minnesota) for two years prior to entering the Army. He had been a middle-weight wrestling star and a pole vaulter, and he intended to enter jump school at Fort Bragg.

Later records indicate that not only did Kaiser become a paratrooper, he also achieved the rank of sergeant in the Army (119).

His story gets more interesting.

Writer Elizabeth Brown of the *Central Minnesota Catholic* wrote on 14 August 2014 about then-Father Kaiser, who had first become a Catholic priest and who later became a martyr (119).

Kaiser was born in Perham, Minnesota, on 29 November 1932, and attended St. John's Preparatory School followed by St. John's University in Collegeville, Minnesota. He subsequently enlisted in the Army in 1954.

Following his Army service, he joined Mill Hill Missionaries in Mill Hill, England, where he studied philosophy and theology. He continued his studies at St. Louis University in Missouri, and was ordained a priest in 1964, into the Mill Hill Order.

Father Kaiser had been assigned to Kenya, where he spent most of thirty-six years in the Kisii Diocese. A strong man, he was known as "Father Seven Oxen," and not only did he have remarkable physical strength, he also demonstrated moral strength through his criticism of corrupt government officials and for speaking out for the rights of maltreated citizens. This activity, which would bring disrepute on the host government, was dangerous even for a religious leader.

His strong voice for the oppressed may have led to his brutal murder. Father Kaiser's body was found in a ditch on 24 August 2000, with a shotgun wound to the back of his head. Father Kaiser had been quoted as saying, "Nobody will ever frighten me out of my priestly obligation of condemning injustices and evil even if it means being persecuted by those who thrive on earthly powers."

The FBI investigated his death and released their final report on 19 April 2000, having concluded Fr. Kaiser's cause of death was suicide, noting a history of clinical depression. The circumstances surrounding Father Kaiser's death, however, remain controversial (120).

Requiescat in Pace, Father.

The 16 October 1954 edition also posted football results pertaining to Ray Malavasi as a player for Fort Belvoir, noting that Belvoir upset Quantico 16-6 in part due to a strong performance from halfback Bob Haner, the Villanova All-American, who was proficient in finding gaps in Quantico's line.

Belvoir put on a "wonderful display of all-around football" at Quantico's Butler Stadium for their upset victory, making them a strong contender for the championship Poinsettia Bowl.

Notable was the strong and accurate passing from quarterback Don Engels, who completed six of nine for 83 yards and a touchdown. The Belvoir running game was anchored by Jerry Lodge and Bob Haner, both of whom contributed first downs when needed. Belvoir's reliable receiver, Frank DiPietro, caught four for forty-six yards.

Belvoir was successful in containing strong Quantico runners such as Gene Filipski, Bill Tate, and Bill Roberts. Ends George Tarasovich and Peters "handled the flanks without error." Belvoir guard standouts were Joe Tyrell, Ray Malavasi, and Bob Gutt.

Ray Malavasi had an interesting football career before and after his Belvoir Army service (121). *Sports Illustrated* reported on the 1951 West Point cheating scandal, which enveloped approximately 90 young men, including Malavasi.

> What caused 90 young men, some of them generally considered among the finest specimens in the Corps of Cadets, to join together

to conspire to defeat the Honor System in the interest of the football team? – Report of the Bartlett Committee.

The massive West Point scandal preceded by only two years the disgraceful Kentucky basketball game-fixing scandal (11). Once the problems at West Point were brought to light and the investigation was completed, President Truman decided to allow the "90 guilty candidates" to resign; they were not dishonorably discharged.

Malavasi transferred to Mississippi State, and others went to schools like Colorado College or Kansas. Somewhat surprisingly, they were able to return to the military or play competitive sports in college or pros. Gil Reich, for example, became an All-American football player at Kansas and was a starting guard on the basketball team that played in the 1953 NCAA final. Reich had been drafted by the Green Bay Packers, but instead made the decision to join ROTC and enter the Air Force.

Several dismissed players ultimately had great success in the military, one even earned a Medal of Honor, but many "never really got over the trauma."

Malavasi passed away in 1987 due to cardiac arrest, according to the *Los Angeles Times* (122). He was the only coach to have taken the Los Angeles Rams to a Super Bowl (while they were still in L.A.). He had come to the Rams in 1973, working as a line coach and as a defensive coordinator under coach Chuck Knox.

Malavasi had a mixed record with the Rams, but was 12-4 in his inaugural season as head coach. The team was only 9-7 the year they made their way to the Super Bowl, ultimately losing to the Steelers. Malavasi was fired in 1982 and was replaced by John Robinson.

Team owner Georgia Frontiere said upon his death, "He was a wonderful person. I'm terribly saddened by the news."

Malavasi's best player was Jack Youngblood, a Rams defensive end. His obituary noted his having been a player/coach for service teams at Fort Belvoir. He had a wide and varied college and pro coaching career.

Rest in Peace, Mr. Malavasi.

1955

The *Army Times* of 1 January 1955 (123) responded to a letter-to-the-editor regarding service football's inclusion in college football polls. Note, this poll is a rare finding, and possibly one of the few, if not the only, known service football poll in existence:

> We have not started such a rating list because we do not think such a list could be fair and accurate. Frankly, we have never thought much of the wire service college football ratings which receive so much space in the daily newspapers during the football season. Post-season games frequently show up the foolishness of the whole scheme and we can't help but think that it is kinda silly to call one team 89.7 and another 89.6, for example.

> The only nationally known service football rating list is put out by Williamson. The final Williamson ratings found the Fort Sill Cannoneers on top but only by two-tenths of a point over Bolling AFB, the team Sill defeated with little trouble in the Poinsettia Bowl, 27-6.

> The final complete Williamson service football (stateside only) ratings follow:

> 1. Fort Sill, 94.2
> 2. Bolling AFB, 94.0
> 3. Fort Belvoir, 93.2
> 4. Quantico, 93.0
> 5. Fort Jackson, 92.5
> 6. Fort Lee, 92.2
> 7. PhibPac, 92.0
> 8. Fort Ord, 91.7
> 9. Shaw AFB, 91.5
> 10. Fort Eustis, 90.7
> 11. Bainbridge, 90.4
> 12. Pensacola, 90.3

13. Fort Hood, 90.2
14. Brooke Medical Center, 90.1
15. Keesler AFB, 89.9
16. Parris Island, 89.8
17. Fort Monmouth, 89.4
18. MCRD, 89.2
19. Little Creek, 88.6
20. Camp Pendleton, 87.8
21. Camp Lejeune, 87.6
22. Great Lakes, 87.0
23. Camp Carson, 86.2
24. Hamilton AFB, 86.0
25. San Diego Naval Air 84.7
26. Cherry Point, 83.7
27. San Diego NTC, 82.7
28. Eglin AFB, 82.7
29. Sheppard, 83.3
30. Norfolk Navy, 82.2
31. Fort Lewis, 80.3
32. Tyndall AFB, 86.7
33. Alameda Naval Air, 76.3
34. Fort Leonard Wood, 75.5
35. Long Beach Navy, 75.2
36. Barstow, 74.7
37. Point Mugu, 74.4
38. Memphis Naval Air, 73.1
39. Edward AFB, 71.1
40. Treasure Island, 70.7
41. Fort Meade, 70.0
42. Presidio, 69.6
43. Amarillo AFB, 67.6
44. Charleston AFB, 65.4

Army Times of 16 April 1955 reported (124) Fort Eustis' All-Army basketball victory over "courageous Camp Chaffee," 90-88, at Fort Benning, Georgia.

Former Illinois star, Jim Bredar, hit a buzzer-beater from 35 feet to seal the win for Eustis in front of a capacity crowd in Briant Wells Field House. The basket ended Chaffee All-Stars's surging comeback, which had tied the game with seconds left to play.

˙Complete Box of Final Game

FORT EUSTIS	FGA	FG	FTA	FT	PF	TP
Al Antinelli, f	3	2	0	0	2	4
Irv Bemoras, f	17	9	10	8	3	26
Charles Dahlke, c	3	3	2	1	3	7
Jim Bredar, g	14	6	5	5	1	17
Larry Hennessey, g	25	12	13	10	3	34
Dick Strebeck, f	3	0	2	2	1	2
Jim Zacha, f	0	0	0	0	0	0
Charles Seifert, g	0	0	0	0	0	0
Totals	65	32	32	26	13	90
CAMP CHAFFEE						
Will Doehrman, f	6	2	6	6	1	10
Don Spitz, f	17	4	1	0	4	8
J. C. Maze, c	18	9	9	9	2	27
Buck Shackleford, g	12	4	0	0	2	8
John Luttrell, g	17	6	2	2	3	14
Gerard Moore, g	4	3	4	3	3	9
Dick Sharp, f	2	1	4	2	0	4
Larry Whitely, f	3	2	0	0	0	4
Buddy Mueller, g	2	1	0	0	2	2
Jim Loomis, c	2	1	0	0	0	2
Totals	82	33	26	22	17	88

Halftime score: Chaffee 41, Eustis 39.
Key to above (for those who do not follow basketball closely): FGA—field goal attempts. FG—field goals scored. FTA—free throw attempts. FT—free throws made. PF—personal fouls. TP—total points.

Top Ten Tournament Averages

Player, Team	Games	Pts.	Avg.
Win Wilfong, Fort Leonard Wood	6	183	30.5
Irv Bemoras, Fort Eustis	4	109	27.2
Bob Smith, Camp Gordon	5	126	25.2
Larry Hennessey, Fort Eustis	4	92	23.0
Herb Weaver, Fort Belvoir	2	44	22.0
Bill Schayowitz, Alaska	4	87	21.8
Edgar Haynes, Fort Lewis	2	40	20.0
Manuel Whitley, Europe (6th A/C)	4	76	19.0
Jerry Lovett, Europe (6th A/C)	4	76	19.0
J. C. Maze, Camp Chaffee	5	86	17.2

The Eustis win ended the six-day All-Army tournament, which encompassed ten teams and nearly 120 players "from all corners of the world."

The enthusiastic crowd showed their tremendous appreciation for Bredar's efforts, and continued their ovation for Win Wilfong of Fort Leonard Wood as he rose to accept his tournament MVP trophy, presented by Maj. Gen. Joseph H. Harper.

Fort Eustis Wins All-Army; MVP Award to Wilfong

All-Army Champs

(Continued from Back Page)

12. Europe 96 (Manuel Whitley 23), Lewis 94 (Bob Woods 21). Europe won on a last-second field goal by Jerry Lovett. It was close all the way. Whitley scored 21 of 23 points for the winners in the second half. Lewis held a 42-38 half-time lead.

13. Eustis 85 (Bemoras 25), Chaffee 72 (Maze 12). Both teams

THE FORT EUSTIS Wheels, All-Army champions for 1955, are all smiles in their dressing room at Fort Benning, Ga., where the annual tournament was held this year. Front row, from left: John Hefferman, Keith Walker, Maj. Clarence Welch (OIC), coach Bob Frala, Jim Breda and Charles Seifert. Standing: Larry Hennessey, Gene Musolf, Irv Bemoras, Charles Dahlke, Dick Strebeck, Jim Zacha and Al Antinelli.

Photo: Army Times archive, 16 April 1955 (124).

Wilfong was extremely productive in the tournament, having amassed 183 points in six games, giving him a scoring average of 30.5 PPG. Unfortunately for Wilfong and his fans, Wood was eliminated by Chaffee in a semi-final game.

"The final battle had all the earmarks of a championship game." Eustis hit 49.2 percent of their shots, while Chaffee made 40.2 percent of their own. Stars for Eustis included J.C. Maze (17 points), Larry Hennessey (17 points), and Irv Bemoras (26 points).

Other notable players were Don Byrd from Belvoir, Bob Smith from Gordon, Bill Schayowitz from Alaska, Jerry Lovett from Europe, Manuel Whitney from Europe, Edgar Haynes from Lewis, Bob Kreighauser from Chaffee, Burr Carlson from Dix, Phil Vukecevich from Far East, Herb Weaver from Belvoir, and Andy McGowan from Dix.

Other participating teams included Fort Leonard Wood, Fort Dix, Fort Belvoir, 40th AAA Brigade from the Far East Command, Alaska Command, and 6th Armored Cavalry of the European Command.

Also in the 16 April edition was the "Inside Sports" column from Cpl. Lee Neumann, in which he highlighted the amazing athletic talent of Alex Litman. Not only had he received football offers from the Cleveland Browns, New York Giants, and Philadelphia Eagles, he was also a track star in his own right.

SFC Litman was "Army's top dash man since 1951," and had his sights set on the upcoming Olympics. Despite his seasoned age of 35, he managed 9.5 seconds in the 100-yard dash and 20.8 in the 200-meter race.

Litman had unusual size for a runner of that time – 6 feet and 195 pounds; he "looked more like a football player than a track star." In fact, he *had* been a football star for Brooke Army Medical Center the previous few years.

Litman had also been spotted at a Far East Command coaches clinic at Fryar Gym in Yokohama (he was being transferred to 229th Quartermaster unit in Pusan, Korea), along with Ohio State's Larry Snyder and Penn State's Chuck Werner, both of whom coached the 1952 Olympic track and field team.

Litman had fallen just short of qualifying for the 1952 Olympics with his fourth place finish in the 200-meter tryouts, though he managed to beat football great Ollie Matson in the All-Army track competition in 1954.

SSG Litman, a veteran of WWII, Korea, and Vietnam, passed away on 18 June 2000.

Rest in Peace, hero.

Defending Armed Forces football champions, Fort Sill Cannoneers, announced their nine-game schedule for the 1955 season, which would include Fort Ord and Fort Belvoir in the 7 May 1955 *Army Times* (125). Opponents Ord, Belvoir and Bolling AFB had been "perennial powerhouses."

The schedule was said to provide opponents that "were a better cross-section of service football leaders." The previous year Sill didn't have much of a problem sweeping their regular season opponents, and they met Bolling in the Poinsettia Bowl. Though Bolling had been the favorite, Sill produced a decisive victory, 27-6.

Former Oklahoma All-American and Washington Redskins pro star, Lt. Leon Heath, would be the new coach following a serious injury that knocked him out of contention as a player. He had big shoes to fill, as the previous coach, Lt. Fred Smith (militarily reassigned), had compiled a 19-1-1 record over two years.

Sill had lost several important players from the championship squad, but would still have talent to spare in Billy Vessels, Buck McPhail, Merrill Green, Joe Romona, Marv Matuszak, and Bert Clark, among others.

On 10 June 1955, columnist Robert W. Bowie reported that the Air Force Academy would enter collegiate competition for the first time in October (126). Assisting with the transition was Capt. Julius Battista, who had been with the Fifth Air Force in Nagoya, Japan, and had been named "Coach of the year in the Far East." Other staff included Byron Gillory and Jesse Bounds, both of whom coached with Hamilton Field in 1952, the year in which Hamilton handed the mighty Fort Ord team its only loss of the year despite efforts of the great Ollie Matson.

The 30 July 1955 *Army Times* (127) reported. "All-Army End Joins Eagles." Winifred Tillery had been discharged from the Army earlier in July and had since joined the Philadelphia Eagles training camp in Hershey, Pennsylvania. As reported in *The Forgotten Athletes of the American Forces Far East* (11),

Tillery had been named to the All-Army Second Team in 1954 as an end, along with end Stan Wacholz out of Fort Ord (*Pro rights: 49ers*).

The Steelers' Parker considered Marv his "whole defense"

Photo: Marv Matuszak - from Fort Sill to the Steelers (14).

Army Times noted that Tillery caught 27 passes for 732 yards-gained in 1954. The Eagles discovered him by way of the All-Army poll results, which had been compiled by Army football coaches and sports writers who liked what they saw in Tillery.

The same *Army Times* edition reported on page 34 that the Fort Ord Warriors had just demolished the San Francisco 49ers rookies, 24-6; "The Fort Ord Warriors exploded for a touchdown in every quarter." The game was essentially a formal scrimmage, but tested both sides in game-simulation conditions. Notable were performances by Ord's quarterback Rudy Bukich, former Oregon State and Washington Redskin fullback Sam Baker, former USC end Ron Miller, halfback Julian Spence, and former San Jose State guard Bruce Halladay, among others.

Also on page 34, it was noted that Fort Dix did not have a football team the previous year, but "would field a team this fall," and service teams wishing to play Dix in 1955 were encouraged to contact Post Athletic Director, James Ward.

Army Information Digest of September 1955 (128) discussed Army athletes who had competed in the Mexico Pan American Games earlier in the spring, and those who desired to qualify for the 1956 Olympics in Australia. Following the Pan-American Games, "Trophy rooms at many posts ... sparkle(d) with displays of individual medals won" by Army athletes.

However, tryouts were not limited to Pan-American Game participants; "Any man or woman in the Army who feels qualified is urged to try out." The Mexico Games were pivotal in that they were considered a warm-up for the upcoming Olympics.

The Army represented well in Mexico, having earned 13 team awards and 24 individual competition medals. Armed service member's participation in international sports was encouraged by the Secretary of Defense, Charles E. Wilson, through directives which had been based on an appeal from the United States Olympic Committee (USOC). Service athletes of all branches fell under the control of USOC on their path to possible Olympic participation.

There was also a Department of Defense Committee for international sports competitions, showing that the U.S. Military was serious about world-wide exposure for their fine athletes.

Army members who felt they had proper qualifications for Olympic competition were to make an application to the Adjutant General with their details, including their competitive experience. They were required to be an amateur and a U.S. citizen.

Selection of athletes was based on All-Army championships, competitions between major commands, or performance in national or international competitions, such as the Pan-American Games [Army Regulation 28-50 (30 Nov. 1954); DA Circular 28-12 (7 June 1955)].

As a point of interest, it was noted that the first U.S. entrant in the "grueling five sports event" - the pentathlon - was none other than a young lieutenant named George S. Patton, in the 1912 Stockholm Olympics; Patton took fifth place.

The Army utilized their Special Services officers to coordinate tryouts for the 1956 Olympics on every post, with final selections based solely on individual merit/ability. Once selections were made, training for Olympic competition would commence.

The Pan American games atmosphere, and its location in Mexico, were described as pleasant and ideal. The weather was sunny and warm, and English speaking police were available to assist as needed. Athletes stayed on the University of Mexico campus, which was described as beautiful, with "striking" architecture.

Teams from different countries mingled on campus and friendships were formed.

There was one hitch in the program, however, as U.S. teams, due to financial restrictions, did not arrive in Mexico City early enough to acclimatize to the extreme altitude of the city (7300 feet). The baseball team only had two days of practice. The basketball team lost one game, but ultimately won the gold, and one commenter reported: "The Americans are giving the world a lesson in perfect basketball tonight."

American Army gymnast, Pfc. John C. Beckner, won five gold medals – more than any other individual in the Games. Track star Lou Jones set a new World Record in the 400 meter run, at 45.4 seconds.

Col. L.W. Jackson said, "In retrospect, the Second Pan-American Games were a complete success for all concerned … Inter-hemisphere relations were strongly bolstered … the Army … can compete with athletes of other nations on an equal basis."

New York Yankee second baseman Billy Martin wanted to try pro pitching, according to *Army Times* (129), after he returned to Carson from the World Series in order to be released from the Army. He had planned to ask Yankee manager Casey Stengel if he could pitch on their upcoming tour of Japan, based on his 2-0 record pitching for Carson. It is not known if his wish was ultimately approved.

Army Times columnist Tom Scanlon reported on 1 October 1955 (130) that Third Army's Fort McPherson was the winner of the 1955 All-Army baseball championship at Fort Belvoir. The game-winning pitcher was Wilmer "Vinegar Bend" Mizell.

Mizell was described as "The St. Louis Cardinal southpaw," who finished out his Army service with a 9-0 shutout over the Fort Hood Tankers (He was to be released 5 October). This had been the final game in the tournament involving nine championship Army Command teams.

McPherson, ironically, lost the initial meeting with Hood, 2-1, forcing them to work their way up the loser's bracket in the double-elimination tournament. McPherson ended up winning five straight games to set up the rematch with Hood.

In the first game of the day, Hood lost to McPherson's Baltimore Orioles Bonus Baby, Billy O'Dell, 7-1, before the evening rematch (Having lost once to Hood, McPherson then had to beat Hood twice) with Mizell on the mound, where Mizell pitched his one-hitter to take the championship.

Scanlon noted that Mizell had pitched 21 straight games without a defeat, and his ERA was below .050.

Scanlon praised the talent of Hood's team, but said McPherson "had too many pros" - notably their pitchers. The pitching crew included Mizell, O'Dell, and Taylor Phillips, who had previously pushed the powerful Fort Ord team out of the tournament with his victory.

Stars for McPherson included shortstop Billy Moran ($40,000 Indians' bonus baby), third baseman Scott Quackenbush (Chicago Cubs), and left fielder Norm Siebern (future Yankee).

An article by Mike Jaffe published by the *Society for American Baseball Research*, dated 14 January 2022, said 6'3" St. Louis Cardinal baseball player, Wilmer "Vinegar Bend" Mizell entered the Army in 1953, and had been assigned to Fort McPherson, where he was able to continue to test and refine

151

his baseball skills (131). Mizell had been working on his pitching control, having been a league leader in allowing walks.

Mizell was known for his exaggerated windup and unorthodox style, and his time in the Army was successful; he compiled a record of 36-2, which included four no-hitters and 16 shutouts.

During his Army stint he threw 324 strikeouts and walked only 48 batters. He was discharged in October 1955 with the rank of sergeant. Following the Army he played ball in Cuba, where it became known that his professional skills had remained intact throughout his time in the service, though Mr. Jaffe opined that Mizell's time in the service had negatively impacted his statistics.

Mizell later returned to the Cardinals, was eventually traded to the Pirates, and later spent some time with the Mets. He participated in one World Series with the Pirates in which he had mixed results, though he did strike out the legendary Roger Maris.

Mizell entered politics, holding several state and national-level positions. He was well-liked, he didn't cuss, and "always had a smile on his face." He passed away in 1999.

Rest in Peace, hero.

Also in the 1 October 1955 *Army Times* was a notice of Fort Jackson's overall football talent, despite the season-opening 20-19 loss to Pensacola Naval Base. "The Eagles produced so many stars that it is difficult to pick the top Jackson back and lineman." Starring at quarterback was Hal Ledyard and at right guard was John Hammock.

Ledyard threw two touchdowns in his five pass completions, and Jackson utilized the Split-T offense formation which allowed Ledyard to deceive opponents with fakes. Ledyard also caused trouble for Pensacola on defense, playing well both ways. Bob Maddox and Roger Hampton were especially effective in the running game. Hammock was able to find holes in the Pensacola line to jam up their runners.

In other 1 October edition football news, out of Redstone Arsenal, Alabama, the "David among service football's Goliaths" - Redstone Arsenal Rockets – "laid low a goodly number of gridiron giants."

The relatively small number of troops stationed at Redstone at that time (~1000) impressively provided enough talent to compete effectively against post teams with potential talent base twenty times that number.

Rockets coach Maj. Ed Long said his team had been "playing out of our league." He said that installations the size of Redstone usually don't have post football teams, however, Redstone's athletes "like to play the rough ones," which made it more enjoyable when they performed well.

Photo: "Space Capital of the Universe," UAH Archives, Special Collections, and Digital Initiatives, accessed October 17, 2025, https://libarchstor2.uah.edu/digitalcollections/items/show/4926.

What the Arsenal lacked in numbers, it made up for with experience; it had "more than its share" of good athletes, as many had played college ball. Somewhat amusingly the article said that unlike on most posts, very few of them had to do manual work! They spent their time on technical and lab work, which apparently left them with more playing energy when it came time to practice.

The Arsenal relied on strong performers to carry their team, and "every year, these stars seem to crop up." This season (1955), they had a pair of "mammoth tackles" who would likely make roster on any college team in the country. One was Bart Massey, 6-4, 225 pounds, from Texas Tech. The other was Glenn Wasz, 6-3, 230 pounds, formerly a starter with Notre Dame.

Redstone Arsenal was not among the Service Sports giants, but they certainly punched above their weight.

Army Times of 12 November 1955 was loaded with sports updates and information out of Fort Sam Houston, Texas (41).

"Fourth Army's 1956 sports program will be the biggest it had ever conducted." The reason, ostensibly, was to support preparation for the upcoming Olympics "to the maximum." Fourth Army champions in eight sports would compete for spots on the applicable All-Army team. If you were competing in track and field, swimming and diving, boxing, triathlon, basketball and baseball, you had a chance to reach the U.S. Olympic trials.

The Army had a modest goal of one hundred percent participation by military personnel in the Sports Program. Fort Sill, a Fourth Army installation, would handle its share of the tournaments, along with Fort Hood, Fort Sam Houston, Brooke Army Medical Center, and others.

The 12 November edition also reported the "stunning" Fort Hood football defeat of All-Service champion, Fort Sill, 13-7, ending Sill's win streak at nineteen. There was an incredible array of talent assembled, though Heisman Trophy winner, Billy Vessels, had not been available for Sill. All-Army fullback Buck McPhail was a constant threat and end Jerry Janes caught a former New York Giant quarterback Don "Cotton" Gottlob pass for the final Hood score, adding to the points already earned by Hood's Roy Mays on a 31-yard reception.

It was also reported that Fort Eustis had defeated Fort Lee in a close match, 20-14, at Fort Lee on a cold Virginia afternoon. Though the game had been tied at halftime, Eustis put it out of reach by scoring two touchdowns in the third period; a deficit from which Lee did not recover.

Lee coach Tommy Young's crew made a final effort in the fourth quarter on a "beautiful 42-yard pass to pull within six points," but there was not enough time left to get the additional points they needed. Lee quarterback Blair Kramer was later sacked for two long losses, erasing any comeback opportunity.

Eustis had started slow, but then "struck like lightning" in the second quarter, when Dick Gregory, formerly of Minnesota, broke free for a 23-yard touchdown run. Fred Bruney then intercepted a Lea Paslay pass, but Lee was able to hold and eventually tie the game going into halftime.

Starring for Eustis was quarterback, James T. Jones; end, Ed Morgan; halfback, Harland Carl, out of Wisconsin; and the previously-noted defensive specialist, Fred Bruney. Fort Lee's Blair Kramer and Floyd Stollsteimer had been indispensable for the Lee Travellers.

SportspressNW.com reported in 2012 the exploits of "Deadeye" Don Heinrich, two-time All-American quarterback for the Fort Ord Warriors as they faced the semi-pro Seattle Ramblers on 6 December 1955 in brutally frigid conditions in Seattle. Despite temperatures in the 20s and icy rain, 5200 fans turned out to see the action, and they were not disappointed (132).

Fort Ord featured "a dozen players who had spent time in the National Football League as well as several college All-America picks." Heinrich, among others, was waiting to commit to an NFL club once released from military obligations.

Fort Ord's team was no joke: Going into the game, Ord was 9-2, and had accumulated 335 points to their opponents' 37, with the two losses being delivered by the professional Los Angeles Rams and the San Francisco 49ers teams (exhibition games).

Despite the adverse weather, the strong Ord team from California defeated the Ramblers 28-0, and proceeds from the game in the amount of $54,000 were donated to the Queen Anne Magnolia Lions.

The game had attracted "some of the best players in the country to the city." Included was Ollie Matson, a 1952 All-Pro from the Chicago Cardinals, and who was also a track and field Olympian in Helsinki. Matson scored twice and rambled for 122 yards, with a very impressive 13.6-yard average carry.

155

Field House

Photo: Fort Ord Fieldhouse, 1953 (133).

Heinrich played to expectations, which were high, and stayed in for all offensive possessions to please the crowd. Following this strong win, Fort Ord, again led by Matson, went on to crush the Quantico Marines (featuring future Iowa coach Hayden Fry) 44-19 in the Poinsettia Bowl, which in turn led to a Salad Bowl 67-12 win over Great Lakes Navy in Phoenix.

After his Service obligations were met, Heinrich was drafted by the New York Giants, where he completed a 56-game NFL stint. He was selected to be on the Washington Husky's all-time team in 1990 and entered the college football Hall of Fame in 1987.

Football great Don Heinrich passed away on 29 Feb. 1992 due to cancer.

Rest in Peace, hero.

The 24 December 1955 *Army Times* reported on the "Shrimp Bowl" in Galveston, Texas, in which Fort Hood defeated Navy's PhibLant Gators, 31 - 13, in front of 7500 fans (134). PhibLant was "no match" for the Tankers of Fort Hood in the seventh-annual Shrimp Bowl game, and Army won easily, despite having used reserves throughout the game.

NEW YORK GIANTS

Aug. 22 at Los Angeles—8:15 P.M.

Coach: Jim Lee Howell

Home Field: Yankee Stadium

Pub. Director: Robert Daley

1957 Record: W 7 L 5

1958 Schedule
Sept. 28 Cards (A)
Oct. 5 Eagles (A)
Oct. 12 'Skins (A)
Oct. 19 Cards (H)
Oct. 26 Steelers (H)
Nov. 2 Browns (A)
Nov. 9 Colts (H)
Nov. 16 Steelers (A)
Nov. 23 'Skins (H)
Nov. 30 Eagles (H)
Dec. 7 Lions (A)
Dec. 14 Browns (H)

Top Scorers: Ben Agajanian—*(7th) 62 pts., 32 XPs, 10 FGs.
Frank Gifford—(10th-T) 54 pts., 9 TDs.

Top Runners: Frank Gifford—(10th) 136 atts., 528 yds., 3.9 avg.
Alex Webster—(15th-T) 135 atts., 478 yds., 3.5 avg.

Top Passers: Charlie Conerly—(7th) 232 atts., 128 comp., 1712 yds., 11 TDs.
Don Heinrich—(21st) 26 atts., 11 comp., 224 yds., 1 TD.

Top Receivers: Frank Gifford—(4th) 41 for 588 yds., 4 TDs.
Alex Webster—(16th) 30 for 330 yds., 1 TD.
*(NFL Finish)

Hood quarterback Dan Gottlob rang up 151 passing yards and two touchdowns in front of the record crowd. Texas star Carl Mayes accumulated ninety yards for Hood in seven carries. Hood scored immediately, and had notched 14 points before the close of the first quarter.

The Tankers' first score came from a 28-yard run by fullback Steve Meilinger, and the next touchdown was thanks to Don Scullane on an eight-yard pass from Gottlob. Other strong contributors for Hood included George Rosso, Jon Anderson, and Noel Schmidt.

In other news, well-known sports columnist Tom Scanlon provided some post-All Army selection notes, including Buck McPhail's honor of being named outstanding player of the Fourth Army conference to go alongside his All-Army award. McPhail had been picked by opposing teams, including Fort Bliss Falcons, Fort Hood Tankers, Brooke Army Medical Center Comets, and Fort Sill Cannoneers.

Scanlon also said that "Big Jim Schrader," former Notre Dame and first team All-Army selection out of Europe, would return to the Washington Redskins upon his completion of service.

157

Also, the *Armed Forces Press* All-Service team was announced:

First team (appears incomplete)

- ✓ Tackle Bill Quinlan, Fort Carson
- ✓ QB Jimmy Powers, Fort Ord
- ✓ Center Dick Tamburo, Fort Hood
- ✓ Back Buck McPhail, Fort Sill
- ✓ Back Neil Worden, Fort Jackson
- ✓ Guard Steve Eisenhauer, Navy(?)

Second team (appears incomplete)

- ✓ End George Tarasovich, Fort Belvoir
- ✓ Tackle Jack Shanafelt, 24th Div.
- ✓ End Bob McFarland, SACOM
- ✓ Back Billy Wells, Fort Belvoir
- ✓ Guard Marv Matuszak, Fort Sill

Scanlon said that some All-Army picks, such as Paul Cameron and Joe Ramona, did not make the All-Service team. Lastly, Scanlon wrote that Washington Redskins owner George Marshall complained about military teams playing under "one platoon" rules:

> (The rules were) jeopardizing the future careers of many National Football League stars … The armed forces should either cease using pro players altogether, or operate under professional rules with separate defensive and offensive units. It is completely unfair to have boys risk having their future civilian careers wrecked while they are in military service.

1956

A Military memo dated 18 March 1956 from CG SIX AND FT LEONARD WOOD MO to various commands and news organizations, such as *Army Times*, *Stars and Stripes*, and *Armed Forces Press Service*, discussed the results of the All-Army Basketball tournament; "A tired but determined Fourth Army team from Camp Chaffee took a double win from the Sixth Army represented by Fort Lewis to be named All Army Champions" (135).

The Fourth Army overall record in the tournament was six wins and one loss, and the Sixth Army had managed three straight wins prior to the title game.

Photo: Ford Ord Field House, alternate view/date, 1955 Fort Ord Yearbook.

Because the Fourth came up through the loser's bracket, they had to play the Sixth Army twice on the same day. The first game of the day was a decisive

159

Fourth Army victory, 98-72; however, the championship game was much closer, with the Fourth defeating the Sixth, 98 to 95, on the backs of finesse players such as Bill Sarver, Jerry Neff, Don Lance, and Al Bianchi.

Fourth star Sam Jones' clutch play helped his team regain a lead with a timely tip-in, and Jones later hit two important "charity tosses." The memo stated that Sam Jones had been a "hard driving guard" and a "one man show."

In the final game, Fourth dominated the second half on strong play from Jones (27 points total) and Bob Kriegs Hauser (21 points) to ensure victory in overtime, after the regulation time had seen the lead change twice, with five ties along the way.

Starring for the Sixth Army were Marth Zaninovich (18 points), Jim Westbrook, and Bruce Goodrich (24 points), all of whom contributed to help the Sixth Army to a second-place finish at tournament's end.

The memo noted the Fourth Army had reached the championship "the hard way" in the loser's bracket after falling to the Third Army in their opening game.

The 24 March 1956 *Army Times* (136) was loaded with basketball updates and information. Firstly, it was reported that basketball teams had been selected for Olympic tryouts.

The Olympic preliminary tryouts would occur at the inter-service playoffs in Louisville, Ky. and at the AAU meets in Kansas City, Mo.; final tryouts would be 2-4 April in Kansas City.

Fourth Army dominated team selections, having placed eight men from Camp Chaffee on the two teams; five on the AAU team, and three on the inter-service team. Also, Bob Speight from Fort Biles, Tex., was named to the AAU squad.

Camp Chaffee men on the inter-service squad were Bill Sarver, Camp Chaffee; Al Bianchi, Brooke Army Medical Center; and Sam Jones, White Sands Proving Ground.

160

Frank Brickey from the University of Utah would coach the inter-service team, along with Ron Weisner, former Wisconsin player. Omar Manley, who coached Chaffee's All-Army champions would coach the AAU squad.

The inter-service tournament team:

- ✓ **Al Bianchi**, Fourth Army, Bowling Green University
- ✓ **Bill Server**, Fourth Army, Illinois Normal
- ✓ **Sam Jones**, Fourth Army, North Carolina State
- ✓ **Clarence Hannon**, Sixth Army, West Point
- ✓ **Marty Zaninovich**, Sixth Army, Stanford
- ✓ **Larry Dugan**, Second Army, Pepperdine College
- ✓ **Sam Bechman**, Second Army, Idaho State
- ✓ **Frank Bolstroff** (sic; Bolstorff), Second Army, Minnesota
- ✓ **Dick White**, Third Army, Western Kentucky State
- ✓ **Austin Cunkle**, Third Army, Florida
- ✓ **Jim Young**, Third Army, Santa Clara
- ✓ **Larry Ramm**, Fifth Army, Washington
- ✓ **Ralph Wilson**, Fifth Army, Marquette
- ✓ **Don Lance**, Fifth Army, Rice

The AAU squad:

- ✓ **Charles Mueller**, Fourth Army, Millikin
- ✓ **Jim Scott**, Fourth Army, Carthage College
- ✓ **Carrol Sharp**, Fourth Army, Drake University
- ✓ **Richard Gross**, Fourth Army, Wheaton College
- ✓ **Charles Zopf**, Fourth Army, Indiana Central
- ✓ **Bob Speight**, Fourth Army, North Carolina State
- ✓ **William Warden**, Second Army, North Central Illinois State
- ✓ **Jerry Neff**, Fifth Army, Westminster
- ✓ **Richard Tamberg**, Europe, California
- ✓ **Myles Witchey**, Alaska, West Liberty State

The 24 March edition of the *Army Times* continued with more All-Army Tournament coverage: "All-Army Ends In Thriller. Jones Leads Chaffee To Overtime Victory."

Eight championship Army teams participated in the tournament, including two teams from overseas. Chaffee won their second All-Army championship in three years by overcoming an eleven-point deficit with eight minutes to play. Chaffee managed to force the game to overtime, ultimately winning by three, 98-95. Bill Sarver hit two clutch "charity tosses" to create the three-point lead and victory for Chaffee.

Sarver tallied up 31 points in Chaffee's previous day's game against First Army, and Jones contributed half the team's rebounds.

Sam Jones' driving layups and fadeaway shots perplexed the Lewis squad to good effect for the Fourth Army. It was noted that Jones was actually a member of the White Sands Proving Ground team, but had been added to the Fourth Army championship team to facilitate the Olympic tryout. The other Chaffee addition was Al Bianchi from BAMC.

In 24 March football news, Fort Benning's Lt. George Morris, "ranked as the greatest center in Georgia Tech history," signed a pro contract with the San Francisco 49ers. Lt. Morris was CO of Co. B, 78th Bn., 151st Engr. Combat Group. Morris was an *Army Times* All-Army selection, and later had coached the Seventh Division team in Korea, with a record of 7-2-1 (*Author note: Lt. Morris coached my father, Jerry Kingrey, of the 7th Division Bayonets football team in the AFFE/8A conference in 1955*).

The 7 July 1956 *Army Times* discussed upcoming coach and umpire clinics in Atlanta in August. Third Army Recreation Officer, Maj. Stuart Hoskins, said, "We work on a theory that a good ball game, be it football, baseball or otherwise, is only as good as the officials who control the play." He said the annual clinics provide one of the biggest improvements in sports quality for the Army.

Well-known guest teachers to attend included Frank McGuire, University of North Carolina basketball coach; Gomer Jones, line coach at the University of Oklahoma; Warren Geise, South Carolina head football coach; and others.

The same edition said that Fort Carson baseball was led by "Cleveland Indian property," John Shorupski, the only returning starter for the new season. He hit .360 in 1955, playing under Billy Martin at Carson the previous year. Added to the roster was Guy Sparrow, who had been a basketball star at the University of Detroit and a baseball prodigy, having played professionally with the Kansas City Athletics at first base.

Other Carson baseball starters for 1956 included pitcher Neil West, second baseman John Chimento, third baseman Ken Owens, shortstop Ed Miller, right fielder Ken Henkemeyer, and left fielder Lello Carneseca.

In the meantime, Fort Dix 200 lb. centerfielder Bob Mayer hit "one of the longest home runs ever seen at Dix," at 450 feet. He was also batting with a .450 average and had plans to sign with a pro ball team.

The 23 August 1956 *Bayonet* (137) discussed Fort Lewis's search for a quarterback for their newly re-organized 3rd Division team; they lacked a seasoned "Split-T" quarterback. The "Marne Gridmen" were diligently preparing for their 15 September opener against the talented Quantico Marines, at Quantico.

Coach Summer Bornstein was not optimistic.

The Marne offense required a talented field general to "make split-second decisions in trying and confusing circumstances." Jim Greenwood and Al Oszustowls were top choices for starting quarterback for the moment, though neither one had the requisite experience. He also felt his players did not have sufficient experience to match the play of their opponents; "Most service teams are loaded with college men and possibly a few pros," but his team lacked all but a few college players and only two with pro experience.

Fort Lewis's Calvin Allen, a guard out of Memphis State and the Pittsburgh Steelers was one; the other was Ohio State All-American guard, George Jacoby, who was under contract with the Cleveland Browns (*though his obituary says he had been drafted by the Giants*).

Jacoby was described as a 5'11", 230 pounder, who was selected All-American in 1953. Jacoby's obituary (138) said that he had been a two-way player for Ohio State, offensive tackle and defensive nose guard. He was co-captain and MVP of the 1953 OSU team, and was named All-Big Ten twice. He was drafted by the Giants, but chose to forgo the professional football path as he was concerned it would not pay enough to sustain his needs. He found his employment niche, enjoying a long career as an accountant, and he passed away in 2013.

Rest in peace, hero.

Marne would face Quantico and then Eglin AFB, which featured All-American Zeke Bratkowski (*A quarterback under contract with the Chicago Bears in 1954, and 1957-1960*). Following those contests, Fort Lewis would meet Fort Jackson and then Fort Hood.

The 6 September 1956 *Bayonet* (139) discussed the Doughboys' football outlook at the beginning of the season, noting that Head Coach Jim Ingram would become a player/coach to help fortify his 27-man squad. Ingram was a star at Ole Miss, and had been offered a contract by the Philadelphia Eagles which he had to decline due to a knee injury.

The next day, the Benning men were to scrimmage the 3rd Division Gridmen at Doughboy Stadium to get a feel for how the teams would look in a game situation.

The Doughboys lacked experience deeper into the roster, though the first team had "various ex-college stars," including 6'5", 250-pound Lou Sawchik from Ohio State, who Ingram said was one of the best ends he had ever seen. The other end position was up for grabs between either South Carolina's Larry Hollman or South Georgia's Bennet Avero.

The Doughboys line would include Arkansas star Hershel Jones, 6'2", 230 pounds, and Radford Hamilton, at 6', 230 pounds. Other starters for the Doughboys included Kentucky's Neil Lowry and Dale Haupt of Wyoming and the Green Bay Packers. Reserve guards were Russ Zimmerman, Buddy Richardson, and Charlie Wilson.

Western Kentucky star Arnie Oaken was a 6', 205-pound Doughboy center. The quarterback was Jim Matthews. The halfbacks were L.A. Rams player Bob Hoerning, and either Florida A&M's Love Collins or Illinois' Dick Ohl.

Happily for the Doughboys, the 20 September 1956 *Bayonet* reported (140) a 27-14 Main Post Doughboy win over the Quantico Marines on Sunday in the 1956 season opener in South Carolina. Doughboy's Oregon State star, Ken Brown, scored two touchdowns in a strong contribution to the Benning victory. Coach Ingram was pleased with the team's performance, saying, "The boys looked great coming from behind. It was a team victory all the way with outstanding performances displayed by many of the boys."

Benning stars of the game included Brown, Vince Donato on defense, Hoerning, Collins, Larry Gressette, Freddy Holland, and Sawchik.

There was a side article which discussed team star, Kenneth Brown, who had been an outstanding football and track performer with Oregon State. He was the school brigade's Special Services Officer and a valued member of the Doughboy football squad. He graduated Oregon State with a Bachelor of Science, but his plan to obtain a master's degree had been cut short by his service obligation.

The 22 September 1956 *Army Times* (141) discussed the All-Army baseball tournament in Fort Dix, New Jersey, noting that on day four only two teams remained undefeated: Third Army/Fort McPherson and First Army/Fort Devens. Fort Ord, Eighth Army from the Far East, and Brooke Army Medical Center were out of the tournament based on double-elimination results. 2000 fans had been in attendance to watch the Army action.

Eighth Army had been eliminated by Fort Carson (Fifth Army), based on performances by pitchers Neil West and Ray Ripplemeyer. Eighth Army's Don Nuxhall was given the loss. Fort Lee knocked out Brooke Medical Center (Second Army) 9-1 on the pitching of Lawrence Leigh, who went all the way, and was helped by the hot bats of the Emaar twins (Duane and Juane). The game was the second elimination game, as Fort Lee had been beaten 8-0 by Fort McPherson in the opener which came about on the strong pitching of Bill Anderton, "property of the Pittsburgh Pirates." McPherson racked up thirteen hits, four of which came from center fielder Al Spangler. McPherson's win included a triple play in the ninth.

Pitcher Dick O'Keefe gave Fort Devens a narrow victory over Fort Carson 5-4 in the third game of the tournament. Brooke Medical Center's Boston Red Sox pitcher Paul Ayward was pulled in the fourth in Brooke's loss to Fort McPherson, 7-2.

There were twenty-five baseball scouts on hand for the tournament, including Hans Lobert, former scout for the Philadelphia Phillies. "Six top pro umpires, led by American League veteran George Barr, are supervising tournament play." Players on the radar included Al Spangler, (owned by Milwaukee Braves), Ray Rosenbaum (Purdue standout), pitcher Charlie

Heerlein (owned by Red Sox; former Duke star), Lee Mattingson (USARPAC), All-Americans Bill Hogarty and Lee Frank.

The Fort Hood Tankers clipped the mighty Brooke Army Medical Center 21-7 in a Fourth Army Conference win, reported the 27 October 1956 *Army Times* (142).

Hood quarterback Jerry Johnson hit Jerry Janes in the end zone for an eleven-yard scoring toss to start things off. Hood back George Rosso broke the goal line again at two yards to put more points on the board, however, Hugh O'Leary put Brooke in position to score with an intercepted pass, and the Medics converted with a quarterback Billy White short run. Earl Bechtel later ran twenty-one yards into the end zone to clinch the victory for Hood.

The 27 October 1956 issue also reported that some of football's greatest players had been voted onto All-Army teams in the six years of its existence at the time.

> Previous All-Army backfield stars include such as (sic) **Ollie Matson** of Fort Ord (1953); **Dave Mann** of Fort Ord (1953) … **Arnold Galiffa**, HSC, Japan (1952); **Larry Coutre**, Camp Breckinridge (1951-52); and **Billy Vessels** of Fort Sill (1954).

Matson and Mann played professionally with the Chicago Cardinals, and the article said that All-Army teams were "dominated" by college and pro players, though sometimes a non-credentialed player earned All-Army honors, such as Fort Eustis' Sammy Reynolds and Fort Belvoir's Billy Leftwich. Past All-Army linemen included:

- ✓ Fort Leonard Wood's Mike McCormack (1953)
- ✓ Clayton Tonnemaker of Camp Drake (1952)
- ✓ John Michels of Fort Eustice (1954-55)
- ✓ Ray Beck of Fort Jackson (1953)
- ✓ Andy Hillhouse of Camp Polk (1951-52)
- ✓ George Tarasovich of Fort Belvoir (1954-55)
- ✓ Hal Mitchell of Fort Lee (1953-54)

Polls were underway for the next team, which would not be split between First and Second team players; organizers felt it would be a fairer system

166

due to the plethora of great players. All twenty-two players would receive Zodiac watches from the *Army Times*.

Ollie Matson's obituary (143) said that not only was he a professional football player, but he was also an Olympic athlete. The versatile Mr. Matson played in the NFL for the Chicago Cardinals, Los Angeles Rams, Detroit Lions and the Philadelphia Eagles. He was the third pick in the first round of the 1952 NFL draft, selected by the Cardinals, and he went on to run up a lot of yardage while accumulating impressive statistics.

Mr. Matson was raised in San Francisco, where he was a talented athlete. He studied at San Francisco City College and then at University of San Francisco, where he earned All-American honors. Because he excelled at both football and track, he earned a place on the 1952 Olympic team to compete in Helsinki, Finland in the 400-meter (bronze medal) and 4x400 meter (silver medal) races.

Further reported in the 27 October 1956 *Army Times* was Fort Ord's defeat of the Camp Pendleton Marines in the "first major test of the football season." Pendleton fumbled the ball five times on their way to their first loss for the year. Ord quarterback Paul Larson connected with Mal Hammack and Charlie Hardy to put points on the board. Contributing Ord runners included Sam "First Down" Brown and Sam McWhirter. Fort Ord remained the only undefeated team on the West Coast.

The 29 November 1956 *Bayonet* reported that the Main Post Doughboys were post Champions following a Thanksgiving Day victory over 3rd Div. Marne Rockets. Despite the brutally cold day, 4000 fans showed for the Fort Benning Championship, in which the Doughboys defeated the Rockets, 23-7, holding Marne to only ten yards in the second half, including both rushing and passing.

Bayonet Sports Editor Tom Wierzbicki described heroics by Rocket halfback Dave Rogers, who scored with a second quarter 57-yard run, and the play of Doughboy backs, Kenny Brown, Dick Ohl, and Ken Clark, whose capable running set up Lou Sawchik for a 14-yard touchdown reception. Rockets' quarterback Gene Hanson struggled to overcome the tough Doughboy defenses, resulting in low yardage gained and an interception.

Photo: Ollie Matson Football card

The 13 December 1956 *Bayonet* (144) reported that Fort Benning football stars, Dave Rogers (Rockets) and Dale Haupt (Doughboys), were named to the "worldwide" All-Army team for 1956 (See also *Army Times* All-Army Football Poll section). The selections had been made by coaches, writers and "grid fans."

Haupt was a 6', 220-pound guard from the Green Bay Packers, who coach Ingram called "one of the finest linemen to grace the gridiron." His "ferocious" play ensured his inclusion on the All-Army team. Halfback Dave Rogers, on the other hand, was the "main offensive threat" for the 3rd Infantry Division. His tally was nine touchdowns for the season, which is consistent with his history of having been a Big Ten star out of Indiana. His nine touchdowns came on runs ranging from 35 to 64 yards. All-American Rogers' skills led to a professional contract with the Philadelphia Eagles in anticipation of his 13 December separation from the Army.

Following the Doughboys Post Championship victory, a new sports policy was released by the Special Services Council (same edition, page 12), which would, ironically, eliminate post-level competition in order to implement a sports program which would allegedly result in wider military personnel participation.

General Powell, Infantry Center Commander, approved the move authorized by Special Troops Command's Col. Henry M. Zeller, of Dallas, Texas, who reasoned that more military personnel would benefit by holding to a strictly command level of participation. Cost savings was an associated factor. It was acknowledged that the level of play would likely be inferior to that of post-level play.

"Regimental champions in these sports will be augmented by several All-Stars from other teams and will represent Fort Benning in Third Army tournaments and any higher competitions." The new program would be effective until 1 May 1958, unless sooner rescinded or superseded.

Another article, same edition, reported "A former grid pupil of Tennessee head coach Bowden Wyatt, 1st Lt. Dale Haupt, a stalwart guard on the Fort Benning Main Post Doughboys, has been selected on the world-wide All-Army football team for 1956." Apparently it was confusing how a Wisconsin boy played in Wyoming under a (then) present day coach from Tennessee.

Haupt said he graduated high school and did not attend school the following two years while he played for the semi-pro Manitowoc Chiefs of the Wisconsin State Amateur League. He was designated an All-Star in that league, which led to scholarship offers from Wyoming and Georgia.

He chose Wyoming.

Haupt played under Coach Wyatt for three years, and he had nothing but praise for Coach Wyatt, comparing him to Coach Blackbourne of the Green Bay Packers.

The 6', 220-pound Haupt graduated from Wyoming and signed a contract with the Packers, where he hung on through the exhibition season until he was released prior to the regular season. He returned to Wyoming to further his education and helped out with the football team until he was drafted into the service in 1955.

Haupt was assigned to Basic Infantry Officers Course number 44 at Fort Benning. He played Service football out of Benning for two years, and his plan upon completion of his military service was to play pro football and later to coach.

As it turned out, Haupt did become a college coach, working at several schools, until he later became a defensive line coach for the Chicago Bears, winning a Super Bowl in 1985. Following the Bears, he made his way to the Eagles, where he finished out his professional coaching career in 1995 (145).

Dale Haupt passed away 3 April 2018.

Rest in Peace, hero.

The 15 December 1956 *Army Times* (146) reported Fort Hood's football loss to Bolling AFB in the Shrimp Bowl in Galveston, Texas in front of 7500 fans. The Bolling Generals came from behind to beat Hood by scoring two touchdowns and a field goal in the fourth quarter. Hood scores came on a blocked field goal by Adam Baker, who then picked up the ball and ran 70 yards for a touchdown.

Hood's "Jerrys" contributed to help keep Hood in the game - Jerry Johnson passing to Jerry Janes, for more points and the lead in the third period. However, Hood's lead was brief. More scoring through the work of Bolling stars Ralph Gugliemi, Doyle Nix, Eugene Hill, and James Haas put the game out of reach in the fourth, and victory was Bolling's.

The 20 December 1956 *Bayonet* reported (147) that the sports editor of the *Columbus Ledger*, Tom Kinney, spoke at a Fort Benning football dinner on 12 December. Kinney had been covering sports for 20 years, including from the Rose, Cotton, Sugar, Orange, and Gator Bowls. Notably, he expressed disappointment in the elimination of post-level competition for the Infantry Center; "The name Doughboys will be sorely missed from the sports scene."

He said he would miss following the post teams, and if one post team was established to play small college teams, "the money derived from, say three games would foot the bill for the entire post sports program."

1957

1957 America was a time of cultural change, technological advancements, and human accomplishment. For example, the private plane industry started to make inroads into overall aircraft production, which had traditionally been military-use focused. The need for additional air traffic control was evident when a 1957 survey showed 123 planes in the air at one time in and around New York City, and the number was expected to quadruple by 1975. The blockbuster movie, *Ten Commandments*, was made for $13 million and would gross $32 million by 1960 at the same time "drive in" theaters were still 25% of all theaters.

1957 also saw heated resistance to integration playing out, specifically at Central High School in Little Rock, Arkansas, where Gov. Orval Faubus had attempted to prevent the school's re-opening; Faubus' non-compliance invited Eisenhower's forceful federal response.

Overall, 1957 saw America growing more prominent on the world stage, technologically, scientifically, and culturally; and Service Sports athletes continued to compete honorably in this time of American ascent on the world stage.

Stars and Stripes reported (148) in 1957 that 900 Army athletes attempted to qualify for the final Olympic Trials via "All-Army and inter-service elimination competition." Of the major services, Army led the way with 54 individuals qualifying in 14 different events. Air Force, Navy, and Marines combined to qualify 46 athletes. The article did not name the specific events.

Army Times of 1 January 1957 (149) informed us that European Command would not send a team to the All-Army basketball tournament in March (18-

23 March at Fort Monmouth) due to "drastic changes" to USAREUR's sports program.

USAREUR intended to eliminate basketball at the regimental level and to get rid of the USAREUR Commander's Trophy in athletics, though other commands were not expected to do the same. "The new policy was met with considerable dismay by Army athletic officials and regimental team players in Europe." The reason given was to maximize player participation at the lower unit level; basketball at the battalion and company level could now only progress to conference championships.

The Far East Command was committed to sending a championship team to all major All-Army tournaments, including basketball and boxing; Alaska and Hawaii would follow suit. The article said that the decision involving basketball was isolated at that command, and would not impact the overall sports program.

"Athletic spokesmen" doubted the new policy would increase participation, and participation by "really good" players would likely decrease.

This new policy appeared to have originated from a Seventh Army meeting in December, where commanders recommended the change. No players were interviewed to indicate how they felt about the change (*Note: The 19 January edition said it was decided that baseball and football would continue to be played at the regimental level, but basketball would not*).

Also on page 43 of the same edition is an article on Service Sports clinics overseas; "top sports officials" were being sent to provide instruction.

Arranged by the Sports Branch, Special Services, Office of the Adjutant General, the clinics play an important part in the Army's sports program. The baseball clinics would run from 18 February to 1 March, in Japan and Hawaii. The instructors were Florida State baseball coach Danny Litwhiler, a major league veteran, University of Wisconsin Coach Art Mansfield, and University of New Hampshire coach, Henry Swasey.

The same paper announced the Fort Knox basketball team had two All-Americans on their roster: Jules (Julius) McCoy from Michigan State and Frank Ramsey from Kentucky.

New Castle News reported (150) that Julius and brother Jimmy had both been outstanding basketball players in the 1950s. Julius, standing 6-foot-1, scored 1471 points in high school, which includes a remarkable 40-point game. Following graduation, Julius moved on to Michigan State, where he earned All-American designation. "After serving in the U.S. Army, Julius tried out for the NBA Hawks, which drafted him. He made the last cut but was let go (*Author note: There had been credible allegations of racism*)."

Julius McCoy passed away on 4 April 2008.

Rest in Peace, hero.

Frank Ramsey, who played at Kentucky under Coach Rupp (Ramsey was *not* among the accused in the Kentucky point-shaving scandal), was, according to his Basketball Hall of Fame entry (151), "a cerebral player who enjoyed pressure-filled situations; he excelled in the clutch."

Frank Ramsey passed away 8 July 2018.

Thank you for your service, hero.

Photo: Frank Ramsey Photo: Julius McCoy

Army Times of 19 January 1957 reported that Fort Lewis basketball stars, Jerry Bird (Kentucky) and Ed Stube (Loyola of Chicago), were part of a strong regimental team, and that they were expected to shine in the subsequent post league. The Lewis lineup would include Stan Glowalski and basketball legend K. C. Jones.

The *Lexington Herald Leader* (152) reported Bird's passing in 2017, noting that he had played for Kentucky from 1954-1956, which included two Southeast Conference titles and a 25-0 record in 1954. Bird's legacy is a part of the Kentucky Athletics Hall of Fame, and his No. 22 jersey is displayed at Rupp Arena. Bird still holds the record, at the time of this writing, for rebounds in a game, at 24. He was drafted by the Minneapolis Lakers in 1956 and later played a year for the New York Knicks.

Fort Lewis star K.C. Jones was known to be a "hard nose guard," and later Hall of Fame coach of the Boston Celtics; he passed away in 2020 at the age of 88, per *ESPN* (153). Jones played nine seasons for the Celtics, winning eight titles and then adding three more titles as a coach, with benefit of enormous basketball talent such as Larry Bird, Robert Parish, Danny Ainge, Bill Walton, Kevin McHale, and Dennis Johnson. It was said that Jones wasn't flashy or big (only six-foot-one) when he played, but he "gave fits to opposing stars like Jerry West and Oscar Robertson." He dished out those same "fits" to other teams as a coach, though in a gentlemanly way. Larry Bird said that Jones "was the nicest man I ever met, he always went out of his way to make people feel good."

Rest in Peace, heroes.

K. C. Jones   6-1   203   26   1   San Francisco
Although he didn't play football in college, Jones was internationally famous as a basketball star, playing alongside of Bill Russell both at the University of San Francisco and in subsequent cage activity. Jones was named the outstanding basketball player of the 1956 Olympics in Melbourne. Although his basketball contract is owned by the Boston Celtics, Jones has chosen to give pro football his best shot, since he showed great grid potential in high school. He was drafted on the 30th round in 1955 on the speculation that he would want to try football at some future time. His basketball agility and speed make him a natural candidate for a defensive backfield spot.

The 9 February 1957 *Army Times* (154) reported that Fort Jackson, defending Third Army champion, was undefeated and boasted a 17-2 record. Eagle coach Ronald Scheffel lauded his team's scoring ability, which was supported by their remarkable 90.5 points per game average while holding their opponents to an average of 71.6 PPG. Strong rebounding, at a rate of 58.3 per game, frequently allowed Jackson to be in scoring position.

Furman All-American Darrell Floyd averaged 19.6 PPG, supported by reliable rebounding from Mickey Harrington and Millard Harris. Shooting aces were Lee Collins and Rudy D'Emilio.

The Eagles planned to attend the Third Army championships at Fort Bragg early in March, and the All-Army championships at Fort Dix later in March.

2 November 1957 *Army Times* reported (155) that the powerful Carson and Dix football teams remained undefeated; Carson beat Fort Bliss 26-0, and Dix topped Fort Lee 21-7.

The game at Fort Carson featured the running of Carson halfback Bill Fleischman and "a rock-ribbed defense." Even with four starters out of the lineup, Carson made short work of Bliss at home. Fleischman introduced variety to his scoring, earning one-yard and sixty-five-yard touchdowns. Fleischman gained 116 yards on 16 carries with the help of Carson's strong offensive line. Carson's defense held Bliss to just 70 yards, despite star defenders Forrest Gregg and Byron Beams having been out of the lineup.

Army Times' Sports Editor, Tom Scanlon, wrote on 7 December 1957 (156) that Fort Dix deserved a football bowl game. He said that Bolling was considered by many to have been the best service team in the nation that season, and that Bolling would meet the San Diego Marines in the Shrimp Bowl in Galveston, Texas, on December 15. Bolling would lock in the number one position with a win over SDM.

Scanlon argued that in fact Dix should have been considered the top team; "Dix boasts probably the finest team ever in the First Army command. The Burros deserve a bowl bid."

Scanlon also said the All-Army poll produced a "solid, well-rounded ball club," though the vote from Europe was down from the previous year. Still, three Europe-based players made the team. He added that the States produce the heaviest voting in the poll, so for three players from Europe to make the cut shows just how special they were.

ARMY SCOREBOARD

GAMES OCT. 25				
Fort Eustis	0 0 0	0— 0		
Fort Belvoir	7 7 7	7—28		

Fort Myer	0 0 0	0— 0
Lockbourne AFB	6 6 13	0—25

GAMES OCT. 26

Fort Hood	0 21 7	7—35
Fort Wood	6 0 0	6—12
Fort Dix	7 14 0	0—21
Fort Lee	0 0 0	7— 7
Fort Stewart	0 0 0	0— 0
Fort Knox	16 7 6	18—47
Bainbridge	12 0 6	6—24
Fort Monmouth	0 7 0	0— 7
Fort Sill	7 0 0	7—14
Bolling AFB	7 14 7	0—28

GAMES OCT. 27

Fort Bliss	0 0 0	0— 0
Fort Carson	13 6 7	0—26

REGIMENTAL LEAGUES

FORT BENNING, Ga. — (3d Div. League) —15th Inf. over Div. Trains, 47-13. 4th Inf. over 38th Inf., 18-6. 7th Inf. over Combat Support Group, 10-6.

FORT BRAGG, N. C. — 504th Inf. over 505th Inf., 12-7. Corps Arty over Bragg Posters, 32-6. 325th Inf. over Supporting Arms, 21-6.

FORT CAMPBELL, Ky. — 501st Abn. Inf. over Post Units, 6-0. Div. Hawks over 502d Abn. Inf., 38-26.

FORT RILEY, Kans. — Non-Div. Kans. over 26th Inf., 18-7. 121st Signal—1st Engr. Falcons over 16th Inf., 33-7. 69th Armor—4th Cav. Spartans over 18th Inf., 13-7. Arty Caissons over 3d Inf., 12-7. 1st Div. Trains over 28th Inf., 27-12.

OTHER SERVICE GAMES OCT. 26-27
Eglin AFB 13 .... Quantico 6
Dover AFB 24 .... Anacostia Navy 20
Pensacola Navy 81 .... Scott AFB 0
Shaw AFB 26 .... Camp Lejeune 21
San Diego MCRD 41 ... San Diego U. 6
Norfolk Tars 6 .... Little Creek 0

The guard position was the most-overlooked in the poll, according to Scanlon, and Fort Leonard Wood's late organization of a post team hurt their overall showing in poll results, i.e. Abe Woodson deserved better than honorable mention, but suffered a lower position in the poll due to lack of complete playing history in 1957.

The 7 December 1957 *Army Times* (157) reported that with twelve wins and no losses, Hqs. Co. (9222) won the 1957 company championship at Camp Leroy Johnson in New Orleans. Players included Pvt. Joe Matuga, Sgt. Kermit Brazley, PFC Kenneth Hohmann, PFC James Herrie, PFC Dave Crowley, SP3 Vince Harmann, Sgt. Dewey Carle (coach), PFC Hugh Carroll, SP3 Larry Hortin, Pvt. Melvin Botkin, PFC Herman Bruce, SP3 Jack

Weatherly, SP3 Carl Mickelson, and Maj. Carl Manis, Jr. (Company Commander).

The 7 December edition also reported Fort Leonard Wood's "stirring" victory over Fort Riley at Hilltopper Field (Missouri) in 37-degree weather. Despite Wood's mistakes, including fumbles and pass incompletions, and despite active referee whistles, the "Big Red" team managed a come-from-behind 7-6 win on the back of Abe Woodson, who ran 59 yards for the tying score. The extra point conversion put FLW ahead for good.

The game had been the first-ever meeting between the two Fifth Army installations.

Starring for Riley were running back Jerry McArthur, quarterback Hugh Fewin, and fullback Lou Halton. Strong players for Fort Leonard Wood were running back Abe Woodson, halfback Alex Litman, and blocker Sylvester Harris.

Riley and Hood met again a week later in Fort Riley, Kansas for the 1957 Harvest Bowl in front of 5000 fans, and astonishingly duplicated the score of their previous meeting, 7-6; however, this time Fort Riley was the victor.

The first-annual Thanksgiving Day Harvest Bowl had been a "complete success," and was played in "perfect autumn weather." The Riley Sabers scored on their first possession through the efforts of Jerry McArthur (12-yard run) and Michigan State star John Matsko (extra-point kick).

University of Illinois' Abe Woodson was hamstrung by Riley's defense this time, which had been Riley's focus. Riley coach Jim Kincaid had correctly predicted that if they shut down Woodson, they would have certain victory. Though the always-dangerous Alex Litman picked up the slack, it was too little and too late.

On the same day, Fort Dix maintained their undefeated season by crushing the hapless Fort Monmouth Signaleers in front of 5000 fans.

Monmouth unfortunately faced a plethora of college and professional players, such as Harold Davis, Bill Lugar, Jack Stephans of the Toronto Argonauts and Holy Cross, Washington Redskins' George Benedict, guard Mike Nardone of North Carolina State, Maryland All-American end Russ Dennis, and Chicago

Bear guard John Mellakas. Additional talent included Sherm Plunkett of the Baltimore Colts, and Roosevelt "Rosey" Grier from the New York Giants.

1958

The 4 January 1958 *Army Times* (158) announced "Carson Dumps Dix" in the inaugural Satellite Bowl in Cocoa, Florida, 12-6.

The Fort Dix Burros were the only major undefeated team in the Army going into the game, but Carson ruined that distinction by impressively holding the Dix juggernaut to six points. Player/coach Lt. Doug Dickey, a native of Gainesville, assumed the quarterback role for Carson, making an instant impact by throwing two touchdown passes in the first quarter. Both throws were caught by former Iowa halfback, Ed Vincent, who scored on the first one with a five-yard run, and the second one with a forty-six yard run.

Dix was held scoreless until the last quarter, when a John Stephans pass to end Bill Meade resulted in a touchdown.

Dickey had been a star quarterback for the University of Florida, propelling the Gators to a 14-13 Gator Bowl victory over Tulsa in 1953.

Dix's "pro-dominated line" previously helped Dix to a nine game win streak, and Dix had been favored to beat Carson. Carson had come off a rough 1956 season where they won only one in ten games; however, Carson was rebuilt by Dickey and his assistants, Roger Kerns and Buck Priester, resulting in "one of the best service teams in the nation."

Sportswriters and broadcasters at the game named Vincent and Dix end Emerson as the outstanding back and lineman, respectively, of the game. Impressive defensively for Carson were back Don Comstock, tackles Byron Beams and Willie Davis, and guard Forrest Gregg (Davis and Gregg were both All-Army honorees).

A letter to the editor in the same *Army Times* edition discussed, "More on All-Army Ban" (Europe). Letter-writer SP1 Wallace J. Kissel said that the ban on

All-Army sports participation was not done with the proper consideration of authorities, and that the elimination of top-level sports competition incentive was ethically and democratically improper. "Top level sports activities are of vital significance to the masses of Army personnel."

Kissel said that elimination of top level performance opportunity produced a "dangerous precedent," based on the "present day world situation."

In other 4 January 1958 *Army Times* news, Aberdeen Proving Grounds was asserting their basketball dominance, having won six of their first seven games - their only loss having been a heartbreaking 75-74 fall to Eustis. The previous year APG was 25/30 games, and they appeared to be on track for similar success in 1958.

APG won handily against Towson Teachers College, Loyola College, Walter Reed Army Hospital, Fort Ritchie, Martin Bombers, and Deslant.

APG stars included Tom Kapsalis, former Purdue and Fort Rucker player, and William Keller, a 6'6" former Vanderbilt star. Kapsalis and Keller had big shoes to fill, with the loss of Utah All-American, Art Bunte, and Minnesota's Doug Bolstorff, who had averaged 26.5 and 16.7 PPG, respectively, in 1957.

AGM's Ray Zelek (Cornell) and William Hillmeyer (Michigan State) were each 6'5", giving the team unusual height for service ball. Other notable players included Thomas Neppell, Jack Wilkin, and William Shaffer.

AGM would meet the powerful Dix team following the holiday break.

In the 18 January 1958 *Army Times* (159), columnist Tom Scanlon reported "New Sub Rule Helps Army Grid Teams." The changes involved points allowed for conversions and substitution rules based on NCAA rule changes.

Conversions were now two points, "which would undoubtedly encourage teams to take more chances," according to Bolling AFB coach, George Makris. But the new substitution rule was thought to be the change with the greater impact on the game. The rule change would allow players reenter a game once during each quarter. This meant that both starters and substitutes would be able to make two appearances per quarter.

Fort Belvoir's head coach, Sam Puterbaugh, said the substitution rule change would help coaches by allowing them to rest their top players without adverse consequence by having them sit out too long. He said the rule would not impact a team like Bolling AFB as much as weaker teams, because Bolling was so loaded with talent they had essentially two starting rotations.

In the same edition, "Basketball Notes" reported that Fort Myer, Va., broke Andrews AFB five game win streak by defeating the talented Air Force team 96-84. Myer's Paul Covington was high-scorer, tallying 31 points in the game. Also, Fort Belvoir beat Bolling AFB 72-61 on the strong work of Lou Dickman, with 19 points, Ray Lipstas with 16 points, and Maurice George with 15 points.

Fort Leonard Wood named their regimental All-Star squad, to include K. C. Jones, Maurice King, Carl Cain, Joe Bertrand and Murphy Simmons for the first team. The second team included Walt Larkins, Ed Crenshaw, Paul Judson, and John Leonard.

K.C. Jones was named MVP, and the MVP runner-up was Larkins.

Aberdeen Proving Ground was to play Fort Holabird for a March of Dimes benefit; the stars for Holabird were "King" Lear, All-American guard with Temple; Tom Kapsalis, Purdue; Bill Keller, Vanderbilt; and Fred Moeves, Cincinnati.

It was also announced that Arizona's Fort Huachuca opened a "million dollar field house," which would house three basketball courts, a boxing ring, and an exercise room. It was named for Will C. Barnes, an Arizona cattleman, conservationist, writer and telegrapher. Barnes was also a Medal of Honor recipient for actions he took during the Apache uprising in the 1880s. Construction began in July 1956.

The 29 March 1958 *Army Times* reported basketball news, noting that Fort Dix won its sixth consecutive First Army basketball championship game at Fort Monmouth, N.J., by thoroughly dominating West Point, 57-26. Top Army player Si Green put in 19 for Dix, and Al Ferrari scored ten.

In an earlier game, Dix destroyed Fort Devens, 112-72, on the back of Al Ferrari's 30 points; four others reached double figures, including Si Green, Wally Choice, Danny Mannix, and Jack Sheehy.

Si Green's brief obituary (160) shows what a basketball force he was in his day, having been drafted ahead of legend Bill Russell in the 1956 NBA draft.

Mr. Green was born in New York in 1933 and died in Pennsylvania in 1980 at age 47. He was a 6'2" guard from Duquesne University who subsequently played nine seasons in the NBA, scoring 4636 career points. He passed away just 14 years after playing his final NBA game.

Rest in Peace, hero.

Fort Ord moved to a "varied sports program" posture in 1958, according to the 5 April 1958 *Army Times* (161). The unfortunate new policy would replace post teams and All-Army tournaments with "maximum intramural sports," though it's not clear why it had to be either/or. It's not clear why tournaments and post teams in major sports couldn't continue at the same time intramural sports took place, though they planned to allow some sports to "reach Sixth Army-level competition," including boxing, basketball, golf, tennis, and baseball.

At the time of the writing it was noted that basketball competition was still in progress, with 800 players in company teams having competed the post tournament. Top company-team players would proceed to brigade level to compete for a Special Services trophy. The games would be scheduled so as to not interfere with basic training.

No explanation was offered as to what prompted the change at that time, and there is some evidence that reduction plans would later be modified.

ARMY TIMES Weekly Army Football Report
THE MOST COMPLETE SUMMARY OF STATESIDE ARMY FOOTBALL TO BE FOUND IN ANY PUBLICATION

The 29 November 1958 *Army Times* (162) lauded Brooke Army Medical Center for defeating Fort Riley on their way to appearing in the Shrimp Bowl in Galveston, Texas, on 14 December. Brooke was to face the strong Eglin AFB team in the year-end contest between the top service teams.

Brooke was led to victory over Riley by their "swivel-hipped" quarterback, Jim Easton, who started things off with a pair of touchdown passes to receiver Charley Blanton. However, good feelings from those touchdowns were soon tempered when Riley's Jerry MacArthur ran a kickoff 95 yards for an answering score. This was followed by a Riley quarterback Alphonse Bennett 79-yard pass to Henry Bell.

Brooke scored twice more in the second period to ultimately put the game out of reach. Outstanding performers for Brooke included tackle Bill Bishop, who recovered a fumble, Larry Kent, Lou Archambeau, Jim Ford, Jess Washington, Bob Hayes, and Napolean Reid.

It is notable that the 29 November edition also reported on the upcoming Far East service football championship in Tokyo's new 70,000-seat National Stadium, saying that a record crowd was expected for the Rice Bowl game between the two best Far East service teams (*Note: the previous record crowd was said to be 42,000*).

> The gridiron classic in Japan was originally set up as a service game between military all-star teams stationed in Japan and Korea. It has continued each year with the exception of 1951 (Korean War) ...
>
> In 1949 the Rice Bowl became a contest between all-star teams of individual services ... two preliminary games – the Sukiyaki and Kimchi Bowls – are played in Okinawa and Korea, both on 6 December. Winners ... meet in the Rice Bowl to determine the Far East champion.

The general public was invited to attend, and seats were available on a first-come, first-seated basis. The Air Force had been the service with the most Rice Bowl victories at five (since 1946).

In other 29 November news, *Army Times* reported the Army named former Univ. of Nevada star and former Army All-Star, Presidio's Hal Fischer, as Army All-Star basketball team coach. The Army team was scheduled for "top inter-service and AAU competition," with possible player selections for the 1959 Pan American Games team and the 1960 U.S. Olympic team.

As coach of Presidio, Fischer racked up an incredible 174 wins and only 14 losses. He also coached the 1951 Pan American basketball team in Buenos Aires. The Presidio Toreros won the Sixth Army title the previous two years.

27 December 1958 *Army Times* (163) reported that Fort Leonard Wood's exceptional Hilltoppers basketball team earned a place in the AAU National

tournament, finishing fourth despite defeating the number one ranked tournament team. Starring for the Hilltoppers were Carl Cain, K. C. Jones, Paul Judson, and Maurice King*

Another article in the same paper says that Maurice King was named player/coach of the Fort Leonard Wood Hilltoppers basketball team. Mr. King was described as a former Kansas university star, and a very popular player on post. He had been twice All-Big Seven, and was the "floor general" while playing with Wilt Chamberlain. He averaged 30 points a game the previous year with Fort Leonard Wood.

Fort Chaffee won the Fourth Army Title, led by Arnold Short, among others, in their defeat of Fort Sill, 77-64, in the final. Fort Bliss's Lou Estes was named the outstanding tournament player.

Photo: ENTRANCE, FORT LEONARD WOOD, MISSOURI, ca. 1950s (postcard).

"Largest Engineer Training Center in the United States, Fort Leonard Wood is situated in South-Central Missouri, in Mark Twain National Forest and in the Ozarks. The 71,000-acre Military Reservation is located near Waynesville, between Rolla and Lebanon, scenic U. S. Highway 66."

The Third Army champion was Fort Gordon (Ga.), which forced a thriller against Fort Jackson (S.C.); Fort Gordon narrowly defeated Jackson 81-80 in overtime on a two-pointer by Johnny McCarthy. Dave Rickets from Fort Eustis was the tournament's outstanding player for Fort Eustis in Second Army competition.

Fort Dix demolished West Point 57-26 for the First Army title on the backs of workhorses Si Green and Al Ferrari.

TERRAPIN CONNECTION

In the course of researching Service Sports, you start to notice trends. One type of trend is how often the name of a certain college/university comes up in the history or biography of service players or coaches. The University of Maryland is one of those schools which had a reasonably strong bond to 1950s Service Sports.

Ironically, much of my research supporting my Service Sports writing came from National Archives II in College Park, which is almost next door to the Maryland campus (a beautiful area).

As noted in my previous book, *The Forgotten Athletes of the American Forces Far East*, Maryland coach Jim Tatum was one of three big-name football coaches invited to Japan in 1955 to give coaching clinics for service players and coaches, along with Paul "Bear" Bryant, then of Texas A&M, and Hugh Daugherty of Michigan State. The clinics had been open to "all members of the Armed Forces and to all civilians working for the Armed Forces" (11).

> Mr. Tatum was "Coach of the Year" in 1953, and he talked about his "famed split T formation." He also discussed stance, blocking and passing, with emphasis on offensive ends during an "aerial attack." Paul Bryant was described as "The man who put Kentucky on the football map before going to Texas A&M." Mr. Bryant discussed the kicking game, drills, and coaching techniques.
>
> Mr. Daugherty was said to have begun his instruction with defensive line drills and the pass protection "used by his club against Big Ten foes. He was expected to concentrate on his multiple offense as the clinic gets away from fundamentals." The three "grid mentors" would be expected to later travel to Haneda in Tokyo to tutor the FEAF clinic from July 18-22.

Maryland football excellence was evident.

Coach Tatum was a legend in college coaching, having guided the Terrapins to the 1953 National Championship at the young age of 41. He was named Coach of the Year in 1951 and 1953. At Maryland, Coach Tatum compiled an astonishing .815 winning percentage, contributing to his place in the College Football Hall of Fame – 1984 induction (164).

Coach Tatum passed away well before his time, at age 45 in 1959. Rest in Peace, hero.

Tatum Among Noted Coaches Coming to Far East Clinics

A 1955 University of Maryland media guide shows two-time All-American and future Army All-Star (1957), center Bob Pellegrini, on the cover as one of two football co-captains of the Maryland team (165). The same media guide briefly mentioned Coach Tatum's trip overseas: "This summer he was chosen by the government to conduct a month's clinic tour for the Armed Forces in Hawaii, the Far East, and Alaska." It was also noted, interestingly, that Tatum spent time as head coach at Jackson Naval Air Station "during the war." No further support for this item was located, and the dates are unknown.

The Maryland media guide had a detailed biographical sketch for Pellegrini, labeling him a "top flight All-American candidate," indicating that he could "easily be the nation's lineman of the year." He had been moved from the guard to center position to fill a team need, and he handled the position change capably - he was considered to be "one of Tatum's finest products."

As was previously noted in the "*Army Times* All-Army" section, Pellegrini had been named to the 1957 *Army Times* All-Army first-team as a guard. He was described as a player/coach out of Fort Knox, and he was clearly respected by his peers.

Pellegrini was inducted into the College Football Hall of Fame in 1996 (166). His star career also brought him to the NFL, where he was a first-round pick by the Eagles in the 1956 draft, fourth overall. He had a nice run in the NFL, first with the Eagles and then the Redskins from 1956 to 1965.

Mr. Pellegrini passed away on 11 April 2008. Rest in Peace, hero.

Another Maryland Service Sports star was 1956 All-Army selection, Dick Shipley. Shipley was a Terrapin veteran who "called defensive signals for the Terps." He played service football for two years out of Fort Jackson in the tackle position, and not only did he play service ball, his skills were recognized to the extent he was selected as an All-Army team member in 1956.

Though Shipley's All-Army selection biography indicates there were no pro rights for him, other sources indicate he was "once the property of the New York Giants." However, *The NFL's Official Encyclopedic History of Professional Football*, which lists all Giants players up to 1976, does not include Shipley's name (25).

Army Times newspaper of 5 January 1957 reported that Dick Shipley was one of six Service Sports football players to be selected to the prestigious All-Service squad, joining Fred Rody of Fort Sill; Dick Syzmanski of 13th Inf. Regt., Europe; Sam Brown of Fort Ord; Tommy Davis of 1st Cav. Div., Tokyo; and Vincent Drake of CCB, 3rd Armd Div., Europe (167). Selection to this elite group reflects Shipley's special skills, effort, and football reputation.

In the Maryland football media guide for 1954, Shipley was said to be a 5-10, 230-pound senior out of Frederick, MD. He was an "outstanding platoon tackle for his size, both ways." He was strong and fast, and though he excelled on offense he was considered stronger defensively – tough to get by.

Thank you for your service, Mr. Shipley.

Yet another Maryland star made a name for himself in Service Sports football - Russ Dennis - who played for the Terps from 1952-1955. Dennis played professionally from 1956-1958 for the Packers and the Redskins.

In the service, Dennis played football for the mighty Fort Dix squad. *Army Times* of 7 December 1957 described Dennis as a "Maryland All-American end" who helped the Dix Burros crush the hapless Fort Monmouth team 46-0 to remain undefeated in 1957.

Dennis teamed up with quarterback Bill Lugar for pass-and-catch yardage and scoring.

Photo: Bob Pellegrini and coach Jim Tatum, 1955, Dept. of Intercollegiate Athletics. Media Relations records, Box 14, Folder Football 1955 [c10 photos, 1954-55], Special Collections & University Archives, University of Maryland Libraries.

Fort Dix was loaded with talent at that time, including the Colts' Sherm Plunkett, the Giants' Rosey Grier, John Mellekas of the Chicago Bears, and others.

The 21 September 1957 *Army Times* in its "Weekly Football Report" (168) said that Dix may have had the best line in the service, which included All-Pro Grier, Washington Redskin John Miller, the Bears' Mellekas, Dennis from the Packers, and Plunkett from the Colts.

Rest in Peace, Mr. Dennis.

The coach and players mentioned are but a few examples of Maryland's proud contributions of elite-tier football talent to Service Sports football in the 1950s.

POINSETTIA BOWL FOOTBALL CHAMPIONSHIP

San Diego's Poinsettia Bowl, inaugurated in 1952, served as the de facto national championship game for CONUS football. From 1952 to 1955 the Poinsettia Bowl was held at Balboa Stadium, which had a seating capacity in the 1950s of 15,000. The stadium was remodeled in the 1960s, which expanded seating to 34,000 - lasting until the 1970s - at which time it was completely demolished and rebuilt from scratch.

Below is contemporaneous reporting from Poinsettia Bowls past.

Photo: Poinsettia Bowl site, Balboa Stadium, San Diego, 1964, post-expansion (169).

1952	Bolling AFB (USAF)	35	San Diego Training Center (USN)	16
1953	Fort Ord (Army)	55	Quantico (USMC)	19
1954	Fort Sill (Army)	27	Bolling AFB (USAF)	6
1955	Fort Ord (Army)	35	Pensacola Naval Air Station (USN)	13

Photo: Poinsettia Bowl History, 1952-1955 (170).

1952 – Bolling AFB vs. San Diego NTC

The 22 December 1952 *Stars and Stripes* (171) reported that Michigan State alumni Al Dorow led the Bolling AFB Generals in a 35-14 defeat of San Diego NTC in the first-annual Poinsettia Bowl service football championship; Bolling was designated national service champion.

Dorow completed 13 passes for 147 yards and one touchdown.

The *San Diego Union*'s Jack Murphy reported, "Bolling Torpedoes N.T. C., 35-14" (172). The All-American from Michigan State, Al Dorow, and his Bolling team "shocked" NTC with a decisive win.

A crowd of 20,000 was anticipated, but heavy rain kept all but 9000 away. There were many Marine and Navy recruits in the stands, however, to watch the action, and there was a lot of it. The game was also televised nationwide to thousands more, with play-by-play from Tommy Harmon.

Navy entered the game as the number-one service team in the nation, hoping to finish the season in the same position, but Bolling had other plans for Navy; Murphy described Bolling as having pushed Navy around in an embarrassing manner. The same Navy team that had recently "outplayed Southern Cal everywhere but on the scoreboard" wasn't strong enough for Bolling on that day.

Bolling was already up 15-0 with seconds remaining in the first period, and by the third quarter had increased their lead to 35-14, "settling the issue beyond all doubt." Bolling prevailed over San Diego, 35-16.

Bolling stars included fullback Allen Boyd, Dorow, safety Dom Fucci, and others. NTC was led by passer Wilbur Robertson. The game statistics were relatively close, surprisingly, but in the end only the scoreboard mattered.

1953 – Fort Ord vs. Quantico Marines

The 21 December 1953 *Long Beach Independent* reported the Fort Ord Warriors handled the Quantico Marines, 55-19, in the second annual Poinsettia Bowl (173).

To no one's surprise, the great Ollie Matson led the Warriors with a "powerful run attack" which overwhelmed the Marines. Matson wasn't alone chewing up yardage on the field; Lawrence Segovia and Dave Mann each produced long scoring runs to add to the winning point total.

Matson, Mann Pace 55-19 Warrior Victory

Coming into the championship game, Fort Ord had been ranked number one and Quantico was ranked number two. Ord's Armed Services Championship win justified their regular-season position as the best service team in the nation (not to be confused with actual service academies, such as West Point or the Naval Academy, which are essentially NCAA teams).

San Francisco University and Chicago Cardinals star Matson scored twice, with seventy-two and thirteen yard runs. Segovia contributed a score with a seventy-seven yard scoring scramble. Mann, from Oregon State, hit the end zone from 39 and 28 yards to help push Ord out of reach for Quantico.

Other stars for Ord included Bill Roffler from Washington State, who scored on a 14-yard run, and passer Don Heinrich from the University of Washington, who threw an eight-yarder to Ed Hanke from Southern Cal for more points.

192

Quantico's quarterback Jack Fry cf Baylor hit end Fred McKee for an eighteen-yard touchdown, accounting for the Marines' only pass-play score. Quantico scored twice more on runs by Jackson King and Rex Simonds.

1954 - Fort Sill Vs. Bolling AFB

The 25 December 1954 *Army Times* reported that Sill defeated Bolling, 27-6, in the 1954 Poinsettia Bowl (174). The Fort Sill Cannoneers "had little trouble" dispatching the vaunted Bolling Generals in front of 10,000 fans.

Sill earned the national service football title, making it two years in a row that Army had prevailed. Sill's win followed the Ord victory in 1953.

Sill's run-yardage was outstanding – 489 yards gained on the ground, though their passing game was a dud, with 0-5 attempts/completions, "but Sill needed a passing attack like Carter needs liver pills."

Army Times All-Army honoree and former Oklahoma star (and Heisman Trophy winner), Billy Vessels, starred both ways – offense and defense. He intercepted four passes and recovered two fumbles on the day.

The game featured long runs by Sill's Merrill Green, with a 73-yarder, and by All-Army team member (1953) Dan Page, former Texas star, who ran sixty-six yards for a score. For Bolling, Bill Reichart produced a nice 38-yard run to help the Generals' effort.

Sill's defensive line was another positive story, having "bottled up Bolling quarterback Tommy O'Connell, the passing wizard who won *Air Force Times*' Most Valuable Player award this year." O'Connell was under constant pressure from the Sill defense, and it showed in the results.

As if Sill didn't have enough weapons, they also had the services of Bobby Green, a "9.5 100-yard dash man," who "went all the way on the first play from scrimmage." Talented All-Army MVP Buck McPhail gave Sill some additional, significant yardage on offense.

Dan Page accumulated 123 yards in seven attempts, for an astonishing average of 17.5 yards per run. McPhail had 97 yards in 17 carries. O'Connell completed 14 of 22 passes for 155 yards. O'Connell's backup, Jimmy Lear, went 6 for 12.

Sill finished the year with twelve consecutive victories, which is not surprising given the level of talent they brought to the field in 1954.

1955 - Fort Ord Vs. Pensacola NAS

The 1 December 1955 *Stars and Stripes* announced, "Ft. Ord Accepts Poinsettia Berth" (175) for the "mythical" Armed Forces football championship. The article said the Warriors would meet the winner of the 10 December playoff game between Fort Sill and Bolling AFB at Fort Sill (*yet Ord's opponent would actually be Pensacola*).

Bolling was the only undefeated team in the nation. Ord had a 10-1 record, and Sill had a 6-1 record. Sill's only loss came at the hands of Fort Hood.

Ord, Hood Win Bowl Games

The *San Bernardino County Sun* reported 18 December 1955 (176) that Fort Ord "pummeled" Pensacola for the Poinsettia Bowl win and the national service championship.

Fort Ord achieved two touchdowns in the first quarter for a quick start to their national championship victory game in the fourth-annual (and final 1950s) Poinsettia Bowl.

UCLA and Pittsburgh Steelers star, Paul Cameron, drew first blood, scoring on a 19-yard run early-on. University of Arizona's Al Dattola helped bring the Ord score to 14 with an interception/run-back 70 yards for the score, with 32 seconds remaining in the first quarter.

Pensacola scored six points in the second period with a 36-yard pass from Naval Academy's Dick Echard to Chuck Wenzlau. Ord scored again before the half when former USC and 49ers' player Jim Powers tossed one to Ron Miller for the touchdown.

Other Ord contributors were Alex Burl and Bob Reinhart, among many others on the star-packed team. "Gerald Perry, former California and Detroit Lions player, kicked four extra points for Fort Ord, and Paul Larson, one-time California star, accounted for the other."

Army Times provided a detailed report of 1955 Poinsettia results, written by SFC Bob McClintic (177). "The infantry blue sparkled brightly here at Balboa Stadium last Saturday afternoon as the pro-studded Fort Ord Warriors shot Pensacola, Fla., Naval Air Station out of the clouds and scuttled the Navy Goshawks ... before 10,000 awed partisan fans."

Notable was Ord's defense, which shut down Pensacola's quarterback, Dick Echard, with their "airtight defense." 1955 All-Army and former UCLA halfback, Paul Cameron, and back Alex Burl of Colorado A&M led the way on the ground for the Warriors.

Cameron racked up seventy-one yards with eight carries; Burl had thirteen carries for 81 yards. Assisting with scoring was All-Army Ron Miller, who ran a pitched ball ten yards for a touchdown. Also notable was Pensacola's halfback John Weaver grabbing a one-handed catch from Echard for a score.

This would be the final Poinsettia Bowl game in the 1950s.

HISTORICAL NOTES ON
INSTALLATIONS

Fort Ord played a major role in CONUS Service Sports in the 1950s, particularly with their football program. The 26 October 1953 to 19 December 1953 *Fort Ord Yearbook* (133) gave a brief history of Fort Ord, which consisted of 28,000 acres on the Monterrey Peninsula on the California coast. Ord was closed in 1994 due to a Base Realignment and Closure program decision.

Photo: Fort Ord 6th Infantry Division HQ, 1953 (133).

"The picturesque Presidio of Monterey, first a Spanish and a Mexican military establishment, has its history interwoven with that of the nation and of California." The fort had been named for Major General Cresap Ord, who "was prominent in the early history of the region." Ord was initially activated in 1940 under General Stilwell, a.k.a. "Vinegar Joe."

Many soldiers received WWII training at Fort Ord, and following the war, no large scale operations took place until the Fourth Infantry Division was activated in 1947; however, it wasn't long before the Fourth was moved to Fort Benning, Georgia (1950), having been replaced by the Sixth Infantry Division – including the 1st, 20th, and 63rd Infantry Regiments.

At the time Fort Ord was only one of ten Infantry basic training facilities in the country.

Another prominent military installation vis-a-vie Service Sports was Fort Benning, Georgia. According to the Fort Benning yearbook of 1936, the facility was named after General Henry L. Benning, C.S.A., a native of Georgia (Fort Benning and Fort Bragg, at the time, were the only two posts named after Confederate officers).

The fort began with the establishment of an Infantry School, and as the Army was reviewing possible sites, they took into account several considerations: Suitable climate for year-round training, centrally situated to "our country's population," and proximity to a seaport and rail facilities.

The site selection members decided in September 1918 to situate the Infantry School near Columbus, Georgia. 115,000 acres were available to be purchased for $3,600,000. The troop capacity was to be 24,000. Following the conclusion of WWI, however, the plans were modified (8 March 1919) to instead purchase 98,000 acres for $2,600,000. At the time, the slightly-smaller purchased acreage would still be "one of the largest tracts of land ever bought by the government of any nation."

The new installation would accommodate "5000 officers and men." Construction cost would not exceed $6,600,000.

Over the years instruction had been given to varying numbers of Regular Army, National Guard, and Reserve Officers.

To this day, Fort Benning remains an integral part of America's military resource and capability infrastructure, "assisting the finest youths of the land to become proficient in training and steeped in the tradition of zealously-guarding and preserving the principles, resources, and ideals which a gallant race of forebears has entrusted to their care" (46).

CONCLUSION

To say it has been fun researching and writing about this very interesting time in sports/military sports history would be an understatement. It's technically work, but it doesn't feel like it. I've learned a lot, met some great people, and have traveled to and experienced some amazing places.

This book follows *The Forgotten Athletes of the American Forces Far East*. Both titles cover U.S. Military Service Sports in the 1950s, but the first one covers more of the nuts and bolts of the Service Sports system – it is a comprehensive review of Service Sports, primarily overseas (but CONUS also), and is intended to be a reference for future research and general interest.

This book is meant to be less technical, with a focus on the great Service Sports stories and personalities of that time in America. It is also a reference, however, and is intended to also be useful for research and general interest.

Service football, in particular, in the Far East, was of course very similar to the CONUS program. The *Army Times* All-Army team selections drew from the Far East, CONUS, and Europe; there was no differentiation in talent levels between each of those areas. The regular seasons were similar in nature, but where the Far East and CONUS differed was in the post-season, specifically for football.

CONUS football was a bigger operation as a general rule in the regular season, including a greater number of teams, games, and average fan attendance. However, results diverged in the post-season playoffs. To put it bluntly, playoffs and championship games in the Far East just seemed like a bigger deal. Far East media coverage was more extensive than it was for CONUS, and the Far East football playoffs simply seemed to be more important to the command staff and to the overall operation of the leagues.

The East/West football championship game in the United States (Poinsettia Bowl), matching the nation's strongest service teams, took place in Balboa Stadium in San Diego, as previously noted, but Balboa only had a seating capacity of 15,000 in the 1950s. In the Far East, the Rice Bowl drew crowds of 40,000 - 50,000, and when the new Japan National Stadium became available in 1958, the Rice Bowl game was moved there, drawing 70,000+ fans – standing room only.

Despite the differences, all commands are on the same team, and we respect and celebrate them all.

Thank you to the people responsible for keeping and maintaining historic sports venues, such as Doughboy Stadium at Fort Benning, which is even more impressive in that they allow the general public to access the stadium in person as part of Benning's "Historic Trail." That's the way it's done!

My hope in writing *The Forgotten Athletes of the American Forces Far East,* and this follow-up book on the CONUS version of Service Sports, is that people will remember and honor those who came before us. Preserving cultural memories and the history of some of our Greatest Americans is one of our highest callings as a nation - let's not let them down!

ARMED FORCES SPORTS ALMANAC

An amazing publication from 1954, the *Armed Forces Sports Almanac*, published by Military Service Publishing Company of Harrisburg, Pennsylvania, author C. O. Kates, provides exceptional details on U.S. Military Service Sports players and teams generally from 1951 to 1954 in the Far East, Europe, and CONUS (178). This book is rare; I was only able to identify approximately six or seven copies in America, housed at some universities, military facilities, and at the Library of Congress.

The Almanac is a large book covering many different Armed Forces sports. Christopher Malpass of the Interlibrary Loan and Document Services at UNC Wilmington, North Carolina, graciously provided scanned copies of the 264 pages pertaining to football and basketball Service Sports.

This incredible publication gives team names and rosters, game scores, All-Army team selections, Service All-Star selections, Service All-American selections, and more. Selected pages pertaining to CONUS teams are reproduced below.

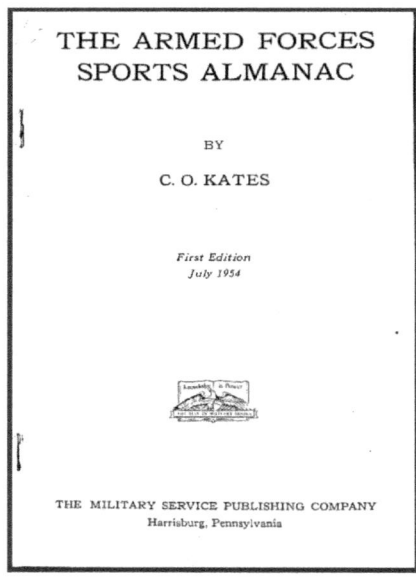

FOOTBALL

SERVICE ALL-STARS

Selected in a poll conducted by the Armed Forces Press Service

1952

FIRST TEAM:

Offense

Andy Hillhouse, Camp Polk, re
Bill Pearman, Ft. Belvoir, rt
Bob Griffis, NTC San Diego, rg
George Radosevich, Parris Island, c
Ted Daffer, Ft. Eustis, lg
Jim Weatherall, Quantico, lt
Jim Mutscheller, Quantico, le
Al Dorow, Bolling AFB, qb
Bill Hayes, Parris Island, fb
Larry Coutre, Camp Breckinridge, hb
Bill Wade, PhibPac, hb

Defense

Bob Schnelker, Parris Island, re
Jack Stroud, Camp Drake, rt
George Weatherly, Ft. Sam Houston, rg
Irv Holdash, Ft. Eustis, c
Joe Palumbo, Ft. Eustis, lg
Don Coleman, Camp Atterbury, lt
Harrison Frasier, Camp Lejeune, le
Verl Lillywhite, NTC, San Diego, qb
Ken Shobe, Ft. Sam Houston, fb
Bob Boyd, NTC, San Diego, hb
Jim Glisson, Ft. Jackson, hb

1953

FIRST TEAM:

Frank McPhee, Quantico, e
Leo Sugar, Ft. Lee, e
Jack Esslinger, NAS, Norfolk, t
Hal Mitchell, Ft. Lee, t
Gil Bucci, Parris Island, g
Don Trevisano, NAS, Pensacola, g
Ray Beck, Ft. Jackson, c
Bob Williams NTC, Bainbridge, b
John Petitbon, Quantico, b
Ollie Matson, Ft. Ord, b
Al Dorow, Bolling AFB, b

SECOND TEAM:

Nick De Rosa, Cherry Point, e
Ed Bell, Ft. Monmouth, e
Gene Lipscomb, Camp Pendleton, t
Jim Mahoney, Little Creek, t
Jim Simmons, Burtonwood AB, g
Joe Skibinski, Ft. Monmouth, g
Paul Hatcher, PhibPac, c
Don Heinrich, Ft. Ord, b
Hank Lauricella, Ft. Belvoir, b
Bob Meyers, Quantico, b
Bill Reichardt, Bolling AFB, b

SERVICE ALL-AMERICAN TEAM

Based upon the Williamson 1953 Service All-American Balanced Poll

FIRST TEAM:

Bucky Curtis, NTC, San Diego, e
Gene Schroeder, Great Lakes, e
Jim Weatherall, Barstow, t
Roscoe Hansen, Quantico, t
Pat Cannamela, Ft. Ord, g
Ted Daffer, Ft. Eustis, g
Glen Graham, Camp Lejeune, c
Billy Wade, PhibPac, qb
John Petitbon, Quantico, qb
Zippy Morocco, Ft. Jackson, hb
Ollie Matson, Ft. Ord, fb

SECOND TEAM:

McPhee, Quantico, e
Jessup, NTC, e
McCormick, Ft. Leonard Wood, t
Boggan, Camp Lejeune, t
Forrester, Hamilton AFB, g
Beck, Ft. Jackson, g
Morris, Ft. Belvoir, c
Bonar, Bainbridge, qb
Smith, Pensacola, hb
Dorow, Bolling AFB, hb
Brunson, Ft. Jackson, fb

THIRD TEAM:

Langas, Ft. Belvoir, e
Martin, Ft. Sill, e
Kimmell, Ft. Lee, t
Anderson, Bainbridge, t
Eggers, Ft. Belvoir, g
Bucci, Parris Island, g
Fuller, Brooke AMC, c
Page, Ft. Sill, qb
Preston, MCRD, hb
Kinek, Cherry Point, hb
Hansen, Little Creek, fb

HONORABLE MENTION:

End: Henke, Ft. Ord.
Tackles: Duca, Cherry Point; Feldner, Ft. Hood; Griffis, PhibPac.
Guards: Kapral, Ft. Sam Houston; Cahill, Little Creek.
Centers: Evans, Barstow; Hatcher, PhibPac.
Quarterbacks: Harding, Camp Polk; Kissel, Ft. Belvoir; Brown, Camp Pendleton.
Halfbacks: Goode, El Toro; Carodine, Camp Pendleton.
Fullbacks: Piscuskas, Camp Polk; Mann, Ft. Ord.

91

ARMY

United States

ALL-ARMY TEAMS

Selected by the readers of ARMY TIMES

1951

FIRST TEAM:

Andy Hillhouse, Camp Polk, e
Denver Mills, Ft. Eustis, e
Jack Stroud, Ft. Jackson, t
Joe Mlinarich, 2d Armd. Cav., t
Gerald Weatherly, Ft. Sam Houston, g
John Helwig, Ft. Ord, g
Bob McCullough, Camp Breckinridge, c
Nat Taylor, Ft. Campbell, qb
Red Jenkins, Ft. Jackson, hb
George Fisher, 1st Div Arty, hb
Larry Coutre, Camp Breckinridge, fb

SECOND TEAM:

Harry Kina, Nurnberg, e
Joe Zuravleff, MDW, e
Nick Bolkovac, Ft. Jackson, t
Archie Finn, Ft. Knox, t
Ronald Gonier, Ft. Eustis, g
Joe Ethridge, Brooke AMC, g
Pete St. Clair, Indiantown Gap, c
Bob Elliott, 14th Armd. Cav., qb
Wally Triplett, Camp Polk, hb
George Sims, Ft. Ord, hb
Hercules Harris, Ft. Richardson, fb

1952

FIRST TEAM:

Andy Hillhouse, Camp Polk, e
Frank Rascoe, Ft. Sam Houston, e
Bill Pearman, Ft. Belvoir, t
Tom Palmer, Ft. Jackson, t
Ray Romero, Indiantown Gap, g
Chuck Asher, Camp Breckinridge, g
Clayton Tonnemaker, Camp Drake, c
Arnold Galiffa, HSC, Japan, qb
Larry Coutre, Camp Breckinridge, hb
Sammy Reynolds, Ft. Eustis, hb
George Lagorio, Ft. Ord, fb (Most
    Valuable Player Award)

SECOND TEAM:

Mike Roarke, Indiantown Gap, e
Barry Deetz, Indiantown Gap, e
Jack Stroud, Camp Drake, t
John Helwig, Ft. Ord, t
Ted Daffer, Ft. Eustis, g
Joe Palumbo, Ft. Eustis, g
Les Richter, Camp Cooke, c
Rocco Calvo, Ft. Lee, qb
Randall Clay, Brooke AMC, hb
Dan Washelesky, Camp Polk, hb
Ken Shobe, Ft. Sam Houston, fb

1953

FIRST TEAM:

Leo Sugar, Ft. Lee, e
Bob Langas, Ft. Belvoir, e
Mike McCormick, Ft. Leonard Wood, t
Hal Mitchell, Ft. Lee, t
Ted Daffer, Ft. Eustis, g
Ray Beck, Ft. Jackson, g
George Morris, Ft. Belvoir, c
Ed Soergel, Camp Atterbury, qb
Dave Mann, Ft. Ord, hb
Billy Sanders, Brooke AMC, hb
Ollie Matson, Ft. Ord, fb

SECOND TEAM:

Ralph Thomas, Ft. Bliss, e
Entee Shine, Camp Atterbury, e
Pat Sarnese, Ft. Belvoir, t
Marion Campbell, Ft. Bliss, t
Pat Cannamela, Ft. Ord, g
Rudy Andabaker, Ft. Lee, g
Harry Riley, Ft. Lewis, c
Dan Page, Ft. Sill, qb
Jim Leftwich, Ft. Belvoir, hb
Jim Roshto, Ft. Sill, hb
Billy West, Ft. Sill, fb

THIRD TEAM:

Wayne Martin, Ft. Sill, e
Cliff Livingston, Ft. Ord, e
Benton Bumgarner, Brooke AMC, t
Stan Campbell, Ft. Ord, t
Frank Kapral, Ft. Sam Houston, g
Bill Pearman, Ft. Belvoir, g
Guy Fuller, Brooke AMC, c
Ron Morris, Ft. Lee, qb
Don Pinhey, Ft. Leonard Wood, hb
Burrell Shields, Ft. Monmouth, hb
Duncan McCaulley, Ft. Hood, fb

ABERDEEN PROVING GROUND, MD.

1953

CO. D, 1st TECH TNG BN
Champions, ORTC

Team

Nick Carchidi, lhb, capt   William Firebaugh, lg
Richard King, le   Ervin Easterling, lg
George Black, re   Pasty Deo, rhb
Lester Grossman, rg   Joseph Policastro, qb
Paul Clements, e   Sylvester Simons, fb
Earl Gerdiman, le

ARMY CHEMICAL CENTER, MD.

1953

Ft. Monmouth 6-47
Bolling AFB 2-51
Ft. Meade 13-8

Team

A. Graham, coach   Don Earich
George Receveur, qb   Ray Starsinic, re
Tony O'Brochta, rt   John Georges, lhb
    (All-American)   Al Lightheart, fb
Joe Carr, lg   Aldo Tremonti, rhb
Bob Prout, rg   Bart Polizzotti, g
Don Molino, c   Herb Cook, le
Cliff Parks   Sam Mullins, lt

CAMP ATTERBURY, IND.
(CARDINALS)
1952
Team

Don Coleman, coach
A. Plant, asst coach
J. Coolsby, asst coach
Joe Silverii, hb
Stan Malec, fb
John Coleman, t
Robert Lee, hb

James Ross, e
George Mayfield, e
Merle Leisher, e
Carl Young, g
Marsh Blackburn, g
Smith
Jack Pope, fb

1953
4W, 5L, 1T

Dayton U 6-12
U of Louisville 15-7
Ft. Leonard Wood 20-6
Purdue Jayvees 19-19
NTC, Great Lakes 6-40
Xavier U Freshman 26-13, 41-7
St. Louis Knights 0-14
Camp Lejeune 0-41
Ft. Jackson 13-14

Team

B. Martino, asst coach
Cary Bachman, coach
C. E. Moss, asst coach
Carl Smith, hb
Ed Soergel, qb
(All-Army)
Jerry Carlson, e
Jim Cash, e
Johnny Tracy, e
John Coatta, qb
Bob Schmidt, fb
Neville Feleihan, g
Paul Adams, t
Gus Mancuso, hb
Rodney Andrus, g
Rollie Strehlow, rhb
Fred Krach, t

Dick Carlson, rhb
Tom Horner, t
William Jackson, qb
Entce Shine, e
(2d team, All-Army)
Ira Franklin, t
Monti Frances, t
Chet Lukowski, g
Charles Mitchell, e
George Giovanas, fb
Roy Butterworth, e, rhb
Len Vandehey, e
Bob Lee, hb
Tom Deitlish, qb
Jim Oxenreiter, e
Jim Feest, fb

FORT BELVOIR, VA.
1952

NRS, Wash., D. C. 55-10
NTS, Bainbridge, Md. 34-13
Ft. Eustis 34-7
Ft. Meade 47-0
Ft. Lee 20-7 14-14
Quantico Marines 42-6 (?)
Indiantown Gap 21-7
Carr Credit 47-7
NAS, Norfolk 33-6
Bolling AFB 21-45

Team

Colie Abney, e
Joel Berry, e
John Hoag, e
Robert Miller, e
Carl Sands, e
Glenn Smith, e
Frank Tobin, e
Cliff Storm, e
George Chandler, t
Charles Coppler, t
Thomas Dasher, t
Douglas Gooden, t
James Lors, t
Julius Robinson, t
Wes Thompson, t
John Yeager, t
Alonzo Rodriguez, t
Ronald Neugold, t

Ralph Phillips, e
Roger Schoeppel, e
George Weiser, e
William Conwell, qb
Richard Romansk, qb
William Pomles, qb
Joseph Veltri, qb
Edwin Burgin, hb
Malcolm Byrd, hb
William Cutter, hb
Walter Court, hb
James Leftwich, hb
John Miller, hb
Al Piccirilli, hb
Salvator Pischiotta, hb
Jimmy Robinson, hb
Walter Smith, hb
Willie Bowles, fb

Joseph Acillo, t
Joseph Stromberg, t
William Pearman, t
(All-American)
Michael Cappiello, g
Horace Drew, g
Robert Graves, g
Lawrence Haller, g
William Santel, g
Thomas Skornschek, g
George Cobb, c
Joseph Hince, c
Jess Lowther, c

Joseph Downing, fb
James Jackson, fb
Edwin Kozlowski, fb
Hilton Keith, c
Charles Meyer, fb
Edward Ross, fb
James Saunders, fb
Harry Smith, fb
J. Talley, head coach
D. Gillis, asst coach
R. Lewis, asst coach
Bill Everson, asst coach
A. Weisman, mgr

1953

West Chester State 21-6
Kent State U 7-6
Toledo U 62-13
Marford Marines 48-0
Ft. Eustis 23-0
NAS, Jacksonville 19-0
Bolling AFB 7-19
Ft. Leonard Wood 20-0
Ft. Lee 13-13
NAS, Norfolk 54-0
Quantico Marines 7-28

Team

Al Davis, coach
Bill Everson, asst ch
Dick Romanski, asst ch
John Tutko, asst ch
Billy Coleman, trainer
C. Poff, trainer
Jim Leftwich, hb
Bob Haner, fb
Frank Di Pietro, fb
Bob Shemonski, hb
Charles Meyer, hb
George Tinsley, qb
Hank Lauricella, hb
(All-American)
Ray Williams, hb
Jime Morse, hb
Ed Kissell, qb
Don Engels, qb
Lou Paludi, c
Walt Shononsky, hb
Bobby Ball, lg
Glenn Smith, re
Bob Langas, le (All-Army)
Lou McClelland, re
Frank Tobin, le
Joe DeRose, c
Dave Simon, le

Ed Clemens, lt
B. Pearman, rg, co-capt, (All-American)
Jim Gasiorowski, c
G. Morris, e (All-American), (All-Army)
Pat Sarmese, lt
Dan Sabino, c
Joe Tyrrell, lg, co-capt
Gene Gribble, hb
Pete D'Alonzo, fb
Ralph Curtis, hb
Larry Fones, le
Frank Banas, re
Dick Bergeron, c
Gary Cooper, le
Bob Dominick, lt
Horace Drew, rg
Bobby Gutt, lg
Jim Haslam, rt
Rod Haughey, hb
Jack Knox, rt
Bob Myers, rt
Ralph Phillips, c
Ray Pierce, fb

FORT BENNING, GA.
1952
ALL-POST TEAM

First Team:
Linton Jordan, e
Bill Thurston, t
Fred Felbaum, g
Bill Stetter, e
Bob Strickland, g
Bill Buza, t
Fred Dreyspring, e
Al Buckles, b
Bill Dietz, b
George Bell, b
Ed Hansen, b
Second Team:
Vern Fahrenkrug, e
Wayne McElroy, t

Charlie Beckwith, g
Marvin Green, c
Bob Hunt, g
Bob Ellis, t
Willis Hames, e
Charles Leonard, b
Adam Zubaty, b
Harry Gibbons, b
Dick Raber, b

INFANTRY SCHOOL DETACHMENT

1952

Donaldson AFB 25-6, 25-0
508th AB Inf. Regt. 28-21, 0-25
CTC 13-13, 0-42
Shaw AFB 6-7
Special Troops, Ft. Benning 7-7, 0-18

Team

Harold Manley, coach	Bob Boeh, fb
Jack Faubion, coach	Bob Milgrim
F. Felbaum, asst ch	Jack Hendrix
Buck Adams, lg	Harold Long, rg
Wayne McElroy, lt	Larry Goins, le
Mel Geipert, c	A. Hohland, t
Bob Hunt, rg	Henry Wilson, g
Clyde Ahlborn, rt	Ken Quart, t
Dennis Ensminger, re	James Odom
Frank DePaolo, qb	Otis Ramseur, g
Eddie Hansen, lhb	Raymond Kuentzel, lhb
K. Harris, rhb	Stanford Hughes
H. Mantzouranis, fb	Edward Metke
Neal McNeill, le	Colin Cochrane
Andrew Holland, lt	Theodore Shepard
Lewis, lg	Robert Wark
Crowley, c	William Ruf
Widder, rg	Bob Harper
Marion Teelaw, rt	Raymond Starns
Donald Dunlap, re	Robert Tyndall
R. Dunlap, qb	Vincent Donato
Charles Leonard, qb	Ford Settle

BRIGADE-PMG (RAMS): Post Champions 1952, 1953

1953

Spl Trps, Ft. Benning 51-0, 58-25
Stewart AFB 31-0
CTC, Ft. Benning 13-19, 20-12
508th Abn Inf Regt 35-18
Shaw AFB 40-2
Redstone Arsenal 35-13
Camp Rucker 34-0

Team

Bill Lawrence, coach	Bill Stetter, asst coach
L. Jordan, asst coach	Milt Wilkert, fb
B. Thurston, asst coach	Mike LaSora, le
Norm Rasp, le	Dick Lohman, lt
Bob Ellis, lt	John Middleton, lg
Frank Kush, lg	Bill Cullom, c
Joe McDonald, c	Ronald Price, rg
Ellis Rainsberger, rg	Mike Shrader, rt
Bob Anglin, rt	Cliff Melton, re
Glenn Luker, rg	Bill Allen, qb
Phil Kuger, qb	Chuck Houser, lhb
Ed Crooks, lhb	Tom Lewis, rhb
Ed Hamilton, rhb	Dick Thompson, fb
Joe Fortunato, fb	

COMBAT TRAINING COMMAND (COMMANDERS)

1952

Donaldson AFB 24-0
Special Troops 6-46, 6-34

NAS, Pensacola 0-44
Inf Sch Det 42-0, 13-13
508th Abn Inf Regt 21-7, 6-20

Team

C. Dickerson, coach	Alvin Kennedy, lhb
B. Strickland, asst ch	Junior Schnitkey, b
Santo DeRose, c	Howard McFarland, b
Charles Matthews, e	James Gutherie, fb
Genier, e	Wheeler Davidson, b
William Henley, e	Marrow, b
John Walsh, e	John Yerby, e
William Fuge, t	Clarence Holder, e
Forrest Lowe, t	Harvey Lundy
Bymon Essix, t	Sylvester Bruten
Harley Stewart, t	Paul Iannoccone, g
Jacob Jones, t	Claude Collins, e
William Williams, g	Perry Lott, g
Theron Cross, g	Jack McCluney
Charles Washington, g	Al Willis
Melvin Anglen, g	Wilburn Addison
Marion Gaddy	George Bartholomay
Clayton Doty	Rex Abernathy
Billy Cato, g	Thomas Haverland
Carl Craft, c	John Stillman
Louis Crispo, c	Murray Raynor
George Bell, fb	Robert Bristow
Adam Zubaty, b	Roland Clement
Dick Raber, b	Paul Shover

1953

508th Abn Inf Regt 7-13, 12-6
Tyndell AFB 25-0
Redstone Arsenal 19-0
Brigade-PMG, Ft. Benning 19-13, 12-20
Spl Trps, Ft. Benning 13-16, 13-7
Camp Rucker 7-20
Lawson AFB 13-16, 14-7

Team

Jim Hefti, coach	Edwin Jones, t
W. Mitchum, asst ch	Bryce Holt, le
Bill Groce, le	Bill Williams, lt
Frank Boring, lt	Jere Moore, lg
John Vines, lg	Charles Smith, c
Vester Newcombe, c	Clayton Doty, rg
Andy Myers, rg	Roosevelt Lee, rt
Mel Anglen, rt	Conrad Deskins, re
Bob Smith, re	Bill Atkinson, qb
Hank Tomsic, qb	Leon Collins, lhb
Melvin Boykin, lhb	Charles Williams, fb
Harry Lundy, fb	Clyde Young, qb
Joe Perry, qb	Richard Sally, e
Robert Forbes, rhb	Charles Strickland, hb
W. Daubert, le	Charles Starling, g
William Hennessee, lg	Willy Sharer, hb
Esme Bain, lhb	Fredrick Neger, g
Harry Woodruff, hb	Bobby Moorhead, rhb
Gilbert Gongaware, t	Herb Mallette, rhb
Joseph Oliva, t	Charles Thomas, rhb
Alphonza Hart, e	Gene Harrell, g
Charles McClendon, hb	

SPECIAL TROOPS (RAMS)

1952

Shaw AFB 33-7
82d Abn Div Arty 6-0
Inf Sch Det 7-7, 18-0
508th Abn Inf Regt 26-7, 23-6
CTC 34-6, 46-6
Parris Island 0-49

Team

Gus Dielens, coach	Bob Wood, t
Bill Lawrence, asst ch	Fred Dreyspring, e
B. Thurston, asst ch	Dick Lohman, g
Lin Jordan, asst coach	Ken Miller, g
Vern Fahrenkrug, e	Bill Cawley, g
Bill Brown, e	Bob Ellis, t
Mike Moropoulos, e	Ernest Cates, g

Harry Hilling, qb
Fred Gaines, hb
Cornell Newman, fb
Jack Gray, qb
Gary Maddox, qb

Clark Merriman
Amon Hassen
Travis Case
Vernon Wyland
Davis

406th ENGINEER BRIGADE (BULLDOZERS)
1953

Main Post 6-9
Div Arty 20-13
505th Abn Inf Regt 6-6
503d MP Bn 19-6
Pope AFB 0-36
Corps Arty 0-19
504th Abn Inf Regt 6-26
325th Abn Inf Regt 0-47

Team

Rudolph Ellis, hb
John Wills, qb
James Cowan, fb
Thurmon Peters

Ernest Johnson
William Conner, rg
Paul Martin, re

CAMP BRECKINRIDGE, KY. (EAGLES)
1951
Second Army Champions

Ft. Jackson 7-67
Ft. Wood 14-19
Austin Peay College 21-13, 46-18
Ft. Knox 28-0
Ft. Campbell 30-13
NAS, Memphis 21-6
NTC, Great Lakes 0-20
Camp Atterbury 29-20
Scott AFB 19-0
Arkansas State College 12-46
Indiantown Gap 13-7

Team

Larry Coutre, hb
Ron Clark, hb
Bob Kilfoyle, qb
Gene Nelson, hb
Joe Unfried, fb
Jesse Cruise, fb
Bob McCullough, c
Tom Barnes, hb

Don McClelland, g
Bob Gonia, g
Clem Jarboe, e
Fred Weidig, b
Roy Gentile, coach
Jim Widman, t
Jake Kernekalian, g
Wally Brunswald, hb

1952
(Post Deactivated, 1953)

NAS, San Diego 20-81
Ft. Leonard Wood 33-0
Austin-Peay College 43-0
NAS, Memphis 46-0
Indiantown Gap 34-28, 13-7
Camp Atterbury 45-6
Scott AFB 60-6
Ft. Jackson 47-7
Ft. Knox 45-6
All-Stars, Ohio Valley Conference 42-0

Team

Roy Gentile, coach
W. Crimino, Jr., l coach
Larry Coutre, hb
Bernard Stephens, fb
Bob Kilfoyle, qb
Bob McCullough, c
Chuck Asher, g
Ron Clark, hb

Sid Parker, hb
Frank Guzik, e
Al Winkler, g
Jim Widman, t
Al Bromberg, e
Joe Vadini
Gerald Overley, fb
John Chalapis, t

Jim Moyer, hb
Vern Dunham, e
Bob Tankosh, e
Jack Jordan, t
Stan Wilkins, hb
Norm Beaton, t
Jake Kerneklian
Bob Stachler, g
Jim Dudding, e
Gerald Amundson, g
Nick Shundich, t
Joe Unfried, fb
John Rummel, e
Joe Cascalanda, qb
Gordon Wyatt, hb

Clem Jarboe, e
Ed Olson, e
John Yuhas, e
Robert Opdyke, c
George Medich, t
Robert Costello, t
John Thompson, t
Sam Pope, g
Jim Wolter, g
George Russett, rhb
Mario Nolfi, rg
Vince Kuestner, e
John Bergman, e
Bob Yoakam, t
Bernie Rose, lhb

BROOKE ARMY MEDICAL CENTER, FT. SAM HOUSTON, TEXAS (COMETS)
1950

Barksdale AFB 54-7
Camp Polk 6-33
Randolph AFB 6-6
NAS, Corpus Christi 32-7
Ft. Bliss 24-14
Ft. Hood 19-20

Team

John Kramer, coach
Howard Newman, qb
Wayne Russell
Joe Gonzales
Alex Litman
Gilbert Henda
Charles Ferguson
Wendell Bates
Dick Roby
Douglas Ellison
Melvin Burkhalter
Russell Kenny
Willie Wright
Gideon Johnson
Howard Teves
Earl Schellhammer
Jimmie Brown
Marion Brooks

Phillip Brown
George Parker
Arthur Lynch
Leonard Brown
Charles Brossman
Karl G. Zschah
Whardie Harvey
Homer Acevedo
William Glenn
Tom Shannon
Marvin Miller
George Williamson
Richard Ballard
Don Bates
Bob Beal
Joe Ethridge
Frank Smith

1951

Goodfellow AFB 39-6
Randolph AFB 40-0
Camp Lejeune Marines 20-0 (Cigar Bowl)
Carswell AFB 13-27
San Diego Navy 17-14
Sam Houston State College 54-21
Camp Carson 52-0, 53-0
Ft. Sam Houston 1-0 (forfeit)
NTC, Great Lakes 57-9
Ellington AFB 1-0

Team

John Kramer, coach
Nelson Campbell
Randall Clay, fb
Allan Neveaux, qb
Carl Depasqua, hb
Charles Russell
Alex Litman
Jack Barry, hb
Marvin Diplock
Mel Selph, fb
Jim Cleveland

Don Logue
Joe Ethridge
Bobby Rogers
George Carlisle
Bubba Bowman
Guy Fuller
Sammy Owners
Joe Tidwell
Billy Lowe
Bobby Jones

1952 ⅄⅄✗ (?)
Camp Lejeune Marines 20-0
Camp Polk 40-0
Ft. Ord 6-7
MCRD, San Diego 15-21
Randolph AFB 34-0
Ft. Leonard Wood 6-13
Carswell AFB 13-19
NAS, San Diego 9-0

Team

J. C. Cleveland, e	Rupert Wright, t
Mervin Hill, e	Bobby Beal, g
Bobby Jones, e	William Gunlock, g
Walter R. Miers, e	Frank A. Johnston, g
Charles S. Russell, e	Albert Rech, g
Karl J. Rustman, e	Walter D. Rock, g
Chris Shaw, e	Chester M. Tobey, g
Connie Wright, e	Bubba Wilson, g
Alex Litman, e	John LaSalle, c
Frank J. Cotter, e	Gerard Faccone, c
Paul Dragovich, t	Guy E. Fuller, c
Robert W. Ethridge, t	Wallace E. Tassos, c
V. (Tug) Franks, t	Jack Barry, b
James H. Martin, t	F. (Bubba) Bowman, b
Robert M. Miller, t	George B. Carlisle, b
Richard O'Bregon, t	Randall, Clay, b
Warren Okelberry	John Faragher, b

Team

Robert Handke, b	Bobby R. Rogers, b
Charles A. Jackson, b	Perry Samuels, b
Benjamin Johnson, b	Melvin L. Selph, b
Bill Lowe, b	Ernie Smith, b
John Melligan, b	Richard C. Smith, b
Allen C. Neveux, b	Joe D. Tidwell, b
Sammy Owen, b	

1953 ✗⅄✗
Camp Polk 13-7, 0-23
Ft. Sill 13-7, 45-13
Ellington AFB 19-0
307th MP Bn, Ft. Sam Houston 49-0
Southern Methodist U "B" 0-0
Ft. Hood 20-0

Team

Aubrey A. Blys, e	R. G. Turnure, g
Gordon Duck, e	William Vohuska, g
James E. Ellet, e	Guy E. Fuller, c'
David H. Gregg, e	Walter Ray Perry, c
Daniel E. Peterson, e	Norman Porter, c
C. A. Shaw, e	John D. Rice, c
A. E. Sergienko, e	Peter A. Vendetti, c
Joseph Williams, e	William R. Cody, b
Benton Bumgarner, t	Harold A. Eaton, b
Rainer M. Burke, t	Raymond Gonsalves, b
Paul D. Catalano, t	Gordon E. Larsen, b
Paul Dragovich, t	Alex Litman, b
Thomas Mahin, t	Vincent Mereadante, b
Paul A. Makara, t	George Pasterchick, b
James A. McDonald, t	J. A. Roberson, b
Leslie S. Poole, t	Theodore R. Riggs, b
Gordon Smith, t	David J. Rothman, b
L. G. Bierman, g	Joseph J. Santos, b
William Bogroff, g	Leslie P. Samuels, b
Howard K. Boland, g	Jesse E. Sample, b
Frank J. Cotter, g	William J. Sanders, b
Sherman M. Mynes, g	Charles R. Schwartz, b
A. M. Raccioppe, g	Larry G. Smith, b
Andrew Smith, g	Richard C. Smith, b
Paul F. Schuler, g	Philip K. Sheridan, b
Frank Swiezy, g	M. B. Taylor, Jr., b

FORT CAMPBELL, KY. (ANGELS)

1951 ⅄⅄✗
Scott AFB 19-7
Georgetown College 19-0

Austin Peay College 26-0
Camp Breckinridge 13-30
Ft. Eustis 14-13
Ft. Jackson 14-37
Ft. Knox 20-13
Seward AFB 13-19

Team

Frank B. Noble, coach	Manilus Hall, b
Nat Taylor, qb	Tom Snyder
Don Hugdahl, b	Tate
John Heenan, e	VanHorne
John Pickett, b	Collins
Howard Ferrell, e	Mullins
Alton McCormick, e	Roddam
Dave Logan, fb	Dick Logan
Bill Reichow, qb	Eugene Drost
Joseph Colonna, qb	Herbie Timms, b
Bill Gregory, fb	Bill DuPriest, t

11th AIRBORNE DIVISION SPECIAL TROOPS

1953 ✗⅄✗

Trooper Bowl:
Special Troops, Ft. Bragg 7-33

Team

Bunny Aldrich, b	Charles M. Carroll, b
Norm Waite, e	Franklin T. Craft, t
Robert D. Blair, g	Merle Daum, g
William Blascak, t	Rod Garner, g
Thomas E. Booth, t	Frederick S. Gault, g
Herman H. Brown, e	William C. Goa, e
Mario J. Brescio, t	Alvin A. Goss, b

Team

Ted J. Harenda, b	Malcolm Sands, b
D. L. Higgins, g	Valery Trout, t
Norman Hoeltzel, b	Malcolmn Wadsworth, e
Robert Helmblad, e	Phillip Wall, e
Herbert J. Jones, b	Richard Weiler, g
George Kelepouris, g	George White, b
Joseph Merschen, t	Landgraff, b
William Mullins, t	S. A. Lewis, coach
Lyle Nelson, g	G. J. Isaak, asst coach
James Ralston, g	R. Dunn, asst coach
Donald Raby, b	

188th AIRBORNE INFANTRY REGIMENT

1953 ✗⅄✗

4W, 6L, 2T
XVIII Abn Corps Arty, Ft. Bragg 7-15
Ft. Campbell Post Units 32-12, 13-6
11th Abn Prov Regt 12-0, 13-25
11th Abn Div Arty 13-6, 14-14
Sewart AFB 6-7
503d Abn Inf Regt 0-55, 13-34
511th Abn Inf Regt 7-7, 0-21

Team

Grant Wells, rhb	William Daniels, lt
Mathew Jenkins, re	James Crooks, le
Richard Piontoski, rt	Merrill Warner, qb
Donald Barrett, rg	William Palumbo, rhb
Mitchell A. Sakey, c	Eugene McCarthy, lhb
James Patterson, lg	Herbert Tims, fb
William Branick, lt	Ronald Dimmick, qb
Thomas Anderson, le	Irwin Zucker, b
Warren B. Palmer, qb	Richard Scott, lhb
Earl Blackman, lhb	Camile Zenow, hb
George Hopkins, fb	Richard McManus, e
Norman Rundle, re	Roger Struck, t
Willie Bullock, rt	John Varela, e
Carl Hansen, rg	Joseph McCallister, t
Malcom Grayson, c	Patrick Dolan, e
Charles Lynch, lg	Lawrence Stone, t

Team

C. Moorman, coach
Lou Ciarroccia, hb
Leo Plourde
Horace Sandlin
Ben Linsalatta, hb
Bob Reid
Arky Arkelian, qb
Bob Swanson, e

Peter McDede, le
David Love, lg
Ward Dollander, c
Harry Steuber
George Hutchins, lt
Ernest Franzone, rg
Ralph Catuogno

1953
Team

C. R. Moorman, coach
Louise Ciarrocca, hb
Leo Plourde, fb
Horace Sandlin, hb
Benny Linsalata, hb
Robert Reid, fb
Arky Arkelian, qb
Peter McDede, c
David Love, g
Ward Dahlander, c
Harry Steuber, t
George Hutchins, t
Ernest Franzone, g
Ralph Catuogno, qb

Raymond Moffett, c
Alan Switzer, e
Jack Davies, e
Stuart Spizer, fb
William Emerson, hb
Seth Barrecolough, hb
Robert Heller, qb
Anthony Farano, g
Douglas Collette, e
Daniel Lucas, e
Henry Manken, t
Hugh Sinclair, hb
Dick Geidlin, mgr

47th INF REGT (RAIDERS)
1952

Service Troops 13-6
364th Inf Regt 0-13
39th Inf Regt 0-18, 0-0
9th Div Arty 18-2
Bayonne, NJ 7-0
60th Inf Regt 6-0

Team

R. Maladowitz, coach
Theron Banks, fb
McMullan
Ralph Pellegrini, qb
Vito Slavickis, hb
Ed Neilson
Ed Bianowitz, c
Alan Hoffman
W. Grant, rb
Toni Parisi, g
Ray Schmitz, c
Mueller, t
Victor Aslan, c
Bill Emerson
Fred Wright
E. Werner, lg
J. Grieves, rg

H. Stander, le
C. Krummel, lg
H. Dozier, rt
H. Lamphere, re
J. Letchford, lb
W. Porebski, fb
J. McLaughlin, le
F. Marszalek, qb
P. DiGiacoma, rg
J. Papini, rt
J. Parnum, rt
E. Abrams, qb
J. Vizzi, lb
T. Jones, rb
Sepler, qb
E. Goodman, rg

364th INF REGT (PANTHERS)
1952

Service Troops 13-7
60th Inf Regt 30-6
39th Inf Regt 7-15, 6-13
9th Div Arty 13-13
47th Inf Regt 14-0

Team

Ted Lauer, hb
Dick Boden, qb
Adam Mataloni, lt
Everett Borgess
Richard Quinn, re

Vince Cioeta
Raymond Rodriquez
Carmen Franco
Maboney

60th INF REGT
1953
Post Champions
Team

Richard Sharry, qb
Joseph Gnerre, qb
Richard Waldron, qb

Edward Garrity, c
John Derszak, t
George Sodini, t

John Bruno, hb
Richard Gorton, hb
Frank Teagich, hb
Seymour Mumbord, hb
Donald Murphy, hb
Robert Mrozack, hb
William Miller, fb
Frank McHood, fb
John Brubacker, c
Robert Hand, c
Edward Healy, c
Frank Garabies, e

Otto Fritz, t
George Bazer, t
Robert Gorton, t
Angelo LaQuaglia, g
Edward Wall, g
Alex Levine, g
John Benson, g
George Brady, g
Edward Muhaw, g
Jim Doyle, c
Donald Lenoir, c
David Small, c

EIELSON ARMY, ALASKA
1952
Team

Wyman, coach
Smith
Rehm
Wallace
Bryant
Jennings
Pagnucco
Estrada
Lawhorn
Knight
Smith
Bemke
Meredith
Gilsenan
Calderone
O'Connor
Sommers
Smith
Meddleton

Smith
Fontana
Bergmann
Hernandez
Sutton
Miller
Tilley
Coiteux
Barr
Harrington
Schley
Lukowski
Ravert
Riker
Lebonnite
Hahn
Hanley
Lombardi
Bacey

FORT EUSTIS, VA.
(WHEELS)
1950

Little Creek 0-3, 0-20
Ft. Monroe 19-13, 7-0
Aberdeen PG 40-6, 41-7
Ft. Lee 28-0
Ft. Knox 6-18

Team

Robert Kelley, coach
Dewey Gunter, t
Jimmie Simpson, t
James D. Gata, t
Ted Wood, e
Joe Raub, e
Arthur Green, e
Charles Lewis, g
Jim Holloway, g
Joe Knatyshak, g
Rocco Defratte, b
Earl Morgan, h
Jack James, b
Bill Early, b
Bill Reynolds, b
Charles Fosberg, b
Lawrence Didion, b
James Walsh, b

John Galbary, e
Donald Borman, e
John Perkins, t
Charles Siwtzee, t
Sam Framo, t
Harry Mark, g
Henry Poitras, g
James Gallagher, g
Earl Virgil, g
Earl McDuffie, c
Jenkins Beard, c
Edward Fields, fb
Noah Davis, fb
Myron Peters, fb
James Scalli, rb
E. O. Porterfield, rb
Edward Papciak, rb
Donald Buckshot, rb

1951

Hampton Institute 12-7
Little Creek 14-7
Bolling AFB 25-20
Ft. Lee 27-0, 20-0
Cherry Point 46-14
Ft. Campbell 13-14
Indiantown Gap 28-0
Bainbridge 38-13

207

Team

Hillary Thompson, b	Al Zmijewski, t
Larry Gautier, b	Al Markert, t
Lynn Chewning, b	Len Szafaryn, t
Dick Kovacevich, b	Frank Pittman, t
Howell Gruver, b	Martin Garcia, t
Hal Songin, b	Holland Donan, t
Paul Johnson, b	Douglas Frostick, t
Ray McCourt, b	Bill Cox, g
Milton Bruckner, b	Joe Mark, g
Joe Gulvas, b	Bob Conard, g
John Bartos, b	Ronald Gonier, g
George Johnson, b	Roland Ash, g
Bill Doherty, b	John Sullivan, g
Jack Maloney, b	Freager Sanders, g
Joe Raub, e	Irvin Holdash, c
Denver Mills, e	John DeFranceschi, c
John Kustich, e	Joseph McCutcheon, c
Charles Mott, e	Earl McDuffie, c
Russell Clements, e	Jack James, c

1952 X X X

Cherry Point 28-0
Parris Island 20-13
Little Creek 46-0
Bolling AFB 7-0
Quantico 2-7
Ft. Belvoir 35-7 ?
Camp Lejeune 0-18
Ft. Jackson 23-7
Ft. Lee 33-0
Bainbridge 14-7
Fort Knox 40-7

Team

Russ Skall, coach	Frank Jeffries, t
Bob Bestwick, qb	Frank Middendorf, t
John Gruble, e	Joe Codiano, hb
Chris Warriner, e	Irvin Holdash, hb
Sam Reynolds, hb	Jack Gordon, llb
Gene Shannon	Don Kasparan, fb
Kenneth Clemensen	George Johnson
Howell Gruver, rhb	Fulmer Armstrong, fb
Sammy Rebecca	Alan Pfeifer, e
Dean Davidson	John Vranjis, t
Fran Rogel	Ray Gonier, t
Richard Pont, hb	Robert Conard
Elwood Raborg	John Shearrow, t
Terrell Daffer	Joe Palumbo, g
Joseph Gould, g	Thomas Kelley, g
Joseph McCutcheon, e	Robert Miller, hb
James Sherrill, hb	George Hudak, fb
Earl Holmes, e	Jack Maloney, e
Robert Jinks	

1953 X X X

Bolling AFB 7-0
Amphib. Forces, Little Creek 20-12
USMC, Quantico 0-21
Ft. Belvoir 0-23
Camp Lejeune 0-27
Ft. Jackson 0-34
Ft. Lee 7-0, 9-21
Cherry Point 32-0

Team

Gene Felker, e, coach	Al Batson, fb
Jim Calderwood, qb	Bob Bestwick, qb
Len Kohl, g	John Cassell, fb
Ted Daffer, g (All-American) (All-Army)	Joe Clements, e
	Dick Ernsberger, hb
Ernest Fann, fb	Bill Fishback, g
John Gruble, e	Arnold Fizzano, hb
Jim Hill, hb	Jack Garst, hb
Irv Holdash, e	Jack Gordon, hb
Bob Horton, e	Bob Jinks, e
George Hudak, hb	Tom Kelley, g
Ellsworth Kingery, hb	Jim Lesniak, t
Bill Mason, bb	Dean McKnight, t
	Frank Middendorf, t

Bob Miller, hb	Alan Pfeifer, e (All-American)
Sam Murphy, fb, t	Jim Porter, qb
Bill Oyler, hb	Tom Proctor, hb
Sammy Reynolds, hb	Keith Reiter, hb
Bill Schleisner, fb	Roland Strehlow, hb
Gene Shannon, hb	Bill Swanson, t
Mike Vacchio, hb	Frank Trubits, e
Jerry Williams, t	Dick Willding, hb
Ted Wood, hb	
Dick Zoller, g	

FORT HOOD, TEXAS
(TANKERS)
1953 X X X

Prairie View A&M 6-21
Allen Acad. 38-6
Ellington AFB 35-7
Ft. Sill 7-7, 7-28
Camp Polk 14-14, 0-53
Ft. Bliss 7-7, 7-23
Brooke AMC 6-20, 0-20
307th MP, Ft. Sam Houston 46-0

Team

Jim Lansford, coach	Frank Donaldson, b
Joe Brock, e	Robert Painter, b
Raymond Casey, g	George Smith, e
John Costello, b	Bob Baldwin, e
John Champion, b	Neal Long, c
Bertram Bryant, b	Dominic Migliarese, g
James McCauley, b	Glen Wood, g
James Wise, b	William L. Jones, c
Bob Flippen, b	Oree Banks, g
Ed Berne, b	Harmon Welsh, t
Al Bailey, e	Henry Poole, t
Leo Brown, b	Joe Feldner, t
R. T. Holloman, b	Walter Napier, t
Cliff Jeffcoat, g	Andrew Barbee, g
John D'Arrigo, b	Bob Shetter, e
Ed Young, b	John Harvey, e
Julius Schelhammer, t	Bob Flowers, e
Jim Orn, e	Charles Gelel, e

INDIANTOWN GAP, PA.,
5TH INF. DIVISION
(RED DEVILS)
1951 X X X :

Harrisburg Bears 20-2
NTC, Bainbridge 42-0
White Hill School 43-0, 58-0
Camp Kilmer 53-0
Universtiy of Scranton 13-13
Mil Dist of Wash 27-7
Lebanon Valley College 12-7
Ft. Dix 18-6
Ft. Eustis 0-28
Camp Breckinridge 13-14

Team

Oscar Helm, coach	Ken Flemming, b
A. Gerometta, coach	George Fabray, g
John R. Finley, coach	Tom Milalick, t
Mike Maccioli, b	Arlon McNeil, b
Mike Kaysserian, b	Dick Asquith, b
Russ Kremer, b	Al Corbo, g
Stu Kirtley, e	Al Bozeman
Andy Anderson, b	Charles McCarty, g
Pete St. Clair, c	C. Klopfenstein, b
Barry Deetz, c	Bob Force, fb
Sam Ross, fb	Joe Sansone, e
Paul Phipps, e	Harry Broadway, e
Ed McWhorter, t	Don Dupper, g
Jack Krimmell, t	Ed Kraynak
Tom Mareski, g	Manny Gregg, b
Jack Cobetto, g	Tim Murphy, t

Nunzio Polichene, e   John Kay
Bill Pfaff   Casimir Dylewski, b
Pete Collura, b   Joe Cutillo, t

1952
(Post Inactivated 1953)

Chambersburg Cardinals 34-0, 34-0
Parris Island Marines 13-21
Ft. Belvoir 21-7
Camp Breckinridge 27-34
Quantico Marines 7-48
Harrisburg Bears 53-0
NTC, Bainbridge 19-32
Anthracite Maroons 45-0
Ft. Dix 45-0

Team

Frank Walton, coach   Wes Bradfor, b
Callahan, b, asst coach   Fred Hariston, b
Roland Starr, g   Bob Harding, e
Bob Collins   Willie Russell, b
William Lurty, c   Charles McCarty, g
Ray Romero, g   Garry Princine, b
Mike Roarke, e   L. D. Gallo, b
Carl Leone, qb   C. Renshaw, b
Barry Deetz, e   D. Ryder, e
Don Jones, t   R. Lewter, e
Joe Pascarella, t   F. Erban, e
Jerry Williams, e   A. J. Malm, e
Bernard Hoge, qb   D. McKnight, e
Jim Whitmer, hb   L. M. Krotec, c
Fred Zangaro, b   G. Holinda, c
Jim Curling, b   W. Hosiener, g
Ken Flemming, b   F. D. Turner, g
Chavis, t   E. S. Long, g
B. Scruggs, t   C. S. Detrick, g
Charles Crenshaw   W. C. Drazeck, t
Walt Shonosky, b   F. Gallo, b
Nat Brookins, b

FORT JACKSON, S. C.
RED DEVILS
1950

Camp Stewart 0-6
Camp Lejeune 13-26
Parris Island 33-19
Columbia Green Waves 6-0, 60-0
505th Abn Inf Regt 0-39
Atlanta Gen Dep 36-0
Cherry Point 13-20
Warner-Robins AFB 39-0

Team

Hal Littleford, qb   William Roberts
Eulas Jenkins   Buddy Berry
Eugene Canada   Harry Signer
Dale Hudson   Parmer Freeman, hb

1951
GOLDEN ARROW DIXIES

Camp Lejeune 34-7
Quantico Marines 21-13
Bolling AFB 34-0
Ft. Campbell 37-14
NAS, Jacksonville 63-7
Camp Breckinridge 67-7
Cherry Point Marines 65-0
U of Miami 13-20
Carswell AFB 7-32
Parris Island 27-13
505th Abn Inf Regt 53-13
Shaw AFB 40-0

Team

Gene Ellenson, coach   George Mayfield, e
Dickerson, asst coach   John Shepherd, g
Jack DelBello, qb   Oliver Vaughn, t
Alan Elger   Harry Massey
Colin Anderson, e   Carl Young, g
Nick Bolkovac   Richard Cain, g
Hugh Pepper, fb   Bob Dugan, fb
Clarence Avinger, g   Curtis Witt
Bryce Griffis   Ewell Pope
Jim Baughman, b   Robert Dunningan
Jimmy Clisson, hb   Thomas Palmer
Jim Barron, t   Harry Blanc
Jack Stroud, t   Merle Leisher
Douglas Lockridge, c   Frank Land
Horace McCool, c   Eddie Ware
Eulas Jenkins, hb   Tom Lucia
Fred Land, g   Clint Dyer

1952

Philadelphia Eagles 7-56
Camp Lejeune 13-6
Miami U. 6-14
Cherry Point Marines 64-0
Bolling AFB 14-48
Ft. Eustis 7-23
Quantico Marines 21-42
Camp Breckinridge 7-47
Camp Atterbury 30-6
Parris Island Marines 31-21

Team

Clayton Biddle, coach   Arnold Boykin, hb
John Fleming, coach   Hal Griffin
Fred Land, coach   Spafford Taylor
Cecil Dickerson, coach   Eulas Jenkins
Colin Anderson, e   Ed Bailey
Ken Frantz, e   Barney Gradman
Nick Bolkovac, t   Walter Chwalik
Bob Donaldson, t   Ed Crook, qb
Tom Palmer, t   Charles Phillips, b
Bob Dunningan, g   Jim Carothers, b
Cliff Brookshire, g   Doug Dedeaux, g
Jim Hahn, g   Bill Pierce, c
Doug Lockridge, c   Tom Lee, hb
Jack DelBello, qb   Harry DeLoach
Jim Clisson, hb   Don Hartman, qb
Lukie Brunson, fb   Bob Knight, e
Fred Bergiacchi, fb   Jack Huddle, e
Jack Prater, e   Jim Melton
Davis Melton, e   Garnet Reynolds
Don Simonovich, g   Bill Lloyd
Bill Slate, e   Jack McCauley
Mike Kerwin, e   Joe Victor
Addison Gilbert, e   P. W. Underwood
Bob Holmes, b   Pierce Laurice
Tom Lucia, b   Herb Eiseman
Sam Sewell, b   Sam Cohen
Henry Blanc   Jim Rembe
Alan Egler, hb   Bill Peterson

1953

Amphibious Force, Little Creek 22-13
Cherry Point Marines 25-0
Bolling AFB 20-26
Camp Lejeune 6-6
MCAS, Miami 65-0
Ft. Eustis 34-0
Quantico Marines 9-7
Ft. Leonard Wood 27-7
Parris Island Marines 28-0
Camp Atterbury 14-13

Team

Beattie Feathers, coach   Allen George, g
 (All-American)   P. W. Underwood, g
H. Sullivan, asst coach   Joe Oxendine, e
Bob Davis, asst coach   Dan Law, e
Henry A. Ferris, e   Davis Speed, t

Bobby Knight, e
Bill Hunsucker, e
Edward Evans, e
Terrence R. Boyle, t
Dominic Simonvitch, t
Robert Laughery, fb
Don Lassiter, qb
Zippy Morocco, hb
Gayle Kerr, hb
Gene Rossi, qb
Bill Banks, g
James Melton, hb
C. Puckett, asst coach
Dedeaux, asst coach,
  equip mgr
Claude Bond, trainer
Sal Renaldi, trainer
Charles Moore, scout
Bill Gerdemann, t
Earl Looman, t
Joe Cimini, t
Thurbie Markoe, g
Troy Barnes, t
Charles White, g
Charles Kitchens, t
Charlie Phillips, fb
Allie Robards, g

Carroll McDonald, c
Jack Prater, c
Ray Beck, g, capt
  (All-American, All-
  Army, All-Service)
Ursin Walker, g
Nathaniel Polak, g
Bill Omar, t
Dominic Stala, t
Walter Chwalik, t
Hugh Ballard, e
Dexter Poss, t
Robert Hartman, qb
Samuel McGowin, qb
Ray Thornton, hb
Luke Brunson, fb
Hal Griffin, hb
Howard Derrick, hb
Donald Brenn, e
E. M. Horton
Bill Speight, hb
Bill Megginson, hb
Twillie Bellamy, hb
Leland Leibold, hb
Jim Shirley, fb
Robert Beam, g
James Johnson, e

1953
Team

Luke King, fb
Doc Murphy, wb
Joe Edgley, tb
Bill Bell, e
Fred Pippin, e
James Rogan, e
Ronnie Joyce, g
George Kramer, g

Dennis Acree, g
Bennie Durham, e, c
Bob Heath, g
Hugh Turner, hb
Buddy Craig, hb
Bill Piper, g
Bob Kayler, wb
Lee Terrill, e

FORT KNOX, KY.
(TANKERS)
1950

Second Army Champions, 1948
La Grange Reformatory 26-19
Scott AFB 14-7
Fort Eustis 6-18

Team

Jim Norman, hb
Max Kehoe, rh
Dean Selkon, re
Ed Helmer, rt
Gideon Jarvis, fb
Smith Eggleston, le

Don Long, c
Arch Finn, rg
Wells, lt
Perkins, lg
Michels, qb
Landers, lh

1951

Camp Breckinridge 0-28
Mil Dis Wash 18-24
Georgetown College 14-7
Scott AFB 13-12
Keesler AFB 6-19
Selfridge AFB 19-6
NAS, Memphis 14-14
Ft. Campbell 20-13
U of Kentucky Frosh 6-0

Team

Billy Anderson, hb
Mickey Carter, qb
Joe Yuna, e
Bob Wright
Tom Murray
Joe Chenoweta
Bill Gunlock
Bob Voskuhl
Frank Oyster

Lyle Myrice
Ed Nearing
John Strutcher
Jim Cardi
Ed Kujawa
Archie Finn
Leonard Sheppard
Gus Goritz

1952

LaGrange Reformatory 82-0
Muskingum College 47-26
NAS, Memphis 25-6
NTC, Great Lakes 6-19
Keesler AFB 6-7
Camp Atterbury 0-34
Ft. Leonard Wood 12-29
Scott AFB 0-0
Camp Breckinridge 6-45
Ft. Eustis 7-40

Team

Bob Dowd, coach
J. Uttermueoller, line
  coach
J. Pickarts, line coach
P. Perini, fb team capt
Strati Chipouras, e
Mickey Carter, qb
John Ritchay, lhb
Jack Richardson, hb
Cecil Fair, hb
Bob Grace, le
Jim Jadwin, lhb
Philip Marker, lt
Leo Miller, t
Tom Murray, lhb
Russell Kapusinski
Myron Singhaus, qb
Ned Vukovich

Charles Hood, fb
Bill Monahan, lg
Ed Deegan
Verne Horn, hb
U. McPherson, e
Ralph Brown, e
Joe Stasko, g
Severt, safety
Archie Finn, rt
Frank Beavers, rg
Delbert Hurleck, re
Ed Toliver, e
John Kastan, hb
Robert Thum, rt
Billy Oldham, rhb
Horace White, re
Vernon Scott
Rudy Visnich

3d ARMORED DIVISION
1953

**Combat Command A, Regimental
Champions**
8W, 1L

Team

Milton Luftig, coach
Joe Reed, rhb
Phil White, le
Dave Bueschen, e
Clifford Dickman, re
Earl Simpson, qb
Frank Artino, qb
Willard Dyer, lhb

Paul Pawlikowski, re
James Hill, c
Paul Jones, le
Hal Neighbors, rhb
John Husten, lhb
Robert Bryant, hb
Ken Bauman, e
Dan Sullivan, e

LADD (ARMY), ALASKA
1952

**All-Army Champions, Alaska
All-Alaska Tournament Champions
North of the Range Conference
Champions**

Eielson AFB 55-13
Big Delta AFB 58-0
Ladd AFB 38-6
Eielson Army 25-13
Fairbanks Huskies 39-0
All-Alaska Tournament:
  39th Air Depot Wing, Elmendorf AFB
  0-13

Team

Earl Harvey, coach
Frank Needs, le
Mike Dereta, re
John Zancha, lt
Thomas Tarlton, rt
Truman Long, lg

Conrad Carter, rg
Dun Huml, c
Dave Rake, qb
John Ditz, lhb
Ossie Lavoe, rhb
James Thompson, fb

1953
Alaskan Armed Forces Tournament:
Elmendorf AFB 14-34

Team

T. Green, le	D. Cucinello, re
R. Vanderslice, le	E. Poinsette, re
C. Leadens, le	C. Piasecki, qb
V. Fugira, lt	E. Shaw, qb
T. Campbell, lt	W. O'Brien
W. Brossard, lg	J. DeBoyer, lhb
E. Cornwell, lg	J. Wali, lhb
A. Trowell, c	C. Manning, rhb
T. McCarthy, c	A. Ambrossio, rhb
P. Gaherty, rg	E. McDonald
R. Suleski, rg	H. Clark, fb
B. Pope, rt	T. Long, fb
L. Green, rt	J. Christy, fb

FORT LAWTON, WASH. (BULLDOGS)
1952

Bremerton 19-6
Ft. Worden 24-6
Ft. Lewis 8-20

Team

Thurman Griffin, hb	Dalton Hamilton, e
Darwin Harper, hb	Samuel Nicolosi, g
Samuel Burch, hb	William Gallagher, c
Edwin Gradington, qb	Don Welter, c
William Chappell, fb	Allie Hardeman, t
Robert Fritz, qb	Patrick Mulcahy, e
Calvin Thomas, hb	Thomas Davis, t
Gordon Smith, hb	Thomas Woods, g
Troy Gaines, e	Richard Dewees, c
Carl Jackson, hb	Gerald Rudsdil, e
Donald Evans, c	James Henderson, t
Norman Simms, hb	John Entorf, t
Alex Morrison, hb	Robert J. Smith, g
William Schulman, hb	James Johnson, fb
John Anderson, e	Lucio Bonilla, fb
Denzel Patterson, fb	Robert E. Smith, e
Richard Jordan, hb	George Davis, t
Maury Miller, e	Joe Wasser, coach
Kenneth Haley, g	C. Johnson, asst coach
Bonnie Smith, e	

FORT LEE, VA. (TRAVELLERS)
1951

NRS, Wash, D. C. 21-0
Ft. Monroe 32-0
Mil Dist Wash. 7-20, 19-40
Ft. Eustis 0-27, 0-20
505th Abn Inf Regt 16-27
Parris Island Marines 13-62
NS, Bainbridge 6-35
Amphib. Force, Little Creek 35-0

Team

Joe McCoy, qb	Aldo Bonomi g
Bill Baumgardner	Jesse Joseph, qb
Peroddy	Dwight Osha, t
Pat Giordana	Rex Partridge, t
Johnny Edwards	Dick Raklovits, hb
Merle Houck, fb	John Stefanoff, g
Andy Pavuk	Dick Strait, hb
"Uppy" Sams	Gene Woods, e
Ed McGinn	Walt Young, fb
John Perona, hb	John Tiller, coach

1952

NRS, Wash, D. C. 62-0
NAS, Norfolk 27-0

NAS, Patuxent 39-0
Ft. Belvoir (20-7,) 14-14
NS, Bainbridge 20-7
Cherry Point Marines 40-14
Ft. Meade 59-0
Ft. Eustis 0-33
Amphib. Force, Little Creek 32-18

Team

Morgan Tiller, coach	Jim Mack
N. Peterson, bf, coach	Eric Rodin, lb
R. Porter, line coach	Charles Dankworth, t
B. Johnston, line coach	John Stefanoff, g
Lavelle Edwards, c	Perry Hairston, c
Russ Carroccio, lt	Don Ledrick, hb
Joe McCoy, qb	Frank Lipski, lh
Bill Scazzere, hb	Merle Houck, fb
David Sparks, g	Jesse Joseph, qb
Jim Smith, lt	Walt Young, fb
Don Green, rt	Conrad Jones, hb
Cornelius Hobmann, le	Ed Listopad, rg
Aldo Bonomi, lg	Rudy Andabaker, lg
Louis Corbett, c	Chet Gierula, t
Chet Ostrowski, e	Jim Jerome, g
Leo Sugar, e	Ed McWhorter, g
Rocco Calvo, qb	Jim Garrett, fb
Joseph Strait, hb	Ronald Pemper
Hal Seidenberg, fb	Gene DeFranceschi, rt
Joe Petruzzo, hb	Taylor Pyke
Jesse Thomas, hb	Dick Strait
Art Wolan, c	Bob Johnson
Dick Raklovits, fb	Ray Fasick, lg
Vic Pujo, e, end coach	Benny Cichon
Jack Wilson, re	Tom Selan, t
Gene Woods, e	Richard Wasson, c
Rex Partridge, e	Al Lopez
Charles Williams, t	Hoyt Gideon
Gus Pelizes, hb	Bob Hengartner, t
Pinky Loehr, hb	Paul Dennis, fb
Alan Ackerman, hb	George Encinas, g
Bernard Ponson, hb	John Perona, hb
Dwight Osha, rt	

1953

Ft. Eustis 21-9
Bolling AFB 14-7
NAS, Norfolk 39-0
Camp Lejeune 13-7
Amphib. Force, Little Creek 15-0
Cherry Point 21-7
Ft. Belvoir 13-13
Quantico Marines 0-9
Ft. Monmouth 9-20

Team

Morgan Tiller, coach	Charlie Williams, t
Gierula, asst coach, t	Hank Hengartner, t
Bernard Ponson, fb	Bob Lusk, c
Joe Petruzzo, hb	Hal Mitchell, t (All-Service, All-Army)
Chet Ostrowski, e (All-American)	J. D. Kimmel (1952 All-American)
Leo Sugar, e (All-American, All-Service, All-Army)	Joe Bryant, e
Clarence Smith, qb	Jim Dooley, e
Conrad Jones, hb	Art Wolan, c
Paul Dinan, hb	Lou Corbett, g
Francis Cavanaugh, hb	Dave Fyock, hb
Henry Hill, hb	Hal Seidenberg, fb
Don Green, t	Joe DaLuz, hb
Rudy Andabaker, g (All-Army)	Jim Garrett, fb
Ed Listopad, g	Ben Cichon, g
Dave Sparks, g	Paul (Pinky) Loehr, hb
Bob Brennan, c	George MacArthur, hb
Jack Wilson, e	Ronnie Morris, qb
Cornelius Hohmann, e	Joe Haddrick, hb
Jim Smith, e	Bill Ayers, hb
Walter Brodie, e	Vince Bagonis, g
Russ Carroccio, t	Lee Matera, qb
	Jack O'Malley, e

FORT LEONARD WOOD, MO. (HILLTOPPERS)
1951

Missouri U JV 12-0
Camp Carson 12-7
Scott AFB 0-7, 25-0
Camp McCoy 48-7
Camp Breckinridge 19-14
Keesler AFB 21-7

Team

C. Bauma, asst coach
W. Regian, asst coach
L. Helgeson, coach
Winfard Carter, fb
Fred Tesone, hb
Tom Rowe, g
Ralph McAlister, b
Joe McGill, c
Ray Morelli, e
Charley Marck, hb
Jim Coulter, t
Don Kelloggs, hb
Don Godbold, t
Jack Crittendon, e
Bill King, t

1952

Camp Breckinridge 0-33
Ft. Knox 29-12
Carswell AFB 0-56
Camp Atterbury 7-6
Scott AFB 20-0
Brooke AMC 12-7
Keesler AFB 0-14
Camp Carson 28-0
Lincoln U 20-0
Missouri U JV 34-7

Team

Gerald Kelly, coach
M. Kayserrian, fb, asst coach
Joe Dirigolamo, e
Jack Crittendon, e
Mike McCormick, t
Bill King, g
Rick Hill, c
Fred Tesene, hb
Nick Adduci, hb
Marty Detmer, e
Don Kellogg, qb
Hank Laughlin, fb
Kenny Hopper, qb
H. T. Smith, hb
Bill Rollison, hb
Ferril Morrison, fb

1953

Shaw AFB 59-0
Camp Atterbury 6-20
Granite City, Ill. 69-0
Keesler AFB 35-6
NTC, Great Lakes 15-6
Ft. Belvoir 0-20
Ft. Jackson 7-27
Lincoln U 27-0

Team

Bob Griffin, coach
M. McCormick, line coach (All-American) (Most Valuable Player Award) (All-Army, 1st Team)
Donald Riggs, OIC
Governor Moerder, mgr
Dick Stebbins, trainer
Ken Treadway, trainer
Marlin Craig, t
George Rambour, t
John Trivenovich, t
Wayne Raifsnider, t
Frank Metzke, t
Jim Hill, g
Jim Hicks, g
Howard Jobson, g
Mike Fleming, g
Edward Oldani, g
Ron Barbeck, g
Frank Rago, qb
Bill Taylor, e
Ken Severt, e
Frank Glover, e
Don Beitler, e
Stan Banasik, e
Allan Farber, e
Bob Miller, e
J. W. Loudermilk, e
Jim McConkey, t
Howard Hall, t
Audrey Ford, qb (All-American)
W. C. Polson, qb
Ken Hopper, hb
D. Pinhey, hb (Most Valuable Back Award)
Paul Specia, hb
Leo Chafin, hb
Glen Wild, hb
Don Vemhaus, hb

Hans Heid, g
Charles Bangs, g
Lyle Olsen, c
Ray Birchfield, c
John Kolesar, c
Bob Hansen, fb
Farrel Morrison, fb
Bob Bergman, fb
George Mihailoff, fb
Joe Fosco, hb

FORT LEWIS, WASH. ROCKETS
1952

Bremerton Navy Yard 19-24
Ft. Lawton 20-8, 42-19
Ft. Worden 39-20, 26-32
Central Wash College 6-33
Bremerton Navy Yard 34-0, 13-33
Tacoma Jr. CC 24-19
Tacoma Police & Firemen 19-6
Seattle Ramblers 0-33
Geiger AFB 14-27

Team

R. E. Smith, qb, coach
Charles H. Miller, lh
James E. Snell, g
Donald Justice, g
Willie Caywood, t
Ronald Klingeberg, g
Claude Devers, t
Garland Daniels, t
Frank Williams, c
Chris Kondoff, e
Julian Kanacholo, fb
Hubert C. Johnson, t
William Kelley, c
Robert Brown, c
Donald Lewis, qb
David M. McCoy, rh
Theodore Farrison, t
Waymon Taylor, g
James Holliday, e
Garland Brown, c
William Barker, fb
Carl D. Diggs, rh
George Hale, g
Rayshaw Gaddy, t
Rudolph Perry, e
Alvin B. Johnson, c
Jack Devoughn, g
OK Brown, fb
Albert Cummings, hb
Stanley Hill, c
Gilbert Rowe, c
Stanley Prokop, c
C. Landenburg, hb
James Neison, qb
Gerald Droll, g
Edward Carney, t
Richard C. Beal, hb
Robert Franklin, hb
Thomas Falvey, e
Edward J. Hoke, bb
Jack C. Tidd, hb
W. Gomes, asst coach
J. Elliot, asst coach
N. Richardson, trainer
Robert Fink, mgr

FOUR-BY-FOURS
1953

El Toro Marines 32-19
NAS, Moffett 52-7
Naval Amphib. Base, Calif. 21-34
NTC, San Diego 6-33
PhibPac 21-34
Ft. Ord 0-33, 0-45
Seattle Ramblers 14-15, 6-6
Vancouver, B. C. Lions 14-1
Camp Pendleton 19-26

Team

Les Richter, coach (All-American)
Al Lary, e (All-American)
Ron Pinchback, qb
Gerry Zaleski, hb
Bob Hayes, hb
Len Deutscher, t
Bill Wright, hb
George Brown, qb
Talmadge Vic, e
Bill Cochrane, hb
Jim Tomasky, qb
Bill Parker, fb
Harry Riley, c
Jim Vella, g
Tom Bice, hb
John Batson, e
Don Wood, c
Dave Davis, e
Earl Bye, e
Clint Westemeyer, le
Ralph Yoder, g
Bert Westemeyer, rg
Bill Rosenau, g
Jerry DeFries, e
Doyle Presley, e
Ed Hoover, rt (1951 All-East)
Rhody Heinen, g
Jim Webb, t
Chuck Holems, t
John Cole, lg
Ray Roberson, t
Claude Mabry, hb
Gil Mains, lt (Little All-American)
Ed Sable, c
John Wolak, hb
Phil Peterson, hb

212

L. Plourde, fb (All-
New England)
Tom Coleman, e
Al Fetter, hb
Jim Pockert, fb

Bryon Weaver, hb
Bob Walker, t
Dave Haan, hb
Ed Conine, qb
Jim Workens, hb

FORT MEADE, MD. (GENERALS)
1953

Lincoln U. 0-13
NRS, Anacostia 6-0
NAS, Chincoteague, Va. 13-7
Norfolk Naval Base 20-0
US NAAS 13-7
Ft. Monmouth 0-52
Army Chemical Center 8-13

Team

R. L. Edwards, coach
Sid Carter, asst coach
R. Kaminiski, asst
coach
Charley Linscomb
Jim Montgomery
Bill Hall
Bill Fischer, fb
Bob Kohler
Call
Gamble
Scruggs
Stevenson

Martine
Flynn
Bennett
Rair
Landry
Merritt
Mihlfield
Thomas
Sarnoski
Pettis
Mantague
Hourigan

MILITARY DISTRICT OF WASHINGTON (RIFLES)
1951

Ft. Lee 20-7, 40-19
NS, Bainbridge 7-20
Bolling AFB 14-51
Indiantown Gap 7-26
Westover AFB 47-0
505th Inf Regt 12-38
NAS, Norfolk 34-27
Ft. Knox 24-18
Quantico Marines 6-67

Team

B. Boulware, coach
Morgan Maxwell, e
Ed Kozlowski, fb
Ed Burgin, hb
Jimmy Robinson, hb
Joe Zuravleff, e
Herman Clark, qb
Jim Lors, g, capt
Bob Rodebaugh, c
Johnny Tette, t
Johnny Stucky, g
Billy Musack, qb
Hilton Keith, fb

Leo Hyland, hb
Julius Robinson, t
George Senior, c
Lou Philhower, t
Doug Watson, hb
Lawrence Martin, fb
Charles Long, qb
Sidney Moore, hb
John Watson, t
Dave Oates, t
Johnny Cook, hb
Hal Beachum, g

FORT MONMOUTH, N. J. (SIGNALEERS)
1953

Camp Lejeune Marines 6-20
Coast Guard, Cape May 33-0
Parris Island Marines 32-7
Westover AFB 33-0
Ft. Meade 52-0
Edgewood Arsenal ACC 47-6
Bolling AFB 0-18
Ft. Devens 35-20
Amphib. Force, Little Creek 26-14
Ft. Lee 20-9

Team

C. Lawson, head coach
Leo Jones, asst coach
O. Mehlberg, back ch
L. James, line coach
M. Bailey, end coach
Ed Bell, co-capt, e
B. Shields, co-capt, hb
Orlando Loschiavo, qb
John Jaeckel, qb
Gordon Forbes, qb
Bernie Haberlein, hb
Sanford Goldberg, hb
William Leonard, hb
Larry Hogue, qb
Bill Earley, hb
Tom Ossman, fb
Richard Molen, fb
John Foutty, fb
Phil Gillis, e
Earl Byrd, e

Francis Caonacki, e
Robert Riley, e
Joe McCarthy, e
Theodore Ditillo, c
Charles Stockton, t
Don Bruhns, c
Arthur Adornato, t
Charles Dallum, t
Joe Kowaliski, t
Joe Skibinski, g
Don Dyer, g
Clyde Hart, g
Arthur Hahner, g
Bernard Gilman, g
Harvey Cohen, g
Don Luft, e
Ken Panfil, t
Earl Killian, e
Albert Crow, t

FORT ORD, CALIF. (WARRIORS)
1951

San Francisco Broncos 7-12
Camp Pendleton Marines 21-7
Presidio, S. F. 62-0
Luke AFB 26-19
San Jose Brewers 19-14
Treasure Island Naval Base 19-0
Hamilton AFB 27-0
San Jose State JV 60-6

Team

John Davis, coach
Verdese Carter, t
George Sims
John Helwig, g
Ted Case
Alfred Reynaud
Luther Phillips
Frank Ernaga
Flynn, e
Coval, t
Andrina, e
Tom Baker, g

Oberg, t
Richard Lane, e
Smith, b
George Lagorio
Don Jones
Angelo Padilla
Jim Harryman
John Salvador
Harold Beardsley
John Hock
Roy Muehlberger
Danny Wagster

1952

NTC, San Diego 0-54
Brooke AMC 7-6
NAS, Alameda 27-0
San Francisco Broncos 22-7
Camp Stoneman 55-0
Calif. Ramblers 34-2
San Jose Packers 7-6, 47-0
Camp Pendleton 33-19, 21-19
Hamilton AFB 13-7, 14-13, 27-0
Camp Cooke 33-14
San Diego Pacific Amphib. Fleet 20-19
NAS, San Diego 6-7

Team

Ken Grieve, mgr
Dalton Klaus
Bill Abbey, hb
Pete O'Gara, e
George Lagorio, fb
Luther Phillips, hb
Julian Spence, hb
John Salvador
John Helwig, g
Zolin Milani
George Sims, hb
Jack Wilson
Bob Colette, e
Chuck Cravey, hb

Marv Gelder, fb
Cliff Livingston, e
Dave Marcelli, hb
Ted Watson, t
George VanSant, fb
Matt Vujevich, hb
Carl Hoffman, g
Orville Crane, g
Ted Case, hb
Al Sambrano, g
Bob Payne, e
Steve Harper, e
Alton Taylor, g
Ray Solari, g

213

Earl Putnam, g
Bud Chadwicke, e
Ted Seownes, hb
Fred Robinson, t
Clyde Adkins, t
Ken Scott
Vern Baxter, e
Ray Lutterman, g
Bill Robinett
Jim Kammaana, qb
Bob Brayton, qb
Jack Price, qb
Dick Cummings, e

Jay Phillips, e
Hosie Tenner, hb
Robert Strane, g
Jim Lewis, e
Robert Coffman, t
Bob Hooks, e
Dick Johnson, e
Jim Gibson, t
Frank Sidoti, t
Dave Miller, t
Harry Laubach, t
John Anglin
Don Mitchell

1953
All-Army Champions
Inter-Service Champions

USMC Recruit Depot 33-0
Camp Pendleton 40-0
Hamilton AFB 32-0
Ft. Lewis 33-0, 45-0
Eagle Rock AC 37-0
Calif. Ramblers 40-7
NTC, San Diego 35-7
PhibPac 40-23
NAS, San Diego 39-6
Queen City Bowl:
    Seattle Ramblers 28-0
Poinsettia Bowl:
    Quantico Marines 55-19
Salad Bowl:
    NTC, Great Lakes 67-12

Team

H. C. Springer, coach
R. J. Peterson, line ch
W. L. Abbey, bf coach
Edgar Henke, e
Clifford Livingston, e
Robert Collett, e
Raymond Rhead, e
Jay D. Phillips, e
Eugene Mitcham, e
David Miller, t
James Swan, t
Darrell Delavan, t
Fred Robinson, t
Earl Putnam, t
Marvin Gelder, g
Donald Birren, g
P. Gannamela, g
Kenneth Scott, g
Joseph Negri, g
Richard Craddock, g
Vernon Baxter, e
John Cummins, c
Peter Bello, e

Don Heinrich, qb
Gerald Hamilton, qb
Jack Price, qb
Lee Rounds, hb
Thomas Ryan, trainer
Jerry Robertson, qb
David Mann, hb
William Bare, hb
Laurence Segovia, hb
Charles Holloway, hb
Roy Garland, hb
Ollie Matson, fb
Alfred Matthews, fb
Ernie Bordier, e
Gene Hansen, t
Stanley Campbell, g
Donald Donovan, hb
Ron Maurer, fb
Lou Maurer, hb
William Roffler, hb
Peter O'Gara, e
H. Crockett, eq mgr
J. Riccobono, eq mgr

CAMP POLK, LA.
THUNDERBIRDS
1950
Fourth Army Area Inter-Service
Tournament Champions

Barksdale AFB 19-12, 40-18
Randolph-Bergstrom AFB 43-19
NAS, Corpus Christi 38-0
Brooke AMC 33-6
Ft. Hood 20-6, 27-13
Louisiana College 26-7
    (Cosmopolitan Bowl)

Team

Bob Ewbank
Gene Cook

Herbert Rosen
Ralph Isbell

Robert Pyle
Guy Kiker
Tom Roberts
John Waters
Robert Dill
Barney Gill

Jim Ryan
Dick Coley
Roger Brown
Ted Rupe
Gene Grower

ARMADILLOS
1951

Kessler AFB 0-13
Ft. Sam Houston 18-7, 6-13
Randolph AFB 25-13
San Marcos AFB 25-13, 21-0
Ellington AFB 0-12, 19-0
NAS, Bainbridge 13-35 (Toy Bowl)

Team

Ken L. Gibson, coach
Wally Triplett, hb
Andy Hillhouse, e
Wilson White, hb
Julius Taylor, g
Manuel Morales, fb
Cecil Evans
Buckley Qualls
Jim Fuller
Rainey Varner, qb
Furney Green, e

L. R. Tillotson, t
William Comer, t
Louis Drounant, g
Carl Graft, c
Roland Prejean, qb
L. Hohenfield, c
Oliver Wisch, g
Bill Estes, t
James Bethea, hb
Aleck Thompson, hb
Philip Weideman, hb

All Opponent Eleven picked by Polk
    players:
Ends: Hill, San Marcos; Wetherly, Ft. Sam
Tackles: Cerecke, Keesler, Simpson, Ellington
Guards: Curry, Randolph; Champbliss, Keesler
Center: Qualls, Randolph
QB: Tompkins, Ft. Sam
HBs: Shobe, Ft. Sam; Singley, Ellington
FB: Adams, San Marcos

1952

Chicago Cardinals 7-66 (Exhibition)
Brooke AMC 0-40
Connally AFB 39-0
Randolph AFB 14-13
NAS, Pensacola 6-6
Sheppard AFB 13-9, 0-3
Keesler AFB 7-20
Ft. Sam Houston 13-6
Alexandria AFB 25-7

Team

J. Underwood, coach
Al Wade, fb
A. Hillhouse, e (All-
    Army)
Dick Houck, fb
Ed Trubie, qb
Ray Hamilton
Carl Taseff
Don Shula
Carl Kaplanoff
George Mastersen, e
Robert Zupke, e
Robert Bailey, e
Sammy Morrow, e
James Hermann, t
Robert Gresock, t
Louis Drouant, g
Fred Tomaseck, g
Jack Rynn, g

Tom McTighe, g
Lamont Wilch, g
Richard Bade, e
Bob Nellen, qb
Jim Franklin, qb
Bill Felzenlegen, qb
Phil Weaver, hb
Jim Roysten, hb
Art Kaplan, t
Frank Boulware, e
D. Washelesky, hb
    (All-Army)
Bart Jenniches, hb
Larry Chadzywski, e
Bill Klingensmith
John Bates, hb
Robert Giesey
Marion Woolsey, hb

HAWKS
1953

Ft. Sill 0-27, 6-43
Brooke AMC 7-13, 13-45
Keesler AFB 6-25
Alexandria AFB 57-2
Ft. Hood 14-14, 0-53
Louisiana College 25-24
Sheppard AFB 12-13

Team

R. Stevens, (coach, pre-season)
G. Masterson, asst ch, e
F. Tomaseck, asst ch
J. Grabko, coach, fb
L. Chadzynski, re
Alton Davis, e
David Hallmon, e
Alton Kite, le
Weldon Long, e
John Thein, e
Charles Bachus, t
John Canale, t
Joseph Coppola, fb
Leonard Mazerbo, t
Anthony Navickas, lt
Ivan Stewart, t
William Adkins, g
Charles Haack, rg
Charles Haramis, g
Edwin Juergensen, g
Roy Sauder, g
Fred Tomaseck, g
Benjamin Tyson, lg
Robert Wurm, rt
Herbert Henderson, e
Thomas Lee, t
John Bates, qb-nb
Kenneth Chappell, fb
Lawrence Coan, rhb

Robert Eriksen, rhb
Hollie Hall, g
Harold Jones, hb
William Lanigan, g
Ronald Nall, t
Vitold Piscuskas, fb
Cecil Smith, lhb
Don Nibbet, le
Joseph Riggi, g
Jim Anderson, rt
Tom Stringer, lt
Harold Reed, t
Gerry Murphy, lg
Dick Patry, e
Willie Truss, hb
Clarence Cooper, fb
Dale Marquart, hb
Herb Schoenowitz, fb
Leighton Kinner, hb
Charley Harding, qb
John Canale, t
Joseph Jefferson, g
Gus Lombardo, qb
Jack Hyman, e
Johnny Day, fb
Ron Williams, e
George Semple, e
Mat Hesson, e
Bob Connor, trainer
T. Kueshner, trainer

PRESIDIO OF SAN FRANCISCO, CALIF.

1952
Team

G. Perricone, coach
R. Ottoson, line coach
Robert Rhodes, e
James Giggs, fb
Willie Hopkin, lob
Franklin Karls, rt
Leonard Bates, le
Robert Bava, lt
Kenneth Gordon, qb
R. J. Daigle, lbb
Leonard Hoaglund, lt
John Morse, le
Graham Johnston, rt
Ted Keating
Lewis Brown, qb
Nick Kirby, fb
C. Seafeldt, re
J. Hackathorn, lhb
R. Jackstadt, qb
William Bailey, e

Henry Baranoski, e
William Bentchell, rg
Delane Pankratz, lg
Will McGee, qb
Dallas Lamb, lhb
Armando Priciado, rhb
Charles Roberts
Cooper Alcibiadio
William Albrecht, re
Leo Miller, lt
Leonard Brooks, lg
Edward Bell, qb
Edmond Anderson
Earl Collins
Joseph Marchiano
William Jackson
Leonard Saleski
George Nikana, rhb
T. Busalacchi, rbb
Robert Catlett, rg

RED RAIDERS

1953

Petaluma 26-12, 14-6
Stanford Braves 14-34
Chico State 7-14
UC Ramblers 7-14
NAS, Moffett 20-13
Treasure Island 27-13
NAS, Alameda 43-26
Edwards AFB 40-19
Mather AFB 44-7

Team

S. J. Vincent, coach
R. Daigle, hb, asst ch
W. R. Carey, asst ch
Jack Bridges, hb
John Warren, e
Vince Price, qb
Ralph Spreen, hb
R. Jackstadt, qb

G. Brandstetter, g
Gerald Peterson, e
Ralph Martin, t
Richard Tucker, e
Joe Papp, hb
Jim Fairchild, g
Dave Marcelli, hb
William Decker, t

Robert Sergenian, g
Leonard Hoaglund, t
Thurman Belcher, g
John Wolterbeek, g
Charles Rogers, rhb
Robert Stachowicz, fb
Arthur Coats, t
Frank Kresse, t
Jack Barnes, e
Dick Wilkinson, fb

Roscoe Morris, e
Don Burroughs, qb
Donald Olson, e
Jerry Wilson, e
Dallas Lamb, fb
Harvey Garcia, g
Teresse Tyler, t
Robert Hooks, e
Bob Catlett, t
Don Garrison, t

FORT RICHARDSON, ALASKA
PIONEERS
1950

All-Alaska Armed Forces Champions

57th Fighter Wing 26-0, 14-6
Ladd AFB 26-6
Ft. Lawton 25-0

Team

Bill Fette, e
Joe Caruso, t
Ned Fiaco, g
Bob Brown, e
Cobert Roeder, e
Isaac Oliver, e
Ralph Shaffer, t
Dante D'Sole, qb

H. Harris, fb (Outstanding Player Award, All-Alaska)
Willhite
Hacker
Heffner
Pulaski

1951

39th Air Depot Wing 13-7, 7-19
Alaskan Air Command 0-18, 6-34

Team

Isaac Oliver, e
Morris Hart, e
Bill Fette, e
Ralph Shaffer, t
John Press, e
Al Garza, g
Charlie Mitchell, g

Frank Brown, e
Dante D'Sole, qb
Tom Stich, bb
E. Holland, hb
Stan Rostowski, hb
Herc Harris, fb

1952

39th Air Depot Wing 0-0, 0-35
196th Inf Regt 0-26, 15-0
Alaskan Air Command 7-14

Team

Davis, e
Mitchell, t
Bosco, g
Headle, e
Foss, g
Cloutre, t
Stenard, e
Le Claire, qb
Strickland, hb
Repelski, hb
Warren, fb
Strand, e
McKay, t
Lennon, g

Johnson, e
Kahanakanui, g
Brinson, g
Bullard, g
Bertillotti, e
Schnurrenberger, e
Lindsay, e
Meeker, punter
Jackstadt, qb
Rekowski, hb
Bradshaw, hb
Acklin, hb
Schuler, hb

196th INF REGT (EAGLES)
1951

39th Air Depot Wing 13-13
Alaskan Air Command 6-6, 6-39

Team

Wilbur Turner, e
Ralph Weddle, e
LeRoy Rose, t
Dick Hanetho, e
Carl Andre, qb

Ray Stroka, qb
Art Aiello, hb
Al Piper, hb
Dave Cady, bb

1952

39th Air Depot Wing 0-27, 0-13
Alaskan Air Command 14-19, 6-6
Ft. Richardson 26-0, 0-15

Team

Young, e	Shanning, e
Irish, t	Ridens, t
Krenshelewski, g	Rose, t
Lee Davis, c	Wiesnewski, t
Waldon, g	Cipparone, c
Jensen, t	Douglas, e
Goodwin, e	Varady, qb
Windish, qb	Clutts, hb
Braelish, hb	Wainman, hb
Golhoffer, hb	Parker, hb
Tex Davis, fb	Crowder, hb
Appleby, e	Milkovich, hb
Brennan, e	Bastien, fh

PIONEERS

1953

4W, 1L, 1T

Team

Fred Marlett, e	Paul Golhoffer, b
James Crisp, b	Chuck Mitchell, t
Marion Lampkins, c	Bob DiAgostino, e
Wayne Lumbartis, b	James Starkey, t
Jack Angroves, e	Bob Ross, b
Al Roth, b	John Bullard, g
Don Trussel, e	Larry Spinello, b
Charles Clines, b	Don Barney, g
Matt Lesnicchia, e	Earl Hyder, b
Matt Vujevich, b	Coy Jones, g
Bob Hardin, t	Booker Guthrie, g
Bob Munson, b	Pepper Crane, g
Francis Berger, t	Lee Bolla, g
Don Rekowski, b	Andy Makay, c
Al Varner, t	Larry Brown, c

FORT RILEY, KANSAS

1953

All-Star Team

Dan McBride, e	Mike Hovsipian, g
Hal Brock, c	Bob Weber, c
Rex Linder, t	Tom McNamee, qb
Bill Zimmer, t	Larry Barnes, hb
Dave Wilcox, g	Frank Congiardo, fb

CAMP RUCKER, ALA.

1953

Brigade-PMG, Ft. Benning 0-34
CTC, Ft. Benning 20-7

Team

V. G. Lollar, coach	C. R. Hemmer, e
R. R. Snow, asst coach	James B. Jones, e
C. Bailey, asst coach	James E. King, c
W. A. Schieve, mgr	K. B. Leake, g
T. J. Foczmanski, mgr	William A. Lee
David Kithcart, qb	Don M. Matheson, c
Marshal Wheaton	Michael Medzigan, t
Donald L. Loa, t	Edward Manson, t
Vernon D. Lang, g	Norbert J. Miller
Estus Hood, t	Billy G. Newsome
Claude Cranford	Denton Parker
Charles Aakhus	Joe L. Scallion
Robert Bostad, e	Joe P. Sanks, e
Joe B. Cassidy	Oinest Sartain, e
J. C. Duncan, c	T. D. Tumey, t
Mike Cummings, hb	Roland D. Wilder, t
Thomas J. Ellis, g	Plummer Seward, g
John Fedoric	Vearn Stewart, e
Anthony Folgia, c	

FORT SAM HOUSTON, TEXAS

RANGERS

1951

Goodfellow AFB 5-0
U of Houston "B" 20-12
Randolph AFB 7-13
San Marcos AFB 39-0
Camp Polk 7-18
Ellington AFB 35-6
Carswell AFB 14-55

Team

John Nelson, le	Don Jarvis
Berley Pruitt, lt	James Andres
Darrell Evans, lg	Ken Landaiche
Gerald Weatherly, c	Bob Fisher
John Ennis, rg	James Lloyd
Arthur Hyatt, rt	Raymond Pearson
John Curtis, re	Ken Schobe
Ray Porta, qb	Frank Roscoe
Dub Kelly, lh	Simon Luna
Arthur Ochoa, rh	Bob Burch
E. Braden, fb	H. J. Sauer
Salty Stevens	Bob Campbell

1952

5W, 2L, 1T

(No 1953 Post Team)

Randolph AFB 14-7
Lone Rangers, San Antonio 12-7
Texas A & I 7-6
Goodfellow AFB 29-13
Ellington AFB 19-19
Sheppard AFB 13-6
Abilene Christian College 21-21
Camp Polk 6-13

Team

John Curtis, le	Allen Lingenfelter
Lloyd Danos, lt	Martin Maccioni
Darrell Evans, lg	Joe Brumfield
Gerald Weatherly, c	Joseph Andraka
Raymond Pearson, rg	Don Wood
Bill Webb, rt	Fred Carner
Bob Burch, re	Bernard Crosby
Arthur Boudreau, qb	Fred DelGininori
A. Mittlestead, lh	Elemo Manchester
Cameron Ostrand, rh	Joe Cantaro
Kenneth Schobe, fb	Nelson Rose
Frank Roscoe	Roger Hoss
W. H. Kelly	Jim Ayraud
Lou Price	Dick Weldon
James Lloyd	Douglas Ryan
Louis Griffin	Fred Hernandez
James Stevens	Ray Marinini
Augustus Turk	John Montague
David Dumas	William Edmondson

307th MILITARY POLICE BATTALION

1953

Texas Lutheran U "B" 20-0
Southwest Texas State College "B" 14-39
Texas Lutheran College 13-14
Brooke AMC 0-49
Sheppard AFB 12-33
Ft. Hood 0-59
Southwest Texas State College 6-55

Team

J. Underwood, coach	Bobby Arledge, e
F. Kapral, asst coach	Ronny Richards, t
Dale Gibson, mgr	Vince Cristallo, t
S. A. Davis, trainer	Edgar Bridges, e
Rufus McCarrell, hb	James Rauch, e
Oscar Brookshire, e	Orville Updyke, e
Rex Bailey, qb	Cosmo Bracato, g
Chuck Storey, hb	Harvey Banks, hb
James Harper, hb	Ken Grunewald, fb
Jim Ford, fb	Amerigo Nerone, t
Bill Ejzak, fb	Bob Lichtenberg, t
Bob Bolay, e	Vince Zappone, g
Mongo Edmonson, fh	Ray Lovejoy, e
Bill Quintana, qb	George Olson, t
Billy Dinnell, qb	Al Gossett, t
Bill Kuhn, e	George Morrow, e
Bob Von Briel, g	Chester Calhoun, e

FORT SILL, OKLA.
548th FA BN
1952

Sheppard AFB 0-20
Cameron Jr. College 6-21

Team

Ray Ewing, coach	Lee Failes, g
Henry Evans	Charles Groves, t
Clyde Cass, t	Jesse McMorris, t
Herman Bowick, qb	Henry Evans, t
Percy Ford, qb	Leroy McCall
Herbert Martin	Ikey Sanders
Gerwell Webster, fb	Claude Brown
John Alexander, fb	Robert Huckabee, fb
Hollis Jones, e	Robert Shelton, e
Willy Purifoy, e	Reed, e
Leroy Browder, g, t	Westbrook, e
Benn Hood, g	Tate, e
Irwin Trotter, g	Cladine
Otis Pruitt, g	

1953
CANNONEERS: Fourth Army
Champions

Cameron College 31-7
Camp Polk 27-0, 43-6
NAS, Olathe, Kansas 40-6
Brooke AMC 26-6, 23-0
Ft. Hood 7-7, 28-7
Ft. Bliss 12-7, 13-8
Southern Methodist U. 0-6

Team

Fred Smith, coach	Tom Hinson, fb
Dan Davis, asst coach	Fred Dunlap, hb
D. Page, qb (Little	Bob Stratton, hb
All-American)	Lew Zeigler, t
B. West, fb, co-capt	Saxton Wraith, fb
Del Prones, rhb	Bill Henderson, e
Jimmy Roshto, lhh	Don Adkins, t
Ted Black, e	Ray Berho, hb
R. Wahlmier, t, co-capt	Duane Louis, qb
Chester Dowell, t	Tom Adams, lg
Vince Reed, g	Blackie Howell, e
Jackie Brooks, g	Joe Fair
Wayne Martin, e	Bill Turnbeaugh, g
Harold Sheets, le	Hollis Henry, g
Gene Suen, qb	Bob Robertson, qb
Jack McClairen, e	Chuck Schmitt, t
D. Torbett, asst coach	Bill George, g
Jim McCormack, e	Bob Adams, e
Bill Childers, hb	Art Hamilton, e
Dave King, g	

CAMP STONEMAN, CALIF.
(TRAVELERS)
1953

Treasure Island Navy 6-33
NAS, Alameda, Calif. 0-26

Team

Charlie White, coach	Gene Locke
Clarence Wright	Wayne Shackelford
Walt Speight	Nick Orlando
Gene Scott	Al Weaver

USMA, WEST POINT, N. Y.
1953
7W, 1L, 1T

Furman 41-0
Northwestern 20-33
Dartmouth 27-0
Duke 14-13
Columbia 40-7
Tulane 0-0
North Carolina State 27-7
Pennsylvania 21-14
Navy 20-7

Team

Earl Blaik, coach	Howard Glock, t
L. T. Lunn, capt, lg	Ralph Chesnauskas, g
F. A. D. Attaya, fb	N. A. Chamberlin
M. L. DeLucia	Robt. J. Guidera
K. R. Kramer	W. R. Haff
R. H. Lincoln	J. E. Krause
W. MacPhail	G. A. Lodge, fb
Robt. M. Mischak, re	P. C. Manus
M. W. Rose	J. C. Rogers
Lowell E. Sisson, e	P. Schweikert
J. E. Weaver	Norman E. Stephen, e
Thomas J. Bell, hb	R. G. Ziegler
F. D. Meyers	W. A. Doremus
R. J. Reich	G. Ordway
J. R. Wing	Peter J. Vann, qb
Bob Farris, t	

Europe

FRANKFURT MILITARY POST INVADERS
1950

Team

Paul Hamaska, b	William Ziemann, t
Dick Smith, b	Philip Perrocca, t
John Fiore, b	Rodger Moya, t
Joe Badley, b	George Literal, t
Charles Nizlio, b	Jim Koslowski, t
John Arata, b	Bob Hott, e
Rudy Pitvorec, b	Homer Nelson, e
Loyal Cook, b	George Enchus, e
Vic Soveziak, b	Tom Jordan, e
Arthur Smith, b	Douglas Wilson, e
Jim McChesney, e	Stan William, e
Nick LaNotte, c	Al Trovost, e
Basil Bourque, e	Paul Schibate, qb
Fred Martin, e	Virgil London, hb
Charles Smith, g	Bill Conleey, hb
Joe Caferelli, g	John Thompson, fb
Otis Hannsure, g	B. Haphey, head coach
Carl Young, g	R. Schouten, asst ch
John Gonzales, g	P. Jeffers, asst coach
Mario Cesaratto, g	F. Beardon, asst coach
Tim Kellaway, g	P. Sisario, trainer
Bill Seearatto, g	Paul Wert, mgr
Charles Kuhl, g	Chuck Carroll, OIC

BLACK KNIGHTS
1952

Nurnberg 12-7
Munich Military Post 2-6
Heidelberg 13-19
12th AAA 6-27
Wurzburg 12-14

217

Newton, le
Blackston, fb
Thornborrow, rt
Keene, rhb
Buttorff, lg
Kundick, re
Cartwright, rg
Schappe, le
Perfetti, rhb
Urlage, rg
Miller, c
Wilke, re

Huff, rhb
Stoup, lt
Kopp, lt
Carter, lhb
Hendershot, ie
Weis, rt
Stone, lt
Singleton, re
Gammel, lg
Johnson, iz
Frain, c

NAVAL AMPHIBIOUS FORCE, LITTLE CREEK, VA. (PHIB LANT-GATORS)
1953

NTC, Bainbridge 14-12
NAS, Norfolk (Tars) 26-6
MCAS, Cherry Point 8-7
Ft. Lee 0-15
Bolling AFB 2-20, 13-22
Ft. Eustis 12-20
Parris Island 28-7
Ft. Jackson 13-22
Morris Harvey College 20-0
Ft. Monmouth 14-26

Team

Phil Bucklew, coach
R. W. Meanix, hb
Howard Irvin, hb
Russel Packer, qb
Stuart Tisdale, qb
Frank Branch, qb
James Davis, hb
George Marinkovich, fb
Vern Wynott, hb
Len Toomey, fb
Edwin Spraker, hb
Noel Schmidt, hb
Howard G. Hansen, fb
John Cahill, g
Gerald Klaus, t
John O'Bar, g
Frank Vitale, g
Roy Robbins, c
Clyde Ross, e

Donald Kelley, c
Jack Love, c
John Schneider, e
Robert Jackson, e
Donald McGin'cy, e
Thomas Martin, e
Charles Gaudet, t
Timothy Tamm, t
James Mahoney, t
(Service-All-Star)
William Wallace, t
Vaughnza Whitmore, e
Charles Daniels, e
Robert Pryor, t
Josh Oldham, g
Jack Wagner, fb
William Pearson, g
Robert Smith, g
Frank Martin, qb

NAVAL AIR STATION, NORFOLK, VA. (NAVY TARS)
1953

Bainbridge 0-46
Ft. Lee 0-39
Ft. Meade 21-0
NAS, Jacksonville 12-9
Little Creek 6-26
Cherry Point 6-24
Ft. Belvoir 0-54
Quonset Point 26-6
NavRecSta, Anacostia 0-19

Team

Doug Mac Lachlen, e
Jack Esslinger, t
(Service All-Stars)
Max Kidd, g
Ed Holden
Don Daniels
Pete Williams
Bob Baxter
Stewart, t

Mixon, c
Don McCauley
Ed Kavanaugh
Ted Bittner
Jim Jennings
Odie Posey
Sileo
Dick Claypool
Harmon

USS PHILIPPINE SEA
1953
12th Naval District League: Third Place

12th ND Comm 49-13
Treasure Island 25-18
NAS, Moffet Field 19-0
NAS, Alameda 19-8
Western Sea Frontier 7-0 (Forfeit)
NAS, Oakland 39-37
NSC, Oakland 32-32
Marines, S. F. 13-20
Naval Hosp., Oakland 60-18
Marines, Port Chicago 40-6
Mare Island 32-52

Team

Dale Know, b
John Waters, b
Bob Thompson, b
Robert Smith, b
Toby Maes, b
Ed Harper, b
Jim Glerum, b
Dale Courtney, b
H. Moore

Ira Reitz
Richard Sneese
Ralph Ratfield
Warren Helgerson
Linton Doucet
M. Rentz
W. Isberg
B. Lucas
John Felker

USS SALISBURY SOUND
1953
Team

R. Chase, head coach
L. Doan, asst coach
James E. Miles, e, hb
William Stapp, e
Wilfred H. Block, t
Minor N. Mosier, t
Paul E. Neff, g
Oscar Turrantine, g
Leon R. Fice, c
William Jinnings, fb
Herman C. Bloss, qb
Albert I. Dodd, hb
Sterling W. Smith, qb
George Hagar, trainer

Jimmie Potts, fb
Gerald F. Burch, e
Kenneth E. Darrow, e
James W. Riley, e
Kenneth Elliott, t
Billy J. Renick, e, t
James C. Taylor, g
Gerald G. Wester, g
Joe L. Snead, c
Calvin Harrison, hb
Charles M. Turner, qb
Keith L. Nixon, hb
Herbert Severns, fb
Floyd L. Karr, mgr

MARINES

ALL-MARINE TEAMS
Selected by the sports editors of Marine service publications in a poll conducted by LEATHERNECK Magazine.
1952
Offensive:
Jim Mutscheller, Quantico, e
Bob Schnelker, Parris Island, e
Tex Lawrence, San Diego, e
Rex Boggan, Parris Island, t
Al Viola, Camp Lejeune, g
Carl Plantholt, Camp Lejeune, g
George Radosevich, Parris Island, c
Sam Vacanti, Parris Island, qb
Billy Mixon, Parris Island, hb
Tom Carodine, San Diego, hb
Bill Hayes, Parris Island, fb
Defensive:
Jerry Elliott, Parris Island, e
Harrison Frasier, Camp Lejeune, e

218

Art Davis, Camp Lejeune, t
Roscoe Hansen, Parris Island, t
Dick Lashley, Parris Island, g
Gil Bucci, Parris Island, g
Bob Goode, San Diego, lb
Bob Griffin, San Diego, lb
Orville Williams, Camp Lejeune, db
John Idzik, Parris Island, db
Don Scott, Quantico, safety

1953

First Team:
Frank McPhee, Quantico, e
Rex Boggan, Camp Lejeune, t
Al Viola, Quantico, g
Glen Graham, Camp Lejeune, c
Ray Suchy, Camp Pendleton, g
Sam Duca, Cherry Point, t
Nick DeRosa, Cherry Point, e
Ed Brandenburg, Cherry Point, b
John Petitbon, Quantico, b
Bob Goode, El Toro, b
John Amberg, Quantico, b

Second Team:
Willie Roberts, Camp Pendleton, e
Jim Weatherall, Barstow, t
John Maultsby, Camp Lejeune, g
John Bergamini, San Diego, c
Gil Bucci, Parris Island, g
Ken Huxhold, Camp Pendleton, t
Ken MacAfee, Quantico, e
Ed Brown, Camp Pendleton, b
Ray Smith, Camp Lejeune, b
Reggie Lee, Camp Lejeune, b
Bob Meyers, Quantico, b

Honorable Mention:
Eugene Brooks, Cherry Point, e
Bob Trout, Quantico, e
Walt Viellieu, Quantico, t
Phil Muscarello, San Diego, t
Frank Malack, Cherry Point, g
Tom Roggeman, Quantico, g
Gerald Wenzel, Quantico, c
John Fry, Quantico, b
George Kinek, Cherry Point, b
Arnold Burwitz, San Diego, b
Bob Tougas, Camp Pendleton, b

MARINE DEPOT OF SUPPLIES, BARSTOW, CALIF. (BULLDOGS)

1952

George AFB 28-6
TraPac Navy 27-7
MCAS, El Toro 18-0
Camp Pendleton 13-56
Ft. McArthur 46-7
NOTS, Inyokern 32-6
NAMTC, Point Mugu 6-7
PhibPac 0-53
NAS, Alameda 7-12
NS, Long Beach 20-16
Edwards AFB (Desert Bowl Game) 12-9

1953

NAS, Alameda 20-0
MCAS, El Toro 7-18
Edwards AFB 26-6
NOTS, China Lake 37-0
Camp Pendleton 18-40
NS, Long Beach 19-7
Treasure Island 12-14
NAMTC Point Mugu 6-19
NAD Hawthorne 43-0

Team

Brown, qb, asst coach	Thomas G. Ellery, e
David English, qb	Lloyd E. Longino, e
Edward McKechnie, qb	Herbert L. Mundy, e
Michael Serna, qb	Stanley E. Reed, e
Leo P. Steele, qb	Anthony Wozniak, e
Archie W. Brooks, hb	Clifford Brookshier, t
Edward O. Hicks, hb	George C. Matulich, t
John Kabeiseman, hb	Peter P. Salopek, t
Dorsey Lightner, hb	Frank P. Turner, t
George K. C. Pang, hb	Weatherall, t line coach
Humberto R. Vega, hb	(All-American; All
Jack P. Wages, hb	Marine)
Avery Burton, fb	Howard L. Evans, g
Charles S. Cannia, fb	Lynell C. Clubine, g
Roy Craig, fb	Ernest Cunningham, g
Robert R. Hessler, fb	Upton B. Henderson, g
Calvin O. Randle, fb	Robert F. Salvidio, g
Donald W. Town, fb	John K. Ferguson, c
M. Lisman, head coach	Allen E. Nelson, c
L. Cunningham, trainer	Peter J. Omer, c
Bill Fischer, mgr	Evans, c
Dean Winchell, mgr	

MCAS, EL TORO, CALIF.

1953

Phib Pac, Coronado 0-27
Barstow (Bulldogs) 18-6
MCRD, San Diego 16-21
Camp Pendleton 7-34
NS, Long Beach 26-0
Ft. Lewis 19-32
Eagle Rock, Los Angeles 6-13
NAS, San Diego 2-33

Team

Robert A. Carew, hb	Richard A. Morrow, g
Robert L. Goode, fb	Jack K. Rollins, e
Thomas L. Larson, g, t	Gerald R. Sullivan, e
Walter Richeling, g, t	Dean J. Westgaard, hb
Jimmie F. Meza, g, t	John L. Hilton, qb
Joseph J. Barbagallo, e	Richard L. McKee, t
James L. Ludlow, g	James J. Davis, g, t
Leslie G. Cates, t	D. Fortenberry, g
Daniel J. Labat, t	Jerry J. Kearney, e
Allen E. Riser, hb	Ivan H. Storer, hb
Scipio Spahn, qb, hb	Robert W. Wofford, fb
Gene A. Fodge	Buster W. Chancey, e
Rodney V. Hurich, c	Sammy Kahalewai, fb
Gerbert H. Price, hb	Sammy L. Brown, hb
Lionel A. Sigman, fb	Robert G. Denton, t
R. Watson, coach, t	Gary F. Harvey, g
George A. Murray, t	Jerry A. Matney, hb
Charles E. Ramsey, g	Frank L. Strocchia, t
Raphael B. Cooke, e, t	

MARINE BASE, CAMP PENDLETON, CALIF.

1952

11th Naval District League: Fourth Place
6W, 4L

Ft. Ord 19-39
Camp Cooke 29-11
Luke AFB 40-20

Owen Scanlon, qb
Earl Jackson, fb
George Cordle, e
Andy Thain, b
Bill Ward, c
Bob Berg, b
Tom O'Connor, g
Jim Hull, e
Ken Oberlin, e
Virgil Humphrey, t
Oscar Bly, e
Bill Davis, c
Ed Stanton, g
Leland Chandler, g
Ed Buckingham, t
Nick Phillips, e
B. Jesse, asst coach

Skippy Dyer, b
Pete Ballahan, qb
Bernal Crow, hb
Joe Matesic, t
Bob Miller, b
Bill Costello, c
Lloyd Guillotte, g
Don Scott, e
Dennis Behunick, b
Tom Krupa, t
Charles Nangle, t
Bob Bonapart
Mel Faust, c
Willie McClung, t
Tom Lyons, g
Doug Andreason, e
Alvin Banta, t

MARINE BARRACKS, NAVAL AMMUNITION DEPOT, HAWTHORNE, NEVADA

1953
3W, 3L

Barstow Marines 0-43
NOTS, China Lake 7-12, 13-6
Lassen Jr. College 22-0, 34-0
Mather AFB 13-19

Team

Charles Hall, coach
Donald Bennett, mgr
Lawrence Fields, qb
Robert Rippstein, hb
Richard Heidebrink, hb
Al H. Spriggs, fb
Francis W. Poole, e
George W. Williams, g
Kay McShane, g
Paul J. Rodarte, t
Darryl Thurston, t
Edwin C. Fox, t
Don Garner, e
W. McCormack, qb

John H. Tapscott, qb
Frank D. Thye, hb
George J. Lenston, hb
Levi Matthews, fb
John W. Barth, fb
Richard U. Temple, e
Kenneth B. Roach, g
Ray Brown, g
Richard I. Schuler, t
Charles E. Nyte, t
George Kinmouth, t
Jennings W. Warn, e
Andy Watson, e
Buddy Gettings, e

MARINE CORPS AIR STATION, CHERRY POINT, N. C. (FLYERS)

1953
5W, 6L

Quantico Marines 9-6 (All-Marine Conference)
Little Creek (Gators) 7-8
Ft. Jackson 0-25
Parris Island 19-0 (East Coast Conference)
Bainbridge 6-33
Ft. Lee 6-21
Camp Lejeune 2-7
NAS, Norfolk 24-6
Ft. Eustis 0-32
MCAS, Miami 46-6
Ft. Benning (Green Wave) 54-12
Lawson AFB 50-12

Team

C. Abrahams, head ch
A. Kelly, backfield ch
Guy Campo, end coach
J. Johnson, end coach
Ed Brandenburg, qb
(All-Marine; All Sea Service)

Art Bernardi, g
John McKendrick, e
Bob Benson, e
John Roussos, g
Joe Henderson, e
J. T. Seaholm, t
Frank Malack, g

George Kinek, hb
Nick DeRosa, e
(Service All Stars;
All-Marine)
Sam Duca, t
(All-Marine)
John Cullity, rh
Angelo Lombardo, fb
Eugene Brooks, e
George Foley, t, g

Don Agler, e
Russ Murphy, hb
Bill Pickett, fb
Joe Kelly, qb
John Barnhardt, e
Tom Healy, e
Robert Reed, t
Jim Wheeler, t
Dick Coffey, g
James Kriel, g

MARINE CORPS DEPOT OF SUPPLIES, PHILADELPHIA, PA.

1953

Coast Guard, Cape May, N. J. 6-14
Southwestern A.C. 7-0
Williamston A.C. 13-6
State Teachers College 0-7
NAS, Atlantic City 14-20
Dover AFB 20-20
Ashland Miners 13-26

Team

R. L. Weidner, qb
Len Mengwasser, fb
Jack Goldstein, rhb
H. J. Vincent, lhb
T. A. E. Thom, c
T. M. Fletcher, lg
R. P. Perry, rg
J. M. Tharp, lt
R. Migliarese, rt
W. Conrad, le
R. R. Starr, re
S. Cook, c
V. C. Dutcher, lg
G. R. Tilghman, rg
S. Long, lt
A. J. Florian, rt
W. Qunibar, le
B. G. Ramsey, re

Dorrycott, lhb
J. Glenn, rhb
L. A. Buynum, qb
J. Edwards, fb
E. R. Davis, e
R. H. Wilson, lg
H. Lauche, rg
J. S. Barshatsky, lt
G. H. Ligaic, rt
E. C. Adams, le
R. R. Gellette, re
H. R. Hayes, lhb
Stechishim, rhb
T. M. Forry, qb
W. Payne, fb
J. Morrell, head coach
K. B. Neal, asst coach
John La Placa, mgr

MARINES, QUANTICO, VA. (LEATHERNECKS)

1950

Xavier U 13-34
Bolling AFB 55-0
Va. Polytechnic Institute 61-21
Waynesburg College 41-7
Niagara U 34-13
U of Dayton 7-0
U of Scranton 41-21
Youngstown College 33-14
Camp Lejeune Marines 42-7
Tampa U 48-0
College of Pacific 14-37

1951

Xavier U 7-12
U of Dayton 14-21
HQ Command USAF 28-7
Parris Island Marines 14-20
Ft. Jackson 13-21
St. Bonaventure College 21-14
John Carroll U 35-15
Camp Lejeune Marines 13-20
US Naval Academy JV 13-0
Holy Cross College 14-39
Military Dist. of Wash. 67-6

1952

Bolling AFB 6-14
Xavier U 14-7
Cherry Point Marines 28-0
Parris Island Marines 7-22
Ft. Eustis 7-2
Fordham U 21-8
Indiantown Gap 48-7
Camp Lejeune Marines 2-25
Ft. Jackson 42-21
Holy Cross College 27-18
Ft. Belvoir 42-6

1953

East Coast Service Champions
All-Marine Champions
Xavier College 13-6
U of Dayton 31-0
Holy Cross College 17-0
Ft. Belvoir 28-7
Ft. Jackson 7-9
Bolling AFB 16-12
Ft. Eustis 21-0
Ft. Lee 9-0

Poinsettia Bowl:
Ft. Ord 19-55

All-Marine Championship:
Camp Pendleton 21-14

All-Marine Conference:
Cherry Point 6-9
Parris Island 35-0
Camp Lejeune 3-0

Team

C. Walker, head coach
R. Davis, line coach
A. Thomas, end coach
W. Sigler, backfield ch
Eugene Watto, g
Gerald Wenzel, g, c
Edwin Wood, hb
Tom Payne
Paul Lentz
George Tinsley
Chet Miller
Joe Gleason
Vic Rimkus
Paul Andrew
Labat, fb
John Amberg, fb
    (Service All-Stars;
    All-Marine; All Sea
    Service)
Jim Baldinger, e
Jesse Berry, e
Bob Brady, t
Russel Burns, t
John Coyne, e
Charles Cusimano, g
Tony Dipaolo, c
John Eldridge, g
Jim Erkenbeck, c
John Fry, qb
Dick Grabiak, fb
Roscoe Hansen, t
Charlie Harris, hb
Albert Hoisington, hb
David Hood, e
John Idzik, hb
Merrill Jacobs, e
Anthony Kramer, t
Jackson King, qb
Edwin Lee, t
Robert Loving, c

Kenneth MacAfee, e
    (All-Marine)
Frank McPhee, e
    (Service All-Stars;
    All-Marine; All Sea
    Service)
Robert Myers, g
    (Service All-Stars;
    All-Marine)
Al Viola, g
    (All-Sea Service;
    All-Marine)
Robert Miller, hb
Donald Mitchell, g
John Mounie, hb
Richard Neveux, qb
Robert Norman, t
James Parker, hb
Marvin Peterson, g
Robert Peck, c
John Petithon, hb
    (All Sea-Service;
    Service All-Stars;
    All-Marine)
Steve Piskach, qb
Peter Reich, g
Fred Rippel, fb
Thomas Robinson, t
Thomas Roche, t
Tom Roggeman, g, t
    (Service All-Stars)
Rex Simonds, qb
Peter Simmons, g
Russell Smale, hb
Don Southerland, e
Paul Stephens, t
Bob Stephenson, t
Daniel Stewart, hb
Robert Trout, e
Walter Viellieu, t

MARINE CORPS RECRUIT DEPOT, SAN DIEGO, CALIF. (DEVILDOGS)

1952

National All-Marine Champions
West Coast All-Marine Champions
11th Naval District: Second Place
7W, 1L

El Toro 66-6
NAS, San Diego 45-13
PhibPac, San Diego 39-20
Parris Island 21-12
Camp Pendleton 42-33
San Diego St. 51-21
Brooke AMC 21-15
NTC, San Diego 21-27

Team

Don Taylor, e	(All-Marine)
Bill Lammes, t	Tom Carodine, hb
Camillo Capuzzi, hb	(All-Marine)
Ron Hoenisch, hb	Bob Goode, fb
Arnold Burwitz, fb	(All-Marine)
John B. Bergamini, c	Bob Griffin, hb
Tex Lawrence, t	(All-Marine)

1953

Ft. Ord 0-33
USC Spartans 26-13
Ft. Bliss 7-20
El Toro 21-16
Camp Pendleton 13-13
NAS, San Diego 14-14
PhibPac, Coronado 9-7
San Diego State College 14-7
NTC, San Diego 0-28

Team

A. B. Ramage, coach
R. Lawrence, line ch
J. Delaney, line coach
R. Jacobsen, line coach
Edward G. Alario, fb
William B. Banaga, g
John B. Bergamini, c
    (All-Sea Service;
    All-Marine)
Otis H. Bealmear, fb
Luther V. Borgeson, g
Arnold W. Burwitz, fb
Camillo J. Capuzzi, qb
Stanley S. Carr, hb
Lawrence K. Colley, e
Samuel F. Craig, t
Thomas Danforth, hb
Raymond E. Darling, t
Donald L. Davis, g
Jack O. Davis, t
A. T. DeVaughn, hb
John T. Flippin, e
Frank B. Epstein, g
John Giangiorgi, qb
Ezra L. Gordon, t
Max D. Hawkins, e

Ronald J. Hoenisch, hb
Charles Holliday, hb
Harold I. Jackson, hb
John Kammerman, g
William A. Kellar, fb
George W. Kendall, e
Robert Kirkpatrick, e
William J. Lammes, t
William H. Lehman, t
Joseph E. Logan, g
Jack Lordo, g, t
    (All Sea-Service)
James S. Marinos, qb
Phil Muscarello, t, c
    (Service All-Stars)
Edward Ostrowski, qb
Cecil W. Parker, e
William A. Preston, t
    (All-American)
Donald M. Price, e
Rodger Rosenquist, hb
Ralph D. Studebaker, e
Donald D. Taylor, e
Dewey S. Wade, fb
Joseph A. Young, t
Stevenson, fb

MARINE CORPS BASE, CAMP LEJEUNE, N. C. (LEATHERNECKS)

1952

7W, 3L
Catawba College 56-7
Xavier College 34-21

Ft. Jackson 6-13
Dayton U 23-19
Ft. Eustis 18-0
Quantico 25-2
Cherry Point 62-14
Baldwin-Wallace 32-7
Bolling AFB 6-7
Parris Island 20-54

Team

Al Viola, g (All-Marine)
Carl PlantHolt, g (All-Marine)
Harrison Frasier, e (All-Marine)
Art Davis, t (All-Marine)
Orville Williams, db, (All-Marine)

1953

Baldwin Wallace 32-6
Pensacola 13-12
Ft. Lee 7-13
Ft. Jackson 6-6
Ft. Monmouth 20-6
Keesler AFB 27-0, 33-0
Ft. Eustis 27-0
Bolling AFB 23-27, 6-6
Camp Atterbury 41-0

East Coast Marine Championship:
Parris Island 16-0
Cherry Point 7-2
Quantico 0-3

Team

Walter Bielich, e	Glen Graham, c
Terence Fails, e	(All-Sea-Service, All-Marine)
John Dietz, c	
Carl Dolan, e	Steve Lazarus, c
Richard Layne, e	John Conner, qb
Joseph Rilo, e	Robert Bechtel, qb
W. Samer, e, end coach	Ronard Byrd, qb
Melvin Yeshnik, e	Hugo Rosell, qb
Kenneth Barfield, t	Jerry Fouts, hb
Rex Boggan, t,	William Hawkins, hb
(All-Sea-Service; All Marine; Most Valuable Player Award)	James Lee, hb (Service-All-Stars; All-Marine)
Louis Golic, t	Frank Nastro, hb
Fred Lippard, t	Leon Robertson, hb
John Maultsby, t, g (All-Marine)	Ray Smith, hb (All-Sea-Service; All-Marine)
Loyd Spencer, t	
William Sutherland, t	Joseph Caprara, fb
Tony Anton, g	William Hayes, fb
Charles Booth, g	Howard Hostetler, fb
Henry Doak, g	Donald Scardami, fb
Frank Rindoni, g	John Crawley, coach
Charles Scott, g	W. Jones, line coach
Richard Steber, g	H. Henson, line coach
William Stovall, g	C. Killeen, backfield ch
Bennie Davis, c	

MARINE CORPS RECRUIT DEPOT, PARRIS ISLAND, S. C.
1952
East Coast Marine Champions
Team

Bob Schnelker, e (All-Marine)	(All-Marine)
George Radosevich, c (All-Marine)	Rex Boggan, t (All-Marine)
Billy Mixon, hb (All-Marine)	Sam Vacanti, qb (All-Marine)
Jerry Elliott, e (All-Marine)	Bill Hayes, fb (All-Marine)
Dick Lashley, g (All-Marine)	Roscoe Hansen, t (All-Marine)
John Idzik, hb	Gil Bucci, g (All-Marine)

1953

Ft. Monmouth 7-32
Southern Mississippi 0-40
Quantico 0-35 (All-Marine Conference)
Wofford College 6-19
MCAS, Miami 28-28
Cherry Point 0-19
Little Creek 7-28
Ft. Jackson 0-28
Camp Lejeune 0-16 (East Coast Marine Championship)
Gen. Supply Depot, Atlanta 59-12

Team

B. Andruska, head ch	Jimmy Ray, fb
B. Maiden, back coach	Gene Wasniewski, fb
W. Beard, line coach	Jim Finn, hb
Gil Bucci, g (Service All-Stars; All-Marine)	Fred Gurgis, qb
	Teddy Bates, e
	Will Overgard, t
John Ilari, g	Dick Bobo, g
Rod Lash, qb	Glen Derr, c
Ed Tokus, t	Herbert Price, b
Bob Lewis, e	Allen Rizer, b
Joe Wasilewski, e	Albert Sigman
Tom Edwards	

COAST GUARD

US COAST GUARD ACADEMY, NEW LONDON, CONN.
(BEARS)
1953
4W, 2L, 1T

Colby 13-0
Wesleyan 6-6
Amherst 7-21
Worcester Poly Tech 0-9
Trinity 25-14
Rensselaer Poly Tech 12-6
St. Michael's 7-6

Team

Nels Nitchman, coach	William Boyle, e
*Guy Mizell, capt, fb	Eric Foster, c
*William Tillo, t	Bob Hollingsworth, qb
*George Seaman, t	Henry J. Rochner, hb
Daniel C. Olson, t	Ross Day, hb
Steve Dasovich	Richard Nielsen, hb
Kirk Kellogg, t	Roger Shannon, b
Dick Groepler, t	James Rivard, b
*John Mosely, g	Henry Suski, b
Vic Robillard, g	Ernest Allen, hb
Bob Bristol, g	Neal Benjamin
*Charles Hahn,e	Richard Kibbey, b
Dwight E. Ramsay, e	Ralph Paganetti
Lloyd Maracks, e	George Bergman
Terry Blair, c	

* All-Star Team, Small Colleges, Conn.

UNITED STATES COAST GUARD RECEIVING CENTER, CAPE MAY, N. J.
1951
8W, 1L., 1T

Clayton AC 15-0
NTC, Bainbridge 13-12

Camp Kilmer 12-0
Zumi AC 13-0
Rider College 6-27
Wildwood Islanders 15-0
NAS, Chincoteague 27-6
U. of Penn Frosh 0-0
Millville AC 12-6
NAS, Atlantic City 19-0

Team

R. Clark, head coach	Wesley West, b
F. Smith, asst coach	Lynn Streiff, b
Robert Connor, b	Gordon Gobel, b
Allison, e	Bob Stelle, b
Gayle Rowe, c	Dick Kennedy, b
Bill Conley, e	John Lombardi, e
Junie Sica, b	Ross Keith, b
Edward Stevens, e	Drummond, g
Reich, t	Shorts, b
Tom Illi, e	Jacoby, e
Vance, e	Ronald Fluegel, g
Vita Clapp, b	Dan Casey, b
Weingarten, g	Don Legg, g
Maynard Wolfe, b	Bill Hawley, t
Foster Campbell, b	Stephen Dalina, t
Richard Novak, e	Bross, g
Fuller, t	Frank Palmisano, g
Fischer, t	Maropis, e
David Thome, t	Perrin, g
Smith, g	Goldsmith, b
Harry Slaine, b	

1952
7W, 1L

Cape May Rockets 6-0
NTC, Bainbridge 0-27
NSD, Bayonne 19-0
NAS, Chincoteague 27-0
NAS, Atlantic City 29-0
Princeton U JV 19-7
USCG Port Securtiy 38-0
Dover AFB 13-0

Team

R. Clark, head coach	Marcus Hill, e
Norman Caribo, b	F. Smith, asst coach
Anthony Diamente, b	Robert Connor, b
Frank Franklin, b	Joseph Dooley, b
Emund Harvey, b	Carl Gimber, b
Donald Mansfield, b	Peter Longo, b
Guy Railey, b	Billy McKinnon, b
Junie Sica, b	Henry Sorelle, b
Arnie Weber, b	Edward Turon, b
Alfred Adkins, e	Edward Wieland, b
H. M. Sage, e	Charles Batway, e
Edward Stevens, e	Arnold Stern, e
John Waggoner, e	Donald Transue, e
James Beckett, t	John Wengrocki, e
Stephen Dalina, t	John Coleran, e
James Whiting, t	Donald Econe, t
Frederick Attebury, g	Salvatore Santaniello, t
William Crooks, g	Harold Wilson, t
Charles Offutt, g	Donald Coleman, g
Russell Adams, e	John Gotich, g
William Bischoff, e	Donald Sullivan, g

1953

Cape May Rockets (semi-pro) 6-0
Ft. Dix 7-6
Dover AFB 20-7
Ft. Monmouth 0-33
Princeton JV 13-6
NTC, Bainbridge 14-34
NAS, Atlantic City 7-14
Marine Depot, Phila. 14-6

Team

James Andrews, b	Wells, t
Luther Brinson, b	Beck, g

Mathew Carr, qb
John Fini, b
Ralph Huffman, hb
(All Sea Service)
Donald Larson, e
Raymond Lewis, b
Billy McKinnon, b
Kenneth Morrow, b
Walter Scheidhauer, b
Glenn Schoeneck, b
Loreto Sica, tb, co-capt
Guy Tracy, b
Alfred Adkins, e
Wayne DeGraff, e
Thomas Gilmer, e
John Kirby, e
Thomas Schmidt, e
Edward Stevens, e
Donald Warner, e
Maynard, e

William Bartmess, t
Stephen Dalina, t
James Morris, t
James Northrup, t
Orba Puckett, t
Donald Transue, t
Henry Caruso, g
Philip Joyce, g
(All Sea Service)
Eugene Morahan, g
Curtis Neal, g
Charles Offutt, g
Joseph Salter, g
Rodney Wilson, g
William Craver, e
Wallace Gorr, e
W. Van Derveer, e
F. K. Smith, hd coach
R. Connor, asst coach
V. E. Ziegler, trainer

AIR FORCE

United States

ALL-AIR FORCE TEAM

Selected by the readers of
AIR FORCE TIMES

First Team:

Walt Klevay, Bolling AFB, hb
Bill Reichardt, Bolling AFB, fb
Carl Trippeer, Sheppard AFB, qb
Tom Driscoll, Hamilton AFB, e
Dick Brand, Sheppard AFB, c
Joe Moss, Bolling AFB, g
John Myers, Keesler AFB, g
Girard Oliva, Keesler AFB, c
Bob Cunio, Nagoya, g
John Wheat, Hamilton AFB, t
Glenn Lippman, Eglin AFB, hb (Most Valuable Player, USAF)

Second Team:

Leo Martin, Bolling AFB, e
Howard Pierson, Nagoya, e
Robert Martin, Sheppard, t
Don King, Itami, t
Herschel Forrester, Hamilton AFB, g
Don Jackson, Westover AFB, g
Alan Clark, Pope AFB, c
Al Dorrow, Bolling AFB, qb
Billy Tidwell, Keesler AFB, hb
Billy Stevenson, Keesler AFB, hb
Buddy DiMott, Sheppard AFB, fb

Honorable Mention:

Jerome Wilson, Westover AFB, e
Charlie Jones, Bolling AFB, e
Jim Glasgow, Sheppard AFB, t
Dick Adams, Eglin AFB, t
Lonnie Williams, Sheppard AFB, g
Lou Mascola, Hamilton AFB, g
Will Alston, Sheppard AFB, c
Ray Graves, Eglin AFB, qb
John Collis, Westover AFB, hb
Merle Myers, Sheppard AFB, hb
Harry Hugasian, Hamilton AFB, fb

BOLLING AFB, WASHINGTON, D. C. (GENERALS)
1953

Army Chemical Center 51-2
Quantico Marines 12-16
Ft. Jackson 26-20
Little Creek 20-2
Camp Lejeune 27-23
Ft. Eustis 0-7
Ft. Lee 7-14
Ft. Belvoir 19-7
Ft. Monmouth 18-0
NTC, Bainbridge 35-7

Team

J. Poloncheck, asst ch
Roger Antaya, coach
W. Klevay, hb (All-AF team)
Leon Carrico, c
A. Dorrow, qb (All-AF, 2d team)
B. Reichardt, fb (All-AF team)
Don Wallace, hb
Dick McGinley, hb
Charles Jones, e
John Ignarski, g
Hugh Jacobs, e
L. Martin, e (All-AF, 2d team)

L. Moss, t (All-AF team)
Joe Dudeck, g, co-capt
Red Lawson, t
Bob Lega, mgr
C. Dorsey, trainer
Bob Allwine, g
John Lindsay, e
Mel Groomes, hb
D. Fucci, qb, asst ch
A. Miketa, e, co-capt
George Christiansen, t
Allen Boyd, fb
Fred James, hb
Ed Nickla, t
Roy Martine, c

EDWARDS AFB, CALIF. (JETS)
1953

Eagle Rock AC 0-39
NOTS, China Lake 39-6
Point Mugu 0-15, 0-29
NAS, San Diego 0-46
Barstow Marines 6-26
Hamilton AFB 6-39
Spartan AC 14-0
Spoiler AC 33-6
Presidio, S. F. 19-40

Team

John Slupski, hb
Chan Johnson
Jerry McCafferty, b
L. Weaver, qb
Bill Craft

Jack Rose
Winston Baber
Charlie Walzer
Bob Robinson

EGLIN AFB, FLORIDA
1953

Marine Corps Air Station 15-0
NAS, Pensacola 7-27
Shaw AFB 13-2
Sewart AFB 34-0
Tyndall AFB 26-0
Jacksonville Navy 33-0
Ft. Benning 35-13
Great Lakes Navy 28-12
Keesler AFB 19-8, 21-62

Team

Ben Burke, t
Duane Johnson, g
Ray Thibault, e
Walter Gary, c

Clarence Logan, c
Walt Taylor, e
Mike Fornaro, hb
Ernest Childs, e

A. J. Baker, e, fb
Fidell Gander, fb
Demus Jones, g
Glenn Lippman, hb
Brad Nusbaum, g
Scotty Kobus, hb
Leonard Travis, hb
Roy Dunbar, g
William Wilson, fb
Richard David, qb
Oliver Agramonte, e
Richard Adams, t
Hugh Meyer, e
Quinten Laabo, t
Charles Light, g
Rocco Calabredta, g
Jack Palizay, hb
Art Bischoff, qb
Pasquell Testa, g
Marciano Duron, hb
James Bradford, t
Charlie Nordman, e
David Karr, e
Leroy Fair, e
William Lewis, hb
Joe Peterson, e
Perry Barrington, fb

John Stallings, g
T. Southerland, e
Duane Eliason, e
Harry Bauville, hb
M. Cammarano, hb
Robert Kestner, t
Johnny Miles, e
W. C. Allbritten, qb
Ray Graves, qb
Eddy Michalski, hb
Tom Kingery, e
William Smack, hb
M. Popavach, trainer
John Voltz, qb
John Resnick, t
James Walsh, g
Bill Thornton, g
Frank Reyna, t
D. Norris, head coach
B. Marshall, ath dir
J. P. Lappin, asst ath dir
D. Watts, bf coach
Larry Tucker, line ch
R. McBride, e coach
Larry Hummel, line ch

EIELSON AFB, ALASKA
1953

Elmendorf AFB 6-24

Team

J. Rudd, rt
R. Guyer, e
Sam Rieben, re
Jack Kamisky, lt
C. Bushick, rt
Clarence Dulek, g
Bob Maimaron, e
Joe Franzo, qb
Perry Marsh, rhb
Harry Holstein, fb
D. Dunlap, le
E. Davis, rg

H. Karish, le
A. Lorina, lt
V. Verdura, fb
J. Nesbitt, fb
R. Melchionno, rg
A. Anderson, re
C. White, qb
H. Busky, qb
D. Landerman, lhb
C. Dalton, lhb
M. Banks, rhb

ELLINGTON AFB, TEXAS (FLYERS)
1953

Brooks AMC 0-19
Sheppard AFB 13-34
Ft. Hood 7-35
Alexandria AFB 33-0
SMU, "B" Team 2-27
Goodfellow AFB 7-33

Team

J. J. Cunningham, t
Albert Bass, e
Earl Liberty, g
Travis Simpson, coach
Lloyd Singley, hb
Ernie Frady, rhb
D. G. Graham, e
Don McGivney, hb
J. J. Jones, hb
Roger DeRosans, bf
Willie Perkins, fb
L. D. Wilborn, e
Randolph Hall, g
Thomas Nelson, e
Guido Forte, t
Charles Pittman, fb
James Smith, g
Kay Bernson, qb
Wes Abbey, qb

Bob Hileman, e
Joseph Regan, g
Aldo Bredolo, g
L. H. Newhaus, t, g
K. Cullinan, g
Joseph Yanovich, e
Harrison Epperly, g
C. H. Schoneck, t
Ben Dallas, e
Raymond Hendrix, e
Austin Tredway, hb
Mitchel Stefanski, t
Joe Blackwell, g
B. G. Smith, g
Roger Craner, t
Joe Ciampa, e
Roger Dersoano, hb
Billy Hall, g

BASKETBALL

WORLD-WIDE ALL-STAR TEAM
(ARMED FORCES PRESS SERVICE)
1953

First Team:
Paul Arizin, f, USMC, Quantico
Dick Schnittker, f, Army, Ft. Meade (All-American)
Ed Roman, c, Army, Ft. Eustis (All-American)
Paul Unruh, g, Army, Camp Breckinridge (All-American)
Don Sunderlage, g, Air Force, Chanute AFB (All-American)

Second Team:
Zeke Sinicola, f, Army, Camp Breckinridge
Ray Ragelis, f, Army, Ft. Lee
Carl McNulty, c, Navy, Great Lakes (All-American)
Sam Ranzinon, g, Army, MTC, Korea
Leroy Smith, g, USMC, Camp Lejeune

Honorable Mention:
Arnold Galiffa, HSC, Japan
Kermit Weiske, Indiantown Gap
Ted Shiro, Camp Chaffee
Frank Kuzara, Camp Kilmer
Tom O'Keefe, Ft. Myer
Rip Gish, Quantico
George Dempsey, NTC, Bainbridge
Ernie Barrett, Sandia Base
Sal Scalfani, Albrook AFB
Ron MacGilvray, Ft. Dix
Ron Minson, AmpPac
Ken Murray, Camp Drake
Chuck Stevesky, Sampson AFB
Jim Walsh, Quantico
George Yardley, Los Alamitos

1954

First Team:
Paul Arizin, Quantico, f
Johnny O'Brien, Aberdeen Proving Ground, f
Ernie Beck, NTC, Bainbridge, c
Dick Groat, Ft. Belvoir, g
Bobby Watson, Andrews AFB, g

Second Team:
Bill McCullum, Lockbourne AFB, f
Chuck Stevesky, Sampson AFB, f
Carl McNulty, NTC, Great Lakes, c
Larry Hennessey, Ft. Eustis, g
Richie Regan, Quantico, g

Honorable Mention:
LeRoy Smith, Camp Lejeune
Ray Ragelis, Ft. Lee
Stan Albeck, Ft. Ord
Harry Folk, Yokota AB
Don Byrd, Ft. Belvoir
Eddie O'Brien, Aberdeen Proving Ground

Dick Knostman, Andrews AFB
Jack Clark, Scott AFB
Al Roth, Ft. Monmouth
Ron MacGilvray, Ft. Dix

INTER-SERVICE CHAMPIONSHIP TOURNAMENT
1954
Great Lakes, Ill.

CHAMPIONS: Andrews AFB, D. C.
NTC, Great Lakes, Ill.
  Camp Chaffee 90-84
  Andrews AFB 66-91
Andrews AFB, D. C.
  Quantico 81-77
  Great Lakes 91-66
Camp Chaffee, Ark.
  Great Lakes 84-90
  Quantico 80-89
Quantico Marines, Va.
  Andrews AFB 77-81
  Camp Chaffee 89-80

ARMY

ALL-ARMY CHAMPIONSHIP TOURNAMENT
1950
Ft. Belvoir, Va.

CHAMPIONS: Ft. Knox, Ky., Second Army (1949: Brooke AMC)
SECOND PLACE: Ft. Richardson, Alaska
Second Army (Ft. Knox):
  Alaska 57-38, 56-52
  Fourth Army 54-48
  USFA 53-39
  Fifth Army 68-55
First Army (Ft. Monmouth):
  Third Army 60-59
  Alaska 48-59
  Fifth Army 54-58
Third Army (Ft. Jackson):
  First Army 59-60
  USFA 58-36
Sixth Army (Ft. Lewis):
  Pacific 60-68
Pacific (Schofield Barracks):
  MDW 53-69
  Sixth Army 68-60
Fifth Army (Ft. Riley):
  Far East 50-82
  First Army 58-54
  Second Army 55-68
Alaska (Ft. Richardson):
  Second Army 38-57, 52-56
  Fourth Army 60-45
  MDW 68-55

323

Far East 48-36
First Army 59-48
Fourth Army (Brooke AMC):
Second Army 48-54
Alaska 45-60
Far East 69-50
USFA (796th MP Bn):
Third Army 36-58
Second Army 39-53
Far East (H & S Group, Tokyo):
Fourth Army 50-69
Alaska 36-48
Military District of Washington (Ft. Myer):
Alaska 55-68
Pacific 69-53

1952
Ft. Sam Houston, Texas
CHAMPIONS: Fifth Army (Ft. Leonard Wood)
Mil. Dist. of Wash. (Ft. Belvoir):
Fifth Army 68-71
First Army 77-60
Alaska 86-50
Sixth Army 70-77
Second Army (Ft. Eustis):
Fourth Army 82-53
First Army 69-63
Sixth Army 61-74
Fifth Army 62-64
Third Army (Ft. Bragg):
Fourth Army 71-69
First Army 88-66
First Army (Ft. Dix):
Third Army 66-88
Second Army 63-69
MDW 60-77
Fourth Army (Ft. Sill):
Fifth Army 69-71
Third Army 69-71
Second Army 53-82
Fifth Army (Ft. Leonard Wood):
MDW 71-68
Fourth Army 71-69
Sixth Army 54-50, 53-55
Alaska 79-47
Second Army 64-62
Alaska (Ft. Richardson):
MDW 50-86
Fifth Army 47-79
Sixth Army (Camp Roberts):
Second Army 74-61
Fifth Army 50-54
MDW 77-70
Fifth Army 55-53

1953
Ft. George G. Meade, Md.
CHAMPIONS: Ft. Belvoir, Va. (MDW)
SECOND PLACE: Fifth Army (Ft. Leonard Wood, Mo.)
Military District of Washington (Ft. Belvoir):
Fourth Army 78-67

Fifth Army 76-64
Third Army 75-70
Second Army 90-77
First Army (Ft. Monmouth):
Second Army 77-84
AFFE 78-71, 70-77
USARPAC 75-71
Second Army (Camp Breckinridge):
Fifth Army 63-68
First Army 84-77
MDW 77-90
Sixth Army 87-85
Third Army (Ft. Jackson):
Sixth Army 83-94
MDW 70-75
Fourth Army (Ft. Sill):
AFFE 73-53
Fifth Army 68-67, 61-81
MDW 67-78
Fifth Army (Ft. Leonard Wood):
Second Army 68-63
USARPAC 77-62
Fourth Army 67-68, 81-61
MDW 64-76
Sixth Army 81-77
Sixth Army (Camp Roberts):
Fifth Army 77-81
Third Army 94-83
Second Army 85-87
AFFE (1st Cav Div):
First Army 71-78, 77-70
Fourth Army 53-73
USARPAC (Schofield Barracks):
First Army 71-75
Fifth Army 62-77

1954
Fort Lewis, Wash.
CHAMPIONS: Camp Chaffee, Ark.
SECOND PLACE: Fort Ord, Calif.
Fort Belvoir, Va. (MDW)
Ft. Ord 61-89, 86-90
Camp Kilmer 79-77
Ft. Leonard Wood 87-86
WACom 80-74
Camp Kilmer, N. J. (First Army)
Ft. Ord 62-88
Ft. Belvoir 77-79
Ft. Leonard Wood 77-79
Aberdeen Proving Ground, Md. (Second Army)
Camp Gordon 63-81
Ft. Ord 87-92
USARPAC 89-82
Camp Gordon, Ga. (Third Army)
Aberdeen PG 81-63
Ft. Ord 68-78
Camp Chaffee 70-91
Camp Chaffee, Ark. (Fourth Army)
Ft. Leonard Wood 76-69
Ft. Ord 113-76, 87-79
Camp Gordon 91-70
Fort Leonard Wood, Mo. (Fifth Army)
Camp Chaffee 69-76

Camp Kilmer 79-77
Ft. Belvoir 86-87
Fort Ord, Calif. (Sixth Army)
  Camp Kilmer 88-62
  Ft. Belvoir 89-61, 90-86
  Camp Chaffee 76-113, 79-87
  Aberdeen PG 92-87
  Camp Gordon 78-68
WACom (USAREUR)
  Ft. Belvoir 74-80
USARPAC
  Aberdeen PG 82-89

ALL-ARMY TOURNAMENT TEAM

(Coaches' Selections)

1953

First Team:
  Dick Groat, Ft. Belvoir
  Jack George, Ft. Belvoir
  Zeke Sinicola, Camp Breckinridge
  Don Byrd, Ft. Leonard Wood
  Joe Smyth, 1st Cav Div
Second Team:
  Gene Smith, Camp Breckinridge
  Fred Christ, Ft. Monmouth
  Jim Wuenker, Ft. Belvoir
  George Macuga, Ft. Sill
  Dave Mayfield, Ft. Leonard Wood
  Charlie Shoptaw, Ft. Sill
Honorable Mention:
  Dick Baumgartner, g, Ft. Leonard Wood
  Lloyd Sandstrom, Ft. Jackson
  Jim Cooke, Ft. Jackson
  Stan Albeck, g, Camp Roberts
  Jerry Pease, c, Camp Roberts
  Buddy Donnelly, Ft. Belvoir
  Bob Wheeler, c, Camp Roberts
  Bato Govedarica, 1st Cav Div
  Don Solinsky, g, Ft. Leonard Wood
  Dick Gomard, Schofield Bks
  Jim Loscutoff, Camp Roberts

FIRST ARMY CHAMPIONSHIP TOURNAMENT

1952

CHAMPIONS: Men—Ft. Dix (2d, Camp Edwards)
Women—Ft. Dix (2d, Ft. Devens)

1953

CHAMPIONS: Men—Ft. Monmouth
Women—Ft. Dix
Team Standings (Men):
  1. Ft. Monmouth
  2. Ft. Dix
  3. Camp Kilmer
  4. Ft. Devens
  5. Camp Drum
  6. Ft. Hamilton
  7. New York Port of Embarkation

  8. West Point
  9. Ft. Jay
  10. Ft. Banks
  11. Ft. Slocum
Team Standings (Women):
  1. Ft. Dix
  2. Murphy Army Hospital
  3. Ft. Jay
  4. Camp Kilmer
  5. Ft. Monmouth
  6. Ft. Devens
  7. Ft. Hamilton
  8. West Point
Small Installation Trophy: Ft. Slocum

1954

Camp Kilmer, N. J.
CHAMPIONS: Camp Kilmer, N. J.
SECOND PLACE: Fort Dix, N. J.
Fort Monmouth, N. J.:
  Ft. Dix 76-69, 85-89
  Camp Kilmer 75-82
  Ft. Jay 93-47
Fort Dix, N. J.:
  Camp Kilmer 95-87, 70-78
  Ft. Monmouth 69-76, 89-85
  Ft. Devens 80-68
  Ft. Niagara 108-72
Fort Devens, Mass.:
  Ft. Dix 68-80
  Ft. Jay 81-46
  Camp Kilmer 67-82
Camp Kilmer, N. J.:
  Ft. Dix 87-95, 78-70
  Ft. Monmouth 82-75
  Ft. Devens 82-51
  Ft. Niagara 89-51
Fort Jay, N. Y.:
  Ft. Devens 46-81
  Ft. Monmouth 47-93
Fort Niagara, N. Y.:
  Ft. Dix 72-108
  Camp Kilmer 51-89
Small Installation Tournament:
  Champions: Ft. Jay, N. Y.
  Second Place: Ft. Niagara, N. Y.

WOMEN'S DIVISION

CHAMPIONS: Fort Monmouth, N. J.
Fort Monmouth, N. J.:
  Camp Kilmer 39-31
  Murphy AH 29-23
  Ft. Dix 39-30
Fort Devens, Mass.:
  Camp Kilmer 34-35
Fort Dix, N. J.:
  Ft. Monmouth 30-39
Camp Kilmer, N. J.:
  Ft. Monmouth 31-39
  Ft. Devens 35-34
Murphy Army Hospital, Mass.:
  Ft. Monmouth 23-29

227

SECOND ARMY CHAMPIONSHIP TOURNAMENT
1954

Aberdeen Proving Ground, Md.
CHAMPIONS: Aberdeen Proving Ground, Md.
SECOND PLACE: Fort Knox, Ky.
Aberdeen Proving Ground, Md.:
  Ft. Lee 81-85
  Columbus Gen Dep 116-45
  Ft. Meade 82-80
  Ft. Eustis 94-88
  Carlisle Barracks 91-85
  Ft. Knox 112-88, 95-89
Army Chemical Center, Md.:
  Carlisle Barracks 75-94
  Camp Pickett 64-94
Carlisle Barracks, Pa.:
  Army Chemical Center 94-75
  Ft. Lee 69-100, 88-81
  Ft. Ritchie 79-60
  Aberdeen PG 85-91
Columbus General Depot, Ohio:
  Maryland Mil. Dist. 61-49
  Valley Forge AH 42-71
  Aberdeen PG 45-116
Camp Detrick, Md.:
  Ft. Knox 55-73
  Maryland Mil. Dist. 70-52
  Ft. Ritchie 67-72
Fort Eustis, Va.:
  Camp Pickett 78-71
  Ft. Ritchie 82-69
  Ft. Lee 64-74
  Aberdeen PG 88-94
Fort Knox, Ky.:
  Camp Detrick 73-55
  Ft. Meade 84-69
  Valley Forge AH 86-54
  Ft. Lee 69-63
  Aberdeen PG 88-112, 89-95
Fort Lee, Va.:
  Aberdeen PG 85-81
  Carlisle Barracks 100-69, 81-88
  Ft. Eustis 74-64
  Ft. Knox 63-69
Maryland Military District:
  Columbus Gen. Dep. 49-61
  Camp Detrick 52-70
Camp Pickett, Va.:
  Ft. Eustis 71-87
  Army Chemical Center 94-64
  Ft. Meade 69-105
Fort Meade, Md.:
  Ft. Knox 69-84
  Camp Pickett 105-69
  Valley Forge AH 99-52
  Aberdeen PG 80-82
Fort Ritchie, Md.:
  Ft. Eustis 69-82
  Camp Detrick 72-67
  Carlisle Barracks 60-79

Valley Forge Army Hospital, Pa.:
  Columbus Gen. Dep. 71-42
  Ft. Knox 54-86
  Ft. Meade 52-99

THIRD ARMY CHAMPIONSHIP TOURNAMENT
1952

CHAMPIONS: Ft. Bragg, N. C.
Ft. Jackson:
  Camp Rucker 77-46
  Ft. Benning 99-81
  11th Airborne Div 79-67
  Ft. Bragg 66-55, 68-65
Ft. Bragg:
  Ft. McPherson 82-59
  Atlanta Gen. Dep. 74-50
  Ft. Jackson 55-66, 65-68
Atlanta General Depot:
  Redstone Arsenal 70-43
  Ft. Bragg 50-74
  Ft. Benning 80-64
  Ft. McPherson 67-65
11th Airborne Division:
  Camp Stewart 60-46
  Ft. Jackson 67-79
  Ft. McPherson 56-64
Camp Rucker:
  Ft. Jackson 46-77
  Camp Stewart 61-27
  Ft. Benning 55-59
Ft. McPherson:
  Ft. Bragg 59-82
  Redstone Arsenal 80-65
  11th Airborne Div 64-56
  Atlanta Gen Dep 65-67
Redstone Arsenal:
  Atlanta Gen Dep 43-70
  Ft. McPherson 65-80
Camp Stewart:
  11th Airborne Div 46-60
  Camp Rucker 27-61
Ft. Benning:
  Ft. Jackson 81-99
  Camp Rucker 59-55
  Atlanta Gen Dep 64-80

1953

CHAMPIONS: Ft. Jackson, S. C.
Ft. Jackson:
  Camp Stewart 94-64
  Ft. Bragg 67-65
  Ft. Campbell 52-45
  Ft. Benning 60-48
  Camp Rucker 85-65
Ft. Benning:
  Camp Rucker 62-57, 61-79
  Camp Gordon 86-60
  Redstone Arsenal 69-61
  Ft. Jackson 48-60
Ft. Campbell:
  Atlanta Gen. Dep. 75-73

Ft. Jackson 45-52
Camp Rucker 56-74
Redstone Arsenal:
Ft. McPherson 76-64
Ft. Benning 61-69
Ft. Bragg 61-81
Ft. Bragg:
Ft. Jackson 65-67
Camp Stewart 87-83
Redstone Arsenal 81-61
Camp Rucker 69-92
Camp Stewart:
Ft. Jackson 64-94
Atlanta Gen. Dep. 72-69
Ft. Bragg 83-87
Camp Rucker:
Ft. Benning 57-62, 79-61
Ft. McPherson 92-58
Camp Gordon 81-75
Ft. Campbell 74-56
Ft. Bragg 92-69
Ft. Jackson 65-85
Atlanta General Depot:
Ft. Campbell 73-75
Camp Stewart 69-72
Ft. McPherson:
Redstone Arsenal 64-76
Camp Rucker 58-92
Camp Gordon:
Ft. Benning 60-86
Camp Rucker 75-81

1954

Camp Gordon, Ga.
CHAMPIONS: Camp Gordon, Ga.
SECOND PLACE: Camp Rucker, Ala.

Camp Gordon, Ga.:
Camp Stewart 97-62
Redstone Arsenal 82-52
Ft. Benning 85-78
Ft. Jackson 88-77
Camp Rucker 98-97
Fort Jackson, S. C.:
Camp Rucker 101-88, 70-76
N. C. Mil Dist 112-44
Ft. Campbell 102-81
Camp Gordon 77-88
Fort McPherson, Ga.:
Ft. McClellan 77-86
Redstone Arsenal 60-73
Camp Stewart, Ga.:
Camp Gordon 62-97
Ft. McClellan 72-87
Fort Benning, Ga.:
Ft. McClellan 90-75
N. C. Mil Dist 95-79
Camp Gordon 78-85
Ft. Bragg 78-95
Camp Rucker 70-81
Camp Rucker, Ala.:
Ft. Jackson 88-101, 76-70
Ft. Bragg 73-53, 81-70

Ft. McClellan 98-64
Camp Gordon 97-98
Fort McClellan, Ala.:
Ft. McPherson 86-77
Ft. Benning 75-90
Camp Stewart 87-72
Redstone Arsenal 88-75
Camp Rucker 64-98
Fort Bragg, N. C.:
Atlanta Gen. Dep. 93-78, 83-73
Camp Rucker 53-73, 70-81
Ft. Benning 95-78
N. C. Mil Dist 95-79
Redstone Arsenal, Ala.:
Ft. McClellan 75-88
Camp Gordon 52-82
Ft. McPherson 73-60
Atlanta General Depot, Ga.:
Ft. Bragg 78-93, 73-83
Ft. Campbell 75-70
North Carolina Military District:
Ft. Jackson 44-112
Ft. Bragg 79-95
Fort Campbell, Ky.:
Ft. Jackson 81-102
Atlanta Gen. Dep. 70-75

WOMEN'S DIVISION

Camp Gordon, Ga.
CHAMPIONS: Fort Benning, Ga.
SECOND PLACE: Ft. Jackson, S. C.
Fort Jackson, S. C.:
Ft. Bragg 42-38, 57-48
Ft. Benning 47-57, 42-50
Fort Bragg, N. C.:
Ft. Jackson 38-42, 48-57
Camp Gordon 44-13
Camp Gordon, Ga.:
Ft. Bragg 13-44
Ft. Benning 14-67
Fort Benning, Ga.:
Camp Gordon 67-14
Ft. Jackson 57-47, 50-42

THIRD ARMY ALL-STAR TEAM
1954

Bill Reigel, Camp Rucker, f
O'Neal Weaver, Camp Rucker, c
Gene Smith, Ft. Jackson, g
Nield Gordon, Ft. Jackson, c
Jim O'Brien, Camp Gordon, f
Ed Koffenberger, Camp Gordon, g
Pete Silas, Ft. McClellan, f
Frank Glenn, Ft. Benning, g
Dickie Vann, Ft. Campbell, f
Howard Pigg, Ft. Bragg, g

FOURTH ARMY CHAMPIONSHIP TOURNAMENT

1951

Ft. Sill, Okla.
CHAMPIONS: Brooke Army Medical Center
SECOND PLACE: Ft. Sill
Men

Ft. Sill:
Camp Polk 59-58, 79-69

BIBLIOGRAPHY

1. CSUMB Digital Commons. *Fort Ord Yearbook: Company F, 5th Infantry Div., RFA Regiment, 21 Jan. 1957 - 16 March 1957. Digital Commons @ CSUMB.* s.l. : U.S. Army, 1956. Online archives.

2. U.S. Army; Eighth Army. *Two Years of Progress.* Camp Zama : U.S. Army; Eighth Army, 1957.

3. Lloyd, Mark. *History of the United States Army.* London : Chevprime Ltd., 1988.

4. Rees, David. *The Korean War, History and Tactics.* [ed.] Richard Williams Ashley Brown. London : Orbis Publishing, 1984.

5. Clarence G. Oliver, Jr. *Tony Dufflebag, and Other Remembrances of the War in Korea.* Bloomington : AuthorHouse, 2007. 978-1-4259-3737-5.

6. Schweikert, Larry and Allen, Michael. *A Patriot's History of the United States.* New York : Penguin Group, 2004.

7. U.S. Army. FMWR continues long legacy of caring for Soldiers, families. *U.S. Army.* [Online] January 5, 2012. [Cited: October 1, 2025.] https://www.army.mil/article/71514/fmwr_continues_long_legacy_of_caring_for_sol diers_families.

8. Alex A. Akhavan, Keith Kelly. Friday Night Laws: A Primer on the Sports Broadcasting Act of 1961. *The National Law Review.* [Online] September 5, 2025. [Cited: October 1, 2025.] https://natlawreview.com/article/friday-night-laws-primer-sports-broadcasting-act-1961.

9. Halberstam, David. *Playing for Keeps.* New York : Broadway Books, a Division of Random House, 2000. 0-7679-0444-3.

10. Stark, Douglas. *Wartime Basketball.* Lincoln, Neb. : University of Nebraska Press, 2016. 9780803245280.

11. Kingrey, D. Goodrich. *The Forgotten Athletes of the American Forces Far East.* s.l. : Goodrich Fine Books, 2025. 9798218715090.

12. Football Archaeology. *Today's Tidbit... Fort Ord Takes On The NFL - Twice.* October 4, 2022. Football Archaeology. Online archives.

13. Football Archaeology. NFLers Fly High with the 1956 Eglin Air Force Base Eagles. s.l. : Football Archaeology, October 15, 2021. *Football Archaeology.*

14. Sports All Stars. Football 1958. [ed.] Arthur Whitman. *Sports All Stars Maco Football Edition.* 1958, Vol. 1, 2.

15. Headquarters 7th Infantry Division. [ed.] Office of the Commanding General. APO San Francisco, California, USA : s.n., Unknown (1950s). *Welcome to the Bayonet Division.*

16. Staff. Jim Brown (1936-2023) Legendary Cleveland Browns Running Back. *Legacy.com.* [Online] May 19, 2023. [Cited: October 29, 2025.] https://www.legacy.com/news/celebrity-deaths/jim-brown-1936-2023-legendary-cleveland-browns-running-back/.

17. Carlson, Chris. Jim Brown, a Flawed Hero, Made His Case As The Greatest Athlete Who Ever Lived While At Syracuse. *Syracuse.com.* May 20, 2023.

18. Sports Illustrated. Special Football Issue. [ed.] Sidney L. James. *Sports Illustrated.* September 24, 1956.

19. Army Times. 3d Army Cage Tourney Opens. *Army Times.* March 15, 1958. Online archives.

20. Army Times. Campbell Trackmen Win at Benning. *Army Times.* May 31, 1958, p. 35. Online archives.

21. Army Times. 78,000 See Army Lose in Rice Bowl. *Army Times.* December 27, 1958, p. 31.

22. Army Times. Ollie Matson & Co. Meet Marine Champs. *Army Times.* December 19, 1953, p. 29. Online archives.

23. Army Times. Ord's Pro Backfield. *Army Times.* August 21, 1954, p. 28. Online archives.

24. Tiffany White, Doug Kelly. The Rams. *therams.com.* [Online] November 22, 2018. [Cited: September 1, 2025.] https://www.therams.com/news/the-rams-story.

25. National Football League Properties, Inc. *The NFL's Official Encyclopedic History of Professional Football.* s.l. : Prentice-Hall, Inc., 1977. 0-02-589010-7.

26. Cavanaugh, Jack. *Giants Among Men.* s.l. : First Sports Publishing, 2008. 978-1-68358-080-5.

27. Kingrey, D. Goodrich. *The Forgotten Athletes of the American Forces Far East.* s.l. : Goodrich Fine Books, 2025. p. 167.

28. Legacy.com. Robert Moellering Fry. *Legacy.com.* [Online] 2019. [Cited: November 2, 2025.] https://www.legacy.com/obituaries/name/robert-fry-obituary?pid=194447140&page=2.

29. Army Times. Monmouth Wins. *Army Times.* October 9, 1954, p. 30. Online archives.

30. Luchter, Paul S. *luckyshow.org.* [Online] January 22, 2024. [Cited: November 3, 2025.] http://www.luckyshow.org/football/FtMonmouth.htm.

31. U.S. Army. *9th Infantry Division, Fort Carson, Colorade (1955).* Fort Carson : U.S. Army, 9th ID, 1955. Online archives.

32. Army Times. *Army Times.* Online archives.

33. Army Times. Basketball Notes: Carson Loses Nine Men. *Army Times.* December 22, 1956, p. 40. Online archives.

34. Army Times. Pride, Altman Star for Carson in Losing Cause. *Army Times.* May 4, 1957. Online archive.

35. Army Times. Fine Pitching by Isaacs, Ramos, Gives Carson 5th Army Crown. *Army Times.* September 21, 1957, p. 37. Online archives.

36. World Musician Obituaries. Biography: Charley Pride. *World Musician Obituaries.* [Online] September 19, 2025. [Cited: September 19, 2025.] https://worldmusicianobituaries.org/musicians/charley-pride/.

37. Legacy.com. Les Roh. *Legacy.com.* [Online] October 15, 2007. [Cited: September 18, 2025.] https://www.legacy.com/us/obituaries/idahostatejournal/name/les-roh-obituary?id=24684962.

38. Malan, Douglas. *Living HBCU Baseball History with The Legends - George Altman of Tennesee A&I.* May 9, 2019.

39. Castrovince, Anthony. George Altman's Remarkable Globe-Spanning Career. *mlb.com.* [Online] May 19, 2023. [Cited: September 19, 2025.] https://www.mlb.com/news/george-altman-played-in-the-majors-negro-leagues-and-japan.

40. Flickr. Anthony Martinez. *Flickr.* [Online] March 11, 2006. [Cited: September 24, 2025.] https://www.flickr.com/photos/macktruckturner/page88.

41. Army Times. Seventeen 4th Army Tourneys Next Year. *Army Times.* November 12, 1955, p. 38. Online archives.

42. Detroit Free Press. Second Lion Regular, Lary, Gets Army Call. *Detroit Free Press.* May 28, 1954, p. 27.

43. Alchetron. Yale Lary. *Alchetron - The Free Social Encyclopedia.* [Online] [Cited: October 27, 2025.] https://alchetron.com/Yale-Lary.

44. Adam Smith, Megan Tooker, Chelsea Pogorelac, Chris Cochran. *A History of Recreation in the Military.* U.S. Army Corps of Engineers. s.l. : Department of Defense, 2011.

45. Wright, Ben. $1.5 Million Doughboy Stadium Facelift to Revive Football at Fort Benning During Historic Moment. *Ledger-Enquirer.* February 23, 2012.

46. U.S. Army. *The Doughboy.* Fort Benning, Georgia : U.S. Army, 1936.

47. Dye, Pat. *www.army.mil.* [Online] September 19, 2013. [Cited: October 27, 2025.] https://www.army.mil/article/111774/Memorable_day_at_Doughboy_Stadium/.

48. Kingrey, D. Goodrich. *The Forgotten Athletes of the American Forces Far East.* s.l. : Goodrich Fine Books, 2025.

49. Scanlon, Tom. Here's a Surprise: Mitchell, Lee Tackle, All-Army MVP. *Army Times.* December 11, 1954, p. 27. Online archives.

50. Bodani, Frank. The Toughest Pittsburgh Steeler with a Giving Heart. *York Daily Record.* November 7, 2019.

51. Army Times. All-Army 1955. *Army Times.* December 17, 1955, p. 32. Online archives.

52. The Oklahoman. Coleman "Buck" McPhail. *The Oklahoman.* March 8, 2005.

53. Army Times. Army Times All-Army 1956. *Army Times.* December 15, 1956, pp. 54, 55. Online archives.

54. Biographies and Memoirs. *Who was Larry Hartshorn?* s.l. : Biographies and Memoirs, July 23, 2013. Biographies and Memoirs.

55. Fuller Funeral Home. Charles T. Maloy Obituary. *Fuller Funeral Home.* [Online] June 5, 2024. [Cited: September 4, 2025.] https://fullerfh.com/tribute/details/3022/Charles-Maloy/condolences.html.

56. Army Times. All-Army MVP. *Army Times.* December 21, 1957. Online archives.

57. Wendall, George. Auburn University Digital Collections. [Online] October 18, 1955. [Cited: October 22, 2025.] https://content.lib.auburn.edu/digital/collection/plainsman/id/1672/rec/224.

58. Army Times. Congratulations to Fob James. *Army Times.* December 14, 1957, p. 56. Online archives.

59. AL.com. Robert "Bobby" Luna. *AL.com.* [Online] March 15, 2008. [Cited: September 26, 2025.] https://obits.al.com/us/obituaries/huntsville/name/robert-luna-obituary?id=13076205.

60. Army Times. "Fob" James All-Army MVP. *Army Times.* December 7, 1957. Online archives.

61. Roosevelt "Rosey" Grier, Dennis Baker. *Rosey, An Autobiography, The Gentle Giant.* Tulsa : Honor Books, 1986. 0-89274-406-5.

62. Vierra, Brock. Rams Legend Rosey Grier Marks Significant Milestone. *si.com.* [Online] July 15, 2025. [Cited: September 26, 2025.] https://www.si.com/nfl/rams/los-angeles-penn-state-new-york-giants-rosey-grier-.

63. Army Times. Korea's Estrada All-Army MVP. *Army Times.* December 13, 1958, p. 41. Online archives.

64. College of the Holy Cross. *Purple Patcher Yearbook.* 1955. p. 220. Higher Education Commons.

65. North Iowa Today. Former Hawkeye Vincent Passes. *North Iowa Today.* September 5, 2012.

66. Green Bay Press Gazette. Leland Joseph "Lee" Hermson. *Green Bay Press Gazette.* August 16, 2022.

67. Army Times. Football Previews ... It Won't be Long Now. *Army Times.* August 30, 1952. Online archives.

68. Stars and Stripes. Pros Debunk All-Americas. *Stars and Stripes.* October 18, 1954. Online archives.

69. Sports Illustrated/CNN. Pro Football, A Don Shula Timeline. *CNNSI.com.* [Online] [Cited: September 14, 2025.] https://web.archive.org/web/20131104102404/http://sportsillustrated.cnn.com/features/1997/weekly/970728/shula/timeline.html.

70. Miami Dolphins. miamidolphins.com. [Online] May 4, 2020. [Cited: September 15, 2025.] https://www.miamidolphins.com/news/don-shula-rip-1930-2020.

71. Stars and Stripes. Antonelli To Face Brooke; Undefeated Teams Clash in Wichita Quarter-Finals. *Stars and Stripes.* August 30, 1952, p. 12. Online archive.

72. Lawrence Ritter, Donald Honig. *The Image of Their Greatness.* s.l. : Crown Publishers, 1992. p. 239.

73. Pacific Stars and Stripes. Colonials, Ord To Meet In NBC Headline Game; Brooke Bows to MDW. *Pacific Stars and Stripes.* August 31, 1952, p. 12. Online Archives.

74. Grant, Kris. Veterans Memorial to Honor Jerry Coleman. *La Jolla Light.* May 21, 2008.

75. Stars and Stripes. Troy Axes San Diego; Fourth Win. *Stars and Stripes.* Online archives.

76. Stars and Stripes. Troy Axes San Diego; Fourth Win. *Stars and Stripes.* October 12, 1952, p. 14. Online archive.

77. Stars and Stripes. College Football scores. *Stars and Stripes.* November 16, 1953, p. 14.

78. European Stars and Stripes. AF teams to Play Before TV Camera. *European Stars and Stripes.* October 25, 1952, p. 10. Online archives.

79. Scanlon, Tom. Top Service Teams To Meet Dec. 20. *Army Times.* November 29, 1952, p. 30. Online archive.

80. Army Times. Many New Champions Crowned in Army Sports During 1952. *Army Times.* December 27, 1952, p. 30.

81. Army Times. All-Army Candidates in Action. *Army Times.* November 29, 1952, p. 30. Online archive.

82. Sobieski, John. Turner Wows Cage Fans at Brooke. *Army Times.* January 3, 1953, p. 24. Online archives.

83. Peach Basket Society. [Online] August 30, 2019. [Cited: August 28, 2025.] https://peachbasketsociety.blogspot.com/2019/08/jack-turner.html.

84. daycarter.com. [Online] 2014. [Cited: August 28, 2025.] https://daycarter.com/tribute/details/1523/Jackie-Turner/obituary.html#tribute-start.

85. Army Times. *Army Times.* January 17, 1953, p. 29. Online archives.

86. Together We Served. [Online] [Cited: August 29, 2025.] https://blog.togetherweserved.com/paul-arizin-u-s-marine-corps-1952-1954/.

87. Scanlon, Tom. Second Guess . *Army Times.* September 19, 1953. Online archives.

88. Army Times. Second Guess. *Army Times.* December 19, 1953, p. 28. Online archives.

89. Rare 1954 U.S. All-Army Basketball Tournament program. *Internet Archive.* [Online] February 4, 2021. [Cited: September 22, 2025.] https://archive.org/details/RARE-1954-US-ALL-ARMY-BASKETBALL-TOURNAMENT-Program-at-Fort-Lewis-Washington-northtexassports/1.jpg.

90. Missouri Sports Hall of Fame. Inductees: Win Wilfong. *Missouri Sports Hall of Fame.* [Online] [Cited: September 23, 2025.] https://mosportshalloffame.com/inductees/win-wilfong/.

91. Memphis Men's Basketball. *gotigersgo.com.* [Online] [Cited: September 23, 2025.] https://gotigersgo.com/sports/mens-basketball/roster/win-wilfong/4608.

92. Army Times. Fort Ord Dices Up Great Lakes, 67-12. *Army Times.* January 9, 1954. Online archives.

93. Stars and Stripes. Giants Sign 2 Service Stars. *Stars and Stripes.* January 20, 1954. Online archives.

94. Army Times. It's World Series Time in Army Basketball ... *Army Times.* April 3, 1954. Online archives.

95. Hope Star. Kellow (sic) Still in Critical Shape. *Hope Star.* April 7, 1954. Online archives.

96. Virginia Sports Hall of Fame. Junius Kellogg. *Virginia Sports Hall of Fame.* [Online] [Cited: September 23, 2025.] https://vasportshof.com/inductee/junius-kellogg/.

97. Stars and Stripes. Chaffee Downs Gordon, Gains All-Army Finals; Warren AB Tops AF List. *Stars and Stripes.* April 10, 1954, p. 13. Online archives.

98. Stars and Stripes. Ord Earns All-Army Finals Slot; Andrews, Scott Clash in AF Play. *Stars and Stripes.* April 11, 1954, p. 12. Online archives.

99. Stars and Stripes. Chaffee Five Wins Army Tournament. *Stars and Stripes.* April 12, 1954, p. 11. Online archives.

100. Army Times. Championship Army Team Loses In Inter-Service. *Army Times.* April 24, 1954, p. 32. Online archives.

101. Army Times. Army Ball Helped Mays, Says Former Teammate. *Army Times.* August 7, 1954, p. 30. Online archives.

102. Army Times. Ollie Matson Stars Against Rams. *Army Times.* August 14, 1954, p. 24. Online archives.

103. Cobley, John. Roger Bannister. *Racing Past.* [Online] February 7, 2011. [Cited: October 13, 2025.] https://www.racingpast.ca/john_contents.php?id=91.

104. Army Times. All-Army Tournament Opens; Lee, Wood, Jackson Win Opening Games. *Army Times.* September 18, 1954, p. 28 Online archives.

105. Goldstein, Richard. Whitey Herzog, Hall of Fame Cardinals Manager, Dies at 92. *New York Times.* April 16, 2024.

106. Pro Football Archives. Walt Napier. *Pro Football Archives.* [Online] September 26, 2025. https://www.profootballarchives.com/players/n/napi00200.html.

107. Army Times. Fort Ord Wins All-Service. *Army Times.* October 2, 1954. Online archives.

108. UC Riverside. Fort Ord to Meet Rams; Camiamela (sic) Sidelined. *California Digital Newspaper Collection.* July 30, 1954, Vol. 3, 9.

109. Army Times. Ord Wins, 46-0. *Army Times.* October 2, 1954. Online archives .

110. Holloway, Charles R. Chuck Holloway Chronicles. *chuckholloway.com.* [Online] [Cited: October 2025, 2025.] Unable to determine date published. http://www.chuckhollaway.com/.

111. Stanley Woodward's Football 1957. [ed.] Stanley Woodward. *Stanley Woodward's Football 1957.* Vol. 1, 9.

112. Army Times. All-Army '53' Quarterbacks Meet in Carson-Sill Game. *Army Times.* November 6, 1954, p. 35. Online archives.

113. Army Times. O'Connell and Co. Top Belvoir, 48-27. *Army Times.* December 27, 1954, p. 35. Online archives.

114. uwbadgers.com. UW Athletic Hall of Fame - Dave Suminski. *uwbadgers.com.* [Online] https://uwbadgers.com/honors/uw-athletic-hall-of-fame/dave-suminski/212.

115. Findagrave.com. Findagrave. *Findagrave.com.* [Online] March 23, 2014. https://www.findagrave.com/memorial/126765944/tom-o'connell.

116. Army Times. Eighth Army Basketball Aces Get All-Star Team Tryouts. *Army Times.* December 25, 1954, p. 24. Online archives.

117. Army Times. Many Schedules Of Post Teams To Be Revised. *Army Times.* October 23, 1954. Online archives.

118. Army Times. Fort Dix Pvt. is PT Paradox. *Army Times.* October 16, 1954, p. 18. Online archives.

119. Brown, Elizabeth. Remembering Perham missionary priest and martyr Father John Kaiser 25 years after death. *The Central Minnesota Catholic.* [Online] August 14, 2025. [Cited: October 8, 2025.] https://thecentralminnesotacatholic.org/remembering-perham-missionary-priest-and-martyr-father-john-kaiser-25-years-after-death/.

120. The East African. The Final FBI Report on the Death of Father John Kaiser. *The East African.* [Online] May 7, 2001. [Cited: October 8, 2025.] https://web.archive.org/web/20050424150858/http://www.nationaudio.com/News/EastAfrican/20052001/Features/Features.html.

121. Deford, Frank. Code Breakers FIFTY YEARS AGO RED BLAIK'S FOOTBALL POWERHOUSE AT ARMY WAS DECIMATED BY THE LOSS OF PLAYERS WHO VIOLATED THE MILITARY ACADEMY'S HONOR CODE. BUT WHO REALLY ACTED DISHONORABLY? *Sports Illustrated.* November 13, 2000.

122. Roberts, Rich. Malavasi, Ex-Coach of Rams, Dead at 57. *Los Angeles Times.* December 16, 1987.

123. Army Times. Statistics. *Army Times.* January 8, 1955, p. 28. Online archives.

124. Army Times. Clutch Shot by Jim Bredar Wins All-Army for Eustis. *Army Times.* April 16, 1955, p. 32. Online archives.

125. Army Times. Service Grid Champs Announce Good Slate. *Army Times.* May 7, 1955. Online archives.

126. Bowie, Robert W. Chotto Matte Young Eagles column. *Pacific Stars and Stripes.* June 10, 1955, p. 22. Online archives.

127. Army Times. All-Army End Joins Eagles. *Army Times.* July 30, 1955, p. 32. Online archives.

128. Jackson, Colonel L. W. Next Stop - Olympics. *Army Information Digest.* September 1955, Vol. 10, 9.

129. Army Times. Billy Martin Wants to Try Pitching. *Army Times.* October 15, 1955. Online archives.

130. Army Times. McPherson Wins All-Army Baseball. *Army Times.* October 1, 1955, p. 33. Online archives.

131. Jaffe, Mike. Vinegar Bend Mizell. *Society for American Baseball Research.* [Online] January 14, 2022. [Cited: October 17, 2025.] https://sabr.org/bioproj/person/vinegar-bend-mizell/.

132. Rudman, Steve and Eskenazi, David. *Wayback Machine: 'Deadeye' Don Heinrich.* s.l. : SportspressNW.com, October 9, 2012.

133. Fort Ord Yearbook. *Fort Ord Yearbook: Company H, 20th Infantry Regiment, 6th Infantry Division, 26 October 1953 - 19 December 1953.* Fort Ord : s.n., 1953. Online archive.

134. Army Times. Hood Wins, 33-13, In Shrimp Bowl. *Army Times.* December 24, 1955, p. 24. Online archives.

135. HQ AFFE/8A REAR. *Results of All Army Basketball Tournament Sixth and Final Day.* Office of Adjutant General, U.S. Army. Fort Leonard Wood, MO : U.S. Army, 18 March 1956. Memo. National Archives II, 353.8, MRN: 171404Z.

136. Army Times. Teams Picked For Olympic Tryouts. *Army Times.* March 24, 1956, p. 47. Online archives.

137. Wagenheim, Kal. Wanted: Quarterback By 3rd Div. Gridmen. *The Bayonet.* August 23, 1956.

138. Toledo Blade. George R. Jacoby; Buckeye Until the End, Die Watching the Team. *Toledo Blade.* September 3, 2013.

139. Wierzbicki, Tom. Lack of Grid Personnel Causes Head Coach Ingram to Don Pads. *The Bayonet.* September 6, 1956. Online archives.

140. The Bayonet. Doughboys Win Opener Against Marines, 27-14. *The Bayonet.* September 20, 1956, p. 10. Online archives.

141. Army Times. Fort McPherson, Devens Take Lead in All-Army. *Army Times.* September 22, 1956, p. 47.

142. Army Times. Fort Hood Tankers Top Brooke, 21-7. *Army Times.* October 27, 1956, p. 53. Online archives.

143. Find a Grave. *Ollie Matson.* s.l. : Find a Grave, February 19, 2011.

144. The Bayonet. Rocket Star Wins Place On Army Time's Squad. *The Bayonet.* December 13, 1956, p. 12. Online archives.

145. Dignity Memorial. *dignitymemorial.com.* [Online] [Cited: November 4, 2025.] https://www.dignitymemorial.com/obituaries/cary-nc/dale-haupt-7811249.

146. Army Times. Hood Tankers Lose, 29-14, to Bolling in Shrimp Bowl. *Army Times.* December 15, 1956, p. 57. Online archive.

147. The Bayonet. Tom Kinney Speaks at TIC Grid Dinner. *The Bayonet.* December 20, 1956, p. 14. Online archives.

148. Stars and Stripes. 34 Soldiers On Olympic Team. *Stars and Stripes.* January 16, 1957, p. 21. Online archives.

149. Army Times. Europe Ends Regimental Basketball. *Army Times.* January 1, 1957, p. 43. Online archive.

150. New Castle News. Legend Dies: Former Farrell Star Mccoy Dead at 76. *New Castle News.* April 11, 2008.

151. Basketball Hall of Fame. *Frank V. Ramsey.* s.l. : Basketball Hall of Fame. Basketball Hall of Fame.

152. Lexington Herald Leader. Former University of Kentucky Basketball Star Jerry Bird Dies at 83. *Lexington Herald Leader.* July 20, 2017.

153. ESPN. Legendary Boston Celtics Player, Coach K. C. Jones Dies at 88. *ESPN.* [Online] December 25, 2020. [Cited: September 6, 2025.] https://www.espn.com/nba/story/_/id/30595836/boston-celtics-legend-kc-jones-dies-88.

154. Army Times. Fort Jackson Undefeated After 17 Games. *Army Times.* February 9, 1957, p. 51.

155. Army Times. Carson and Dix Still Undefeated . *Army Times.* November 2, 1957. Online archives.

156. Army Times. Sport Ed's Corner. *Army Times.* December 7, 1957, p. 45. Online archives.

157. Army Times. Camp Johnson Champions. *Army Times.* December 7, 1957. Online archives.

158. Army Times. Carson Dumps Dix in Bowl, 12-6. *Army Times.* January 4, 1958, p. 35. Online archives.

159. Army Times. New Sub Rule Helps Army Grid Teams. *Army Times.* January 18, 1958. Online archives.

160. Find a Grave. Si Hugo Green. *Find a Grave.* [Online] December 28, 2013. [Cited: September 18, 2025.] https://www.findagrave.com/memorial/122361104/si_hugo-green.

161. Army Times. Varied Sports Program at Ord . *Army Times.* April 5, 1958, p. 44. Online archives.

162. Army Times. Bowl-Bound Brooke Comets Whip Fort Riley, 46-20. *Army Times.* November 29, 1958, p. 41. Online archives.

163. Army Times. Army Sports 1958. *Army Times.* December 27, 1958, pp. 31, 33. Online archive.

164. National Football Foundation and College Hall of Fame. Jim Tatum. *National Football Foundation and College Hall of Fame.* [Online] [Cited: November 11, 2025.] https://footballfoundation.org/hof_search.aspx?hof=1789.

165. University of Maryland. University of Maryland men's football media guides. *Archive.org.* [Online] [Cited: November 11, 2025.] https://archive.org/details/universityofmary1955univ/mode/1up.

166. National Football Foundation and College Hall of Fame. National Football Foundation and College Hall of Fame. *footballfoundation.org.* [Online] April 20, 2008. [Cited: November 11, 2025.] https://footballfoundation.org/news/2008/4/20/_51958.aspx?path=football.

167. Army Times. Six All-Army Grid Stars Make All-Service Squad. *Army Times.* January 5, 1957. Online archives.

168. Army Times. Fort Dix May Have Best Service Line. *Army Times.* September 21, 1957. Online archives.

169. *The Journal of San Diego History.* San Diego, Calif., USA : s.n. Balboa Stadium, November 1964. ©SDHS, UT #85:E2475, *Union-Tribune* Collection.

170. NCAA. *NCAA.com.* [Online] December 22, 2013. [Cited: November 6, 2025.] https://www.ncaa.com/news/football/article/2013-12-09/history-poinsettia-bowl.

171. Stars and Stripes. Bolling AFB Cops Poinsettia Clash. *Stars and Stripes.* December 22, 1952. Online archives.

172. Murphy, Jack. Bolling Torpedoes N.T.C., 35-14. *San Diego Union.* December 21, 1952. Online archives.

173. Long Beach Independent. Matson, Mann Pace 55-19 Warrior Victory. *Long Beach Independent.* December 21, 1953. Online archives.

174. Army Times. Sill Ground Attack Drives Bolling Airmen Batty, 27-6. *Army Times.* December 25, 1954. Online archives.

175. Stars and Stripes. Ft. Ord Accepts Poinsettia Berth. *Stars and Stripes.* December 1, 1955. Online archives.

176. San Bernardino County Sun. Fort Ord in Poinsettia Bowl Win. *San Bernardino County Sun.* December 18, 1955. Online archives.

177. McClintic, Bob. Ord Wins, 35-13 In Poinsettia Bowl. *Army Times.* December 24, 1955, p. 24. Online archives.

178. Kates, C. O. *The Armed Forces Sports Almanac.* Harrisburg : The Military Service Publishing Company, 1954.

179. CSUMB Digital Commons. *Fort Ord Yearbook: Company F, 63rd Infantry, 3 October 1955 - 26 November 1955.* s.l. : U.S. Army, 1955. p. 31. Online archives.

180. Army Times. Sparks Sill. *Army Times.* October 23, 1954. Online archives.

181. Kates, C.O. *The Armed Forces Sports Almanac.* First Edition. Harrisburg : The Military Service Publishing Company, 1954.

182. *stadiumsofprofootball.com.* [Online] https://www.pinterest.com/pin/balboa-stadium-history-photos-more-of-the-former-home-of-the-san-diego-chargers-nfl-stadium--216172850837009978/.

INDEX

244

245

247

248

University of Illinois, *177*
University of Maryland
  Terrapins, *3, 101, 185, 186, 188*
University of Missouri, *106, 132*
University of Pennsylvania, *58*
University of San Francisco, *24, 50,*
  127, 167
USAREUR, *54, 63, 78, 79, 82, 117,*
  172
Used Books, *Acknowledgements*
Van Brocklin
  Norm Van Brocklin, *17, 18, 19,*
  77
Van Brocklin, Norm, *17, 18, 77*
Van Fleet, Lt. Gen., *3*
Vandersee, Jack, *32*
Vandeweghe, Al, *92*
Vendehey, Van, *138*
Vessels, Billy, *24, 46, 48, 50, 60,*
  127, 134, 135, 147, 154, 166, 193
Veterans Memorial Stadium, *17*
Villanova, *50, 84, 101, 140*
Vincent, Eddie, *81, 84*
Wacholz, Stan, *47, 50, 148*

Warriors
  Fort Ord, *17, 19, 20, 55, 58, 101,*
    102, 104, 110, 115, 116, 123,
    126, 131, 136, 148, 155, 192,
    194, 195
Wartime Basketball, 9
Washington Colonials, *93*
Washington Redskins, *23, 57, 63,*
  117, 131, 147, 157, 158, 177
Washington State, *112, 192*
Watson, Art, *32*
Weiss, Chuck, *118*
Wells, Willie, *34*
West Point, *40, 71, 79, 82, 128, 140,*
  141, 161, 180, 184, 192
Western Kentucky, *97, 98, 104, 132,*
  161, 164
Wheeler, Bob "Wheels", *100*
Wilfong, Win, *105, 106, 145*
Wilson, "Touchdown Tommy", *10*
Woodson, Abe, *176, 177*
Worden, Neil, *36, 158*
Wyatt, Bowden, *169*

D. Goodrich Kingrey lives in the Great State of Alabama with his wife, children, and dog. Mr. Kingrey is thankful for American freedom, as secured by our noble and selfless veterans.